NEW TESTAMENT GREEK AND EXEGESIS

Gerald F. Hawthorne
Photograph courtesy of the Wheaton College Archives

New Testament Greek and Exegesis

ESSAYS IN HONOR OF

Gerald F. Hawthorne

Edited by

Amy M. Donaldson
&
Timothy B. Sailors

WILLIAM B. EERDMANS PUBLISHING COMPANY
GRAND RAPIDS, MICHIGAN / CAMBRIDGE, U.K.

Wm. B. Eerdmans Publishing Co.
255 Jefferson Ave. S.E., Grand Rapids, Michigan 49503 /
P.O. Box 163, Cambridge CB3 9PU U.K.

Printed in the United States of America

07 06 05 04 03   7 6 5 4 3 2 1

Library of Congress Cataloging-in-Publication Data

New Tesament Greek and exegesis: essays in honor of Gerald F. Hawthorne
edited by Amy M. Donaldson, Timothy B. Sailors.
p.   cm.
Includes bibliographical references and index.
ISBN 0-8028-3878-2 (cloth: alk. paper)
1. Bible. N.T. — Criticism, interpretation, etc.
I. Hawthorne, Gerald F., 1925-
II. Donaldson, Amy M.   III. Sailors, Timothy B.

BS2393.N489   2003
225.6 — dc21

2003044952

www.eerdmans.com

Contents

Gerald F. Hawthorne: A Personal Appreciation   viii
    Ralph P. Martin

Abbreviations   xi

Introduction   1
    Amy M. Donaldson and Timothy B. Sailors

I. GREEK AND EXEGESIS

Lexical Glosses and Definitions of Θεραπεύω   11
    David E. Aune

Exegetical Rigor with Hermeneutical Humility:
The Calvinist-Arminian Debate and the New Testament   23
    William W. Klein

Finding the Devil in the Details: Onomastic Exegesis
and the Naming of Evil in the World of the New Testament   37
    Douglas L. Penney

CONTENTS

II. GOSPELS AND ACTS

The Spirit in the Gospels: Breaking the Impasse
of Early-Twentieth-Century German Scholarship   55

    John R. Levison

A Leper in the Hands of an Angry Jesus   77

    Bart D. Ehrman

Liar Liar and "This Woman" in John 7:1–8:59:
From Rhetorical Analysis to Intertextual Rereading   99

    Jeffrey L. Staley

The Spirit and Jesus "on Mission" in the Postresurrection
and Postascension Stages of Salvation History: The Impact
of the Pneumatology of Acts on Its Christology   121

    William J. Larkin Jr.

Moral Character and Divine Generosity:
Acts 13:13-52 and the Narrative Dynamics of Luke-Acts   141

    Bruce W. Longenecker

III. EPISTLES

Philippians 1:28b, One More Time   167

    Stephen E. Fowl

Transformation of Relationships: Partnership,
Citizenship, and Friendship in Philippi   181

    G. Walter Hansen

Ephesus and the Literary Setting of Philippians   205

    Frank S. Thielman

The Meaning of Ἀπείραστος Revisited   225

    Peter H. Davids

Contents

Publications of Gerald F. Hawthorne   241

Contributors   245

Tabula Gratulatoria   249

Index of Modern Authors   253

Index of Scripture and Ancient Literature   255

Gerald F. Hawthorne:
A Personal Appreciation

Many friends and colleagues of Gerald Hawthorne would jump at the chance to pay him some well-deserved tributes. His circle of friends at Wheaton College and far beyond must be extensive, and he has endeared himself to a host of friends by his genial personality and genuine interest in other people's lives. I count myself in that number, and I am glad for the opportunity to speak on their behalf, though of course in an unofficial, unauthorized way.

My mind drifts back across several decades in which our paths have crossed, from the days in the early 1970s when I first met him in connection with the Institute for Biblical Research. The coming together of scholars in Los Angeles when, in conjunction with the Society of Biblical Literature meetings there, the Institute was formed is still a vivid memory. He has been an active and honored member and official of the Institute ever since, repaying the strong debt of friendship with the first president, E. Earle Ellis. That society of evangelical biblical scholars has grown from its early and small beginnings to become an international body rivaling, in a friendly way, the Tyndale Fellowship in the UK. In no small measure the success of IBR may be traced to its early leaders, among whom Jerry holds a special place that has inspired the confidence of the fellows and associates over the years.

A reference to the Cambridge-based Tyndale Fellowship recalls other occasions when our paths have met on the other side of the Atlantic. My wife and I shared the hospitality of his lodging in Cambridge when he and his wife Jane were on sabbatical leave. It was a pleasurable experience for us to escort them to the environs of the university town and in particular to Bedford, where we relived the history of John Bunyan. It has been a fitting tribute to his Anglophilic links that Wheaton College has provided a house for visiting scholars in Cambridge and dedicated it, most appropriately, in Jerry's name. I am sure he took pleasure in this gesture.

Other links with the UK came later when, on a subsequent sabbatical, I was able to entertain him in northwest England. His services as a church-committed believer as well as a scholar were readily enlisted as he spoke at a local church's midweek service in Southport and came across the Pennines to visit the Biblical Studies Department at the University of Sheffield. In some small way I was able to reciprocate this gesture as, on several occasions, I visited Bethany Chapel, his place of worship in Wheaton, and was invited to speak to the Sunday morning Bible study and worship service there. His attachment to and support of this Brethren assembly have been characteristic of his loyalty and desire to place his academic work at the service of the local congregation.

His home in Wheaton has provided a veritable oasis for students at the college and an open door of welcome to greet visiting family and friends, both from afar and from the community. His wife Jane, with her strong missionary associations, has proved a gracious hostess, assuring all who pass through Wheaton of a welcome with thoughtful attention to their needs.

I must move on in my itinerary of occasions when our lives have intersected, to speak of our collaborative endeavor in two notable projects: his writing of a volume on Philippians for the Word Biblical Commentary, and his editorial contribution to InterVarsity Press's *Dictionary of Paul and His Letters*. These enterprises drew us together in a close bond, and I learned to appreciate him even more intimately.

Not that we always saw eye to eye, naturally. I well recall animated conversations and debates over the nuance of the objective genitive in Greek, and on a broader front his espousal of "imitation of Christ" as a motif of Christian discipleship. His published works reflect his careful exegesis of the Greek text and his desire to secure the well-being of his students and other readers. Whenever I felt obliged to part company with his positions (for example, on Phil 2:6-11 or the provenance of Philippians), I did so with a certain hesitation and unease.

The focus of the following essays well highlights Jerry's chief scholarly interest and concern: his passionate handling of the Greek New Testament text, his gracious manner in dealing with inquiries and problems, and his churchly connections. These are well-observed traits, and the essays salute the honor in which he is held by former students.

Yet it is as a friend and fellow worker that I have chosen to write, and to hold up the fine example of a Christian gentleman and a Christian family member (the title "brother" is doubly apropos!) whose influence lives on in the people he has touched and who join (as in Acts 28:15) to thank God for him and take fresh heart.

RALPH P. MARTIN
Professor of Biblical Studies (Emeritus)
University of Sheffield

Abbreviations

AB	Anchor Bible
AGJU	Arbeiten zur Geschichte des antiken Judentums und des Ur-christentums
AJT	*American Journal of Theology*
ANEP	*The Ancient Near East in Pictures Relating to the Old Testament.* Ed. J. B. Pritchard. 2d ed. Princeton, 1969
ANET	*Ancient Near Eastern Texts Relating to the Old Testament.* Ed. J. B. Pritchard. 3d ed. Princeton, 1969
AS	Assyriological Studies
BAGD	W. Bauer, W. F. Arndt, F. W. Gingrich, and F. W. Danker. *Greek-English Lexicon of the New Testament and Other Early Christian Literature.* 2d ed. Chicago, 1979
BBR	*Bulletin for Biblical Research*
BDAG	W. Bauer, F. W. Danker, W. F. Arndt, and F. W. Gingrich. *Greek-English Lexicon of the New Testament and Other Early Christian Literature.* 3d ed. Chicago, 1999
BECNT	Baker Exegetical Commentary on the New Testament
Bib	*Biblica*
BJRL	*Bulletin of the John Rylands University Library of Manchester*
BNTC	Black's New Testament Commentaries
BSac	*Bibliotheca sacra*
BTB	*Biblical Theology Bulletin*
BWANT	Beiträge zur Wissenschaft vom Alten und Neuen Testament

BZ	*Biblische Zeitschrift*
BZAW	Beihefte zur Zeitschrift für die alttestamentliche Wissenschaft
BZNW	Beihefte zur Zeitschrift für die neutestamentliche Wissenschaft
CAD	*Assyrian Dictionary of the Oriental Institute of the University of Chicago.* Chicago, 1956–
CEV	Contemporary English Version
CIL	*Corpus inscriptionum latinarum*
ConBNT	Coniectanea biblica: New Testament Series
CSBR	Chicago Society of Biblical Research
DBI	*Dictionary of Biblical Interpretation.* Ed. J. H. Hayes. 2 vols. Nashville: Abingdon, 1999
DDD²	*Dictionary of Deities and Demons in the Bible.* Ed. K. van der Toorn, B. Becking, and P. W. van der Horst. 2d ed. Leiden, Grand Rapids, 1999
DJD	Discoveries in the Judaean Desert
DJG	*Dictionary of Jesus and the Gospels.* Ed. J. B. Green and S. McKnight. Downers Grove, Ill., 1992
DLNT	*Dictionary of the Later New Testament and Its Developments.* Ed. R. P. Martin and P. H. Davids. Downers Grove, Ill., 1997
DPL	*Dictionary of Paul and His Letters.* Ed. G. F. Hawthorne and R. P. Martin. Downers Grove, Ill., 1993
Ebib	*Études bibliques*
EDNT	*Exegetical Dictionary of the New Testament.* Ed. H. Balz and G. Schneider. 3 vols. ET Grand Rapids, 1990-93
EgT	*Église et théologie,* Ottawa
ET	English translation
ExpTim	*Expository Times*
GBS	Guides to Biblical Scholarship
GELS	J. Lust, E. Eynikel, and K. Hauspie, *A Greek-English Lexicon of the Septuagint.* 2 vols. Stuttgart, 1992-96
HB	Hebrew Bible
HSM	Harvard Semitic Monographs
HTKNT	Herders theologischer Kommentar zum Neuen Testament
HTR	*Harvard Theological Review*
HvTSt	*Hervormde teologiese studies*
IBR	Institute for Biblical Research
ICC	International Critical Commentary
IG	*Inscriptiones graecae.* Editio minor. Berlin, 1924-
Int	*Interpretation*
ITS	*Indian Theological Studies*
JBL	*Journal of Biblical Literature*

JETS	*Journal of the Evangelical Theological Society*
JPTSup	Journal of Pentecostal Theology: Supplement Series
JQR	*Jewish Quarterly Review*
JSJ	*Journal for the Study of Judaism in the Persian, Hellenistic, and Roman Periods*
JSNT	*Journal for the Study of the New Testament*
JSNTSup	Journal for the Study of the New Testament: Supplement Series
JSPSup	Journal for the Study of the Pseudepigrapha: Supplement Series
JTS	*Journal of Theological Studies*
KEK	Kritisch-exegetischer Kommentar über das Neue Testament (Meyer-Kommentar)
L&N	J. Louw and E. A. Nida, eds., *Greek-English Lexicon of the New Testament Based on Semantic Domains*. 2 vols. New York, 1988
LAB	*Liber antiquitatum biblicarum*
LCL	Loeb Classical Library
LEC	Library of Early Christianity
LSJ	H. G. Liddell, R. Scott, and H. S. Jones, *A Greek-English Lexicon*. 9th ed. with revised supplement. Oxford, 1996
LXX	Septuagint
MGWJ	*Monatschrift für Geschichte und Wissenschaft des Judentums*
MM	J. H. Moulton and G. Milligan, *The Vocabulary of the Greek Testament Illustrated from the Papyri and Other Non-Literary Sources*. 1930; repr. Grand Rapids, 1980
MS(S)	manuscript(s)
MT	Masoretic text
NA^{27}	*Novum Testamentum Graece*, Nestle-Aland, 27th ed.
NAB	New American Bible
NAC	New American Commentary
NASB	New American Standard Bible
NCB	New Century Bible
NEB	New English Bible
NIBCNT	New International Biblical Commentary on the New Testament
NICNT	New International Commentary on the New Testament
NIGTC	New International Greek Testament Commentary
NIV	New International Version
NJB	New Jerusalem Bible
NLT	New Living Translation
NovT	*Novum Testamentum*
NovTSup	Novum Testamentum Supplements
NRSV	New Revised Standard Version
NT	New Testament

NTS	*New Testament Studies*
NTTS	New Testament Tools and Studies
OBO	Orbis biblicus et orientalis
OT	Old Testament
OTP	*Old Testament Pseudepigrapha.* Ed. J. H. Charlesworth. 2 vols. Garden City, N.Y., 1983-85
PG	Patrologia graeca. Ed. J.-P. Migne. 162 vols. Paris, 1857-86
PTMS	Pittsburgh Theological Monograph Series
REB	Revised English Bible
RevExp	*Review and Expositor*
RevQ	*Revue de Qumran*
RSV	Revised Standard Version
SBL	Society of Biblical Literature
SBLDS	Society of Biblical Literature Dissertation Series
SCHNT	Studia ad corpus hellenisticum Novi Testamenti
SD	Studies and Documents
SIG³	*Sylloge Inscriptionum Graecarum.* Ed. Wilhelm Dittenberger. 3d ed. 4 vols. Leipzig, 1915-24
SNTS	Studiorum Novi Testamenti Societas
SNTSMS	Society for New Testament Studies Monograph Series
SP	Sacra Pagina
STDJ	*Studies on the Texts of the Desert of Judah*
TDNT	*Theological Dictionary of the New Testament.* Ed. G. Kittel and G. Friedrich. Trans. G. W. Bromiley. 10 vols. Grand Rapids, 1964-76
Them	*Themelios*
THKNT	Theologischer Handkommentar zum Neuen Testament
TLG	*Thesaurus linguae graecae: Canon of Greek Authors and Works.* Ed. L. Berkowitz and K. A. Squitier. 3d ed. New York, 1990
TNTC	Tyndale New Testament Commentaries
TSK	*Theologische Studien und Kritiken*
TynBul	*Tyndale Bulletin*
VC	*Vigiliae christianae*
VT	*Vetus Testamentum*
WBC	Word Biblical Commentary
WTJ	*Westminster Theological Journal*
WUNT	Wissenschaftliche Untersuchungen zum Neuen Testament
ZNW	*Zeitschrift für die neutestamentliche Wissenschaft und die Kunde der älteren Kirche*

Introduction

SIR THOMAS MORE: Why not be a teacher? You'd be a fine
teacher. Perhaps even a great one.
RICHARD RICH: And if I was, who would know it?
SIR THOMAS MORE: You, your pupils, your friends, God. Not a
bad public, that. . . .

Robert Bolt, "A Man for All Seasons," Act One

Gerald F. Hawthorne is a great teacher. We, his pupils, know it, are sure
that it is known to his friends and to God, and wish, by the publication of
this *Festschrift* in his honor, to make it known once more to him. This collection of essays, under the general title *New Testament Greek and Exegesis*,
reflects the diversity within the field of the academic study of the NT — a
field that has been enriched by the life and work of Jerry Hawthorne. This
enrichment is evident not only in his numerous publications and involvement in professional organizations, but also in the desire he has instilled in
his students to engage the text of the NT and, in time, to take on students of
their own — in no small way to emulate their beloved teacher. Thus the diversity of methods and interests in this collection has a theme more unify-
ing than the title of the work: all the contributors to this volume learned
Greek at Wheaton College as students of Jerry Hawthorne and have gone
on to distinguish themselves as teachers of the NT.

Fifty years ago, in 1953, Gerald F. Hawthorne began teaching Greek at Wheaton College. Born August 16, 1925, he matriculated at Wheaton as an undergraduate on September 14, 1949. He had already earned his B.Th. from the Los Angeles Bible Theological Seminary (later known as BIOLA), but Hawthorne found his first year at Wheaton to be "like a year in purgatory," as he validated his transfer credits from Visalia Junior College by examination.[1] Nevertheless, he thrived at Wheaton, becoming a member of the Naitermian literary society (Knights), the Intersociety Council, the Bethany Male Quartet, and the Men's Glee Club, as well as an editor of *Kodon,* the campus magazine. These extracurricular activities, however, did not detract from his success in the classroom. Hawthorne was made a member of the Wheaton College Scholastic Honor Society and was awarded an A.B. in Greek with highest honors on August 17, 1951.

"For your first assignment, read the book of Hebrews through in Greek, make an exegetical outline of the book, and list some of the problems connected with it." It was with these words that Professor Merrill C. Tenney opened his second-semester class in the book of Hebrews at Wheaton College Graduate School in 1952.[2] This "assignment" reflects the nature of the Master of Arts program under Professor Tenney, the program into which Hawthorne enrolled after completing his bachelor's degree. It was during this time, in 1953, after having served as a graduate fellow and while still a master's student, that Hawthorne began teaching Greek as an instructor at Wheaton College. He completed his M.A. in Theology on June 14, 1954, having written his thesis on "The Significance of the Holy Spirit in the Life of Christ." Hawthorne's further work and thoughts on this topic would later be published in *The Presence and the Power.*[3] On June 17, 1955, he married Jane Elliot, a 1953 graduate of Wheaton who would herself spend a lifetime in service to the college, in the finance office, the business office, and the registrar's office. Together they would have three children — Stephen, Lynn, and James.

While continuing to teach Greek at Wheaton, Hawthorne also undertook studies for the Ph.D. at the University of Chicago, in the Department of New Testament and Early Christian Literature. During this time,

---

1. As quoted in Rachel M. Castañeda, "*Jerry's Pub* Draws Professors to Weekly Discussion Session," *Wheaton Record* 120 (April 28, 1995): 7.

2. *Tower* 32 (Wheaton, 1952), 56.

3. *The Presence and the Power: The Significance of the Holy Spirit in the Life and Ministry of Jesus* (Dallas: Word, 1991). See also idem, "Holy Spirit," *DLNT* 489-99.

Gerald F. Hawthorne with Prof. Merrill C. Tenney.
(*Tower* 32 [Wheaton, 1952], 57)

Chicago boasted the presence of scholars such as Allen P. Wikgren, Norman Perrin, Robert M. Grant, Markus Barth, and, as visiting professors, T. A. Burkill, Frederick C. Grant, and Edvin Larsson. Robert Grant, whose career at Chicago spanned thirty-five years, and with whom Hawthorne mostly studied early Christian literature other than the NT, says of his former pupil, "I can state emphatically that he was one of the ablest students ECL had in my time."[4] In 1962, while a doctoral candidate, Hawthorne was awarded the Noyes-Cutter Prize for the best essay submitted to the department. On June 13, 1969, he was awarded the Ph.D. for his dissertation, "Melito of Sardis: His Rhetoric and Theology." In this thesis, written

---

4. Robert M. Grant, personal correspondence, July 14, 2001.

under the supervision of then department chair Allen P. Wikgren, an examination of the historical, cultural, and theological environment of Melito is followed by a thorough rhetorical-critical study of Melito's *Paschal Homily*. The influence of Melito's rhetorical artifices on his theology is then examined.[5] Some of Hawthorne's students would also pursue doctoral degrees in this same department at the University of Chicago: David E. Aune, Francis C. R. Thee, Calvin K. Katter, and (thirty years after Hawthorne) James A. Kelhoffer.

Throughout this time, studying at Chicago and teaching at Wheaton, Hawthorne was active in various professional societies. In 1957 he became an associate member of the Evangelical Theological Society and was a full member by 1967. He has been a member of the Society of Biblical Literature for over forty years, and, since 1965, a member of the Chicago Society of Biblical Research. In 1976 he was elected a member of *Studiorium Novi Testamenti Societas*. But it is his involvement in another society that especially comes to mind. On October 26, 1970, at a New York café across the street from the host hotel of the SBL Annual Meeting, a small group of scholars formed what they called the "Tyndale Committee." This grew out of an interest in the British "Tyndale Fellowship" and the Tyndale House research library in Cambridge. Included in this group were E. Earle Ellis and his former housemate from the master's program at the Wheaton College Graduate School, Jerry Hawthorne. Three years later in Chicago, under the leadership of Ellis and Hawthorne, the "Tyndale Committee" became the Institute for Biblical Research (IBR).[6] Hawthorne eventually served sixteen years as the treasurer of IBR (1973-89) and four years as president (1989-93).

Coupled with an involvement in the academy, however, has always been an involvement in the community and the church — whether as president of the Holmes School PTA or an elder at LaGrange Gospel Chapel or Bethany Chapel in Wheaton. But the community within which Hawthorne is best known is the Wheaton College community. He has served as a faculty freshman counselor, a class sponsor, an advisor for Student Council, an

---

5. The thesis also included the most complete list of Greek words in Melito at the time. Hawthorne maintained an interest in patristics generally, and in Melito and his *Paschal Homily* in particular, as can be seen in many of his essays, articles, and book reviews.

6. On the founding of IBR, and the close association with Tyndale House in Cambridge, see E. Earle Ellis, "Institute for Biblical Research 1973-1993: Prologue and Prospects," *BBR* 4 (1994): 35-40. Additional information has been provided by Prof. Ellis in personal correspondence, October 3, 2001.

advisor for the Foreign Missions Fellowship, and a member of the Red Cross Coordinating Committee. He also served as vice-chair of the faculty for four years (1981-85) and was head of the faculty council during the selection process of President J. Richard Chase as the successor to Hudson T. Armerding. In 1985 Hawthorne was honored by the Wheaton College Alumni Association as Alumnus of the Year in recognition of such service.

Perhaps one of the most memorable ways in which Hawthorne has fostered community at Wheaton has been through "Jerry's Pub." In the mid-1970s, Hawthorne and Arthur A. Rupprecht, his fellow Greek professor and long-time colleague, joined a group of their students late on Friday afternoons for a cup of coffee in the Student Union (the "Stupe"). These gatherings consisted not only of discussions of theological issues and difficult Greek passages, but also light-hearted conversation. In time, the throng outgrew their corner booth in the Stupe. When a new chapel schedule allotted a free hour on Wednedsays, John Ortberg and his housemates invited the group to meet during this time in Windsor House (the faculty were to provide donuts — the Windsor men coffee). Windsor House continued to host this circle of students and faculty from all disciplines until library expansion necessitated its demolition. The meetings next moved to Kay House, then to Hidden House. After more than a decade of this community's life, another change in schedule returned chapel to Wednesdays. Most faculty participants, however, did not wish to surrender this special time for the exchange of ideas and, "with no desire to flaunt chapel, nor to encourage students to 'skip,'" it was decided that all who wished could come to Hawthorne's office at the traditionally designated time. As many as eighteen professors from various departments across the humanities, the arts, and the sciences crammed into his small office for their weekly repast of coffee and donuts. The late Dr. Joe McClatchey, Professor of English, dubbed the place and the congregation "Jerry's Pub," a name it still holds, though it presently meets now on Tuesdays and Thursdays — creating no chapel conflict in Prof. Rupprecht's office. [7]

Throughout his more than forty-year career at Wheaton, the syllabus for Hawthorne's beginning Greek class laid out the three things every student needed to know about the Greek language: Greek is difficult, Greek is

---

7. G. F. Hawthorne, "A Brief Overview of the Pub's History," and A. A. Rupprecht, "Jerry's Pub" (*Jerry's Pub,* special exhibition at Buswell Memorial Library, Wheaton College).

fun, and Greek is important. Teaching his students both to love and to apply themselves to Greek, Hawthorne strove to instill in them a sense of the academic and devotional importance of Greek for the study of the NT. The Wheaton College community has honored his excellence in teaching multiple times. Hawthorne was voted Teacher of the Year in 1963 and 1980 — he was the first faculty member to be awarded both the junior and senior Teacher of the Year awards. His teaching accolades also extended beyond the college. Distinguished for being a scholar-educator, Hawthorne was a Danforth Associate from 1965 to 1975. And in 1990-91 he was awarded the Sears-Roebuck Foundation Teaching Excellence and Campus Leadership Award, "in recognition of outstanding contributions to undergraduate education, student learning, and campus life." Hawthorne also shared his gift as a teacher with seminary students through the position of visiting professor at North Park Theological Seminary of Chicago in 1972 and again in 1981, and at Northern Baptist Theological Seminary (Oakbrook, Ill.) in 1973-74. Even after retirement, Hawthorne's role as a teacher at Wheaton has not ended.

The ideals he propounds in the classroom are also embodied in his own research and writing. Hawthorne's research and publications have covered an array of interests, from early Christian pneumatology to patristics, and from early Christian prophets and prophecy to the Greek text of the NT and its translation.[8] As of 1969, Hawthorne was the author of a column on the Greek language appearing in *Eternity* magazine. He also served as a member of the editorial board for the *New International Version,* was responsible for the notes on Colossians in the *NIV Study Bible,* and acted as a theological reviewer for the *Life Application Bible.* His commitment to publication and research has also been honored. In 1968, 1977, and 1984, Hawthorne was awarded Wheaton Alumni Association Faculty Research Grants. In 1984 his Philippians commentary was selected as *The Bible Newsletter*'s Book of the Year for Academic Commentaries.

When he decided to retire after over four decades of teaching at Wheaton College, it was clear what an impact Professor Hawthorne had made in the lives of his students, colleagues, and friends. That impact has been recognized in a number of ways. One visible example was the standing ovation on Hawthorne's behalf in Edman Chapel upon his retirement in 1995. That same year, in honor of Jerry and Jane Hawthorne's service

---

8. A complete list of Hawthorne's publications is found on pp. 241-44 below.

and through a large, specified donation, Wheaton College established the Hawthorne House. Fittingly situated near Tyndale House in Cambridge, with which Hawthorne has strong ties from many summers and sabbaticals spent there, this house provides a residence for Wheaton professors on sabbatical as they both rest and research in Cambridge. Generous donations by friends and alumni of the college also enabled the Gerald F. Hawthorne Chair of New Testament Greek and Exegesis to be established, a position filled by Scott J. Hafemann (Dr.theol., Tübingen), who has continued Hawthorne's tradition of inspiring students to approach the Greek language enthusiastically as a tool for better understanding Scripture. This *Festschrift*, named for that chair, is intended as one more way of recognizing the incredible legacy of Gerald Hawthorne in the lives of his peers and students.

Throughout the years, over thirty-six hundred students, many more than could contribute to this *Festschrift* or be mentioned herein, have studied Greek at Wheaton College under Hawthorne's tutelage.[9] Dozens of them have subsequently contributed to the study of the NT. Some have greatly enhanced the production of scholarly work in biblical studies through publishing and technology. Several others have since distinguished themselves in other subdisciplines of theology, such as Hebrew Bible, church history, theological ethics, systematic theology, liturgical studies, and philosophy of religion. Still others are known for their work in English literature, history, Egyptology, philosophy, classics or psychology. From university and seminary administrators and faculty, to ordained and lay ministers, Hawthorne's impact, through his students, on both the academy and the church is difficult to overestimate.[10]

Hawthorne has aptly described disciples, teachers, and their relationship as follows:

> A disciple was a learner, a person actively engaged in the process of acquiring a practical skill or theoretical knowledge. The acquisition of such skills and knowledge in antiquity, however, was gained primarily (perhaps exclusively) not from books or scrolls but rather from teachers — that is, from people who were recognized and respected for the ability they possessed as artisans or for the attractiveness of their per-

---

9. Castañeda, "Jerry's Pub," 7.
10. For a sampling of these individuals, see the Tabula Gratulatoria on pp. 249-52 below.

sons and the power of the ideas that they promulgated. There is thus no disciple without a teacher.[11]

Gerald F. Hawthorne is truly an artisan of the Greek language and a man to whom all are attracted for his character and integrity. On this fiftieth anniversary of the inception of his teaching career at Wheaton College, we, his *discipuli,* pay our teacher tribute.

A. M. DONALDSON, *Notre Dame*
T. B. SAILORS, *Tübingen*

---

11. Gerald F. Hawthorne, "The Imitation of Christ: Discipleship in Philippians," in *Patterns of Discipleship in the New Testament* (ed. Richard N. Longenecker; McMaster New Testament Studies; Grand Rapids: Eerdmans, 1996), 163.

Part I

GREEK AND EXEGESIS

Lexical Glosses and Definitions of Θεραπεύω

David E. Aune

The verb θεραπεύω has a number of distinct meanings that belong to several different semantic domains, though the basic meaning is "to render assistance or help by performing certain duties, often of a humble or menial nature," that is, "to help, serve."[1] In this discussion I focus on certain problems presented by those meanings of θεραπεύω that belong to the subdomain of "health, vigor, strength," part of the more comprehensive semantic domain of "physiological processes and states."[2] The proposal for which I argue in this essay is that in the semantic subdomain of "health, vigor, strength," θεραπεύω exhibits three distinct but related semantic meanings, the last two of which can be ambiguously glossed (i.e., given the translation equivalent) "heal, cure": (1) "to nurse or care for someone who is sick," that is, "to nurse, care for"; (2) "to help someone who is sick recover physical health by providing medical treatment," that is, "to cure, heal, treat successfully"; and (3) "to cause someone to recover physical health immediately, without medical treatment or nursing," that is, "to cure, heal" (referred to below as definitions 1, 2, and 3, respectively). These definitions are based on two different sets of ideas, "caring for or treating

---

1. In L&N 1:460, it comes under the subdomain of "Serve," part of the semantic domain of "Help, Care For."

2. Using the convenient categorization of semantic domains presented in L&N 1:268-69.

11

the sick" and "curing or healing the sick." The first set provides the basis for the first definition, the second set provides the basis for the third definition, and both sets are combined in the second definition. I also argue that none of the three definitions has a figurative extension of meaning in the NT.

Greek words for healing have been subjected to a lengthy study by Louise Wells, who placed particular emphasis on comparing and contrasting ἰάομαι and θεραπεύω.[3] Though her work provides fine discussions of many important texts, her lexicographical methodology proves ultimately disappointing. In this article I want to respond to Wells's book by attempting to clarify some of the lexical problems presented by θεραπεύω, to propose some specific definitions of this lexeme, and to critique some of the more vulnerable proposals made by Wells.

Lexical Problems

The term θεραπεύω presents several lexical problems. One involves the categories of meaning proposed by existing lexicons. It is striking, for example, that the premier Greek-English lexicon, Liddell-Scott-Jones-McKenzie,[4] even in its most recent revision,[5] provides no appropriate category for the meaning of θεραπεύω in thirty-seven of forty-one occurrences in the Gospels and Acts. In those NT contexts, θεραπεύω can be glossed "heal, cure," which may be more closely defined as "to cause someone to recover physical health immediately without intervening medical treatment or nursing" (particularly in narrative contexts where θεραπεύω is used to describe or report the healing activity of Jesus or his followers; definition 3).[6] Similarly,

---

3. L. Wells, *The Greek Language of Healing from Homer to New Testament Times* (BZNW 83; Berlin and New York: de Gruyter, 1998).

4. H. G. Liddell and R. Scott, *A Greek-English Lexicon* (rev. H. S. Jones and R. McKenzie; 9th ed.; Oxford: Clarendon, 1940), 792-93. The same can be said for the most extensive of all Greek lexicons, one from which Liddell and Scott derived a great deal of data, H. Estienne, *Thesaurus Graecae Linguae* (ed. K. B. Hase, W. Dindorf, and L. Dindorf; 1865; repr. Graz: Akademische Druck- u. Verlagsanstalt, 1954), 5:321-23.

5. P. G. W. Glare and A. A. Thompson, *Greek-English Lexicon: Revised Supplement* (Oxford: Clarendon, 1996), 150, where two new glosses are added, "of embalming" and "caulk."

6. The following is a list of the thirty-seven occurrences of θεραπεύω that have this meaning: Matt 4:23, 24; 8:7, 16; 9:35; 10:1, 8; 12:10, 15, 22; 14:14; 15:30; 17:16, 18; 19:2; 21:14; Mark

Moulton and Milligan do not have a category for satisfactorily translating these thirty-seven occurrences of θεραπεύω in the Gospels and Acts, a fact explained by the relatively restricted nature of their lexical focus. Observing that William Ramsay (arguing against W. K. Hobart's thesis of the medical language of Luke) maintained that θεραπεύω, as a *medical term,* means strictly "treat medically" rather than "heal," Moulton and Milligan argue that both papyri and inscriptions confirm this judgment.[7] I think that this view is correct, for the use of θεραπεύω in the Gospels is nonmedical in the sense that individuals are healed immediately, apart from the application of an extended medical regimen.

Another problem with the lexicography of θεραπεύω is that it is far from evident when the distinct meaning "to cause someone to recover physical health immediately without intervening medical treatment or nursing" (definition 3) developed, given the tendency of lexicographers to gloss rather than define Greek lexemes, a procedure that fosters unclarity and ambiguity, since both of the definitions of θεραπεύω presented in the preceding paragraph can be translated "cure, heal."

Specific Definitions

At this point I focus on occurrences of θεραπεύω that Wells or others translate ambiguously as "heal" or "cure," in order to discover whether the frequent definition of θεραπεύω in the Gospels and Acts as "to cause someone to recover physical health immediately, without medical treatment or nursing" (definition 3), occurs elsewhere. In her account of how ἰάομαι and θεραπεύω are used in the Septuagint, Wells is generally correct in claiming that ἰάομαι is used of the healing activity of God, while θεραπεύω is used of the activity of humans.[8] She cites Tob 12:3 (MSS AB), in the context of other occurrences of θεραπεύω and ἰάομαι, as a particularly good example of how the meanings of the two lexemes are kept separate:

1:34; 3:2, 10; 6:5; Luke 4:40; 5:15; 6:7, 18; 7:21; 8:2; 9:1, 6; 10:9; 13:14 (bis); 14:3; John 5:10; Acts 4:14; 5:16; 8:7; 28:9.

7. MM, 289.

8. Wells, *Greek Language of Healing,* 103-4.

ὅτι με ἀγείοχέν σοι ὑγιῆ καὶ τὴν γυναῖκά μου ἐθεράπευσεν καὶ τὸ ἀργύριόν μου ἤνεγκεν καὶ σὲ ὁμοίως ἐθεράπευσεν.

Because he led me to you in health and *cured* my wife and he brought my money and he also *cured* you.[9]

According to Wells, the narrator (aware that God is using the heart, liver, and gall of the fish to solve Tobit's blindness and free Sarah of the evil demon Asmodeus) has Tobit use the verb θεραπεύω because Tobit thinks that Raphael is a *human* friend. The narrator, however, uses ἰάομαι (3:17), and, since he knows that Raphael is really an angelic messenger from *God*, has Raphael use the verb ἰάομαι when he speaks of healing (6:9; 12:14).[10] Wells is quite correct in this analysis.[11] However, one significant aspect of θεραπεύω that she does not discuss is the meaning of the gloss "heal" as a translation of the two occurrences of θεραπεύω in 12:3.[12] Other translators prefer the gloss "cure," or even a combination of the two,[13] but these translation equivalents are no less ambiguous than "heal." These two occurrences of θεραπεύω in 12:3 are the only instances in which the editors of *A Greek-English Lexicon of the Septuagint (GELS)* suggest that θεραπεύω should be translated "heal."[14] While these translations are of course not incorrect, they are obviously ambiguous in that they do not reflect a specific definition of the meaning of θεραπεύω. Since the restoration of Tobit's

---

9. Unless otherwise stated, the translations of Greek texts are mine.

10. Wells, *Greek Language of Healing*, 109-10.

11. This point is also made by P. Deselaers, *Das Buch Tobit: Studien zu seiner Entstehung, Komposition und Theologie* (OBO 43; Göttingen: Vandenhoeck & Ruprecht; Freiburg, Switzerland: Universitätsverlag, 1982), 187-89; and by C. A. Moore, *Tobit: A New Translation with Introduction and Commentary* (AB 40A; New York: Doubleday, 1996), 268.

12. Wells, *Greek Language of Healing*, 349.

13. For "cure" in Tob 12:3 see NAB; NJB; F. Zimmermann, *The Book of Tobit: An English Translation with Introduction and Commentary* (New York: Harper & Brothers, 1958), 109; Moore, *Tobit*, 267. Both occurrences of θεραπεύω are translated "cure" in NRSV and REB. These translators preferred, apparently on the basis of English usage, to use "cure" for relieving Sarah of demon oppression and "heal" for restoring the sight of Tobit.

14. *GELS* 1:204. The single gloss "dienen" (representing the basic meaning of θεραπεύω) is given in F. Rehkopf, *Septuaginta-Vokabular* (Göttingen: Vandenhoeck & Ruprecht, 1989), 139. The religious meaning of θεραπεύω in the LXX and its relationship to λειτουργέω are discussed by S. Daniel, *Recherches sur le vocabulaire du culte dans le Septante* (Paris: C. Klincksieck, 1966), 107-8, 112.

eyesight and the freeing of Sarah from demonic influence are accomplished through the medicinal use of the heart, liver, and gall of a fish (6:4, 6-8; 8:1-3; 11:7-8, 11-14),[15] their "healing" is the result of medical treatment,[16] so that in this context θεραπεύω should be defined as "to treat or nurse someone in such a way that they recover physical health," that is, "to treat successfully" (definition 2).

Another text discussed by Wells is the late (160 c.e.) Apellas inscription from Epidauros (*IG²* 1, no. 126), where a key phrase reads:

καὶ τὸν ἱερέα λέγειν "τεθράπευσαι χρὴ δὲ ἀποδιδόναι τὰ ἴατρα."

And the priest said: "You are cured but you must pay up the thank offerings."[17]

In line 20, however, τεθράπευσαι does not mean "you are cured" or "you have been cured," but rather "you have undergone treatment," for Apellas is not yet fully and completely cured. The narrative of his treatment continues in lines 22-31, and only the final "health" formula in line 32 indicates complete restoration to health: χάριν εἰδὼς καὶ ὑγιὴς γενόμενος ἀπηλλάγην, "Full of gratitude, I departed well."[18] Elsewhere Wells observes, in connection with the evidence from the Hippocratic corpus linked to Kos, that "It [θεραπεύω] is rarely used in the aorist tense, and if it appears in the perfect tense it usually describes a present state achieved by long and regular therapies."[19] In a footnote she specifically mentions this occurrence of the verb θεραπεύω in the Apellas inscription.[20]

Another interesting occurrence of θεραπεύω in the Septuagint is in Sir 38:6-7:

---

15. Parallels with treatments for blindness in the ancient Near East are discussed in Moore, *Tobit*, 201-2.

16. Deselaers, *Tobit*, 188n.304.

17. Text and translation from E. J. Edelstein and L. Edelstein, *Asclepius: A Collection and Interpretation of the Testimonies* (2 vols.; Baltimore: Johns Hopkins Univ. Press, 1945), 1:247-48.

18. This inscription is briefly mentioned in MM 289, who propose the translation "treatment has been prescribed for you, and you must pay the physician's fee." They also observe that the actual treatment is to follow.

19. Wells, *Greek Language of Healing*, 82.

20. Ibid., 82n.607.

καὶ αὐτὸς ἔδωκεν ἀνθρώποις ἐπιστήμην
ἐνδοξάζεσθαι ἐν τοῖς θαυμασίοις αὐτοῦ·
ἐν αὐτοῖς ἐθεράπευσεν καὶ ἦρεν τὸν πόνον αὐτοῦ

And he gave skill to men
that he [or they] might be glorified in his marvelous works.
By them he *heals* and takes away pain.

This passage affirms that it is God who works through the physician, for it is God who is the grammatical subject of the verb ἐθεράπευσεν, parallel with the statement a few verses earlier in 38:2: παρὰ γὰρ ὑψίστου ἐστὶν ἴασις, "healing is from the Most High." While ἐθεράπευσεν is glossed "heals," it could more appropriately be glossed "provides treatment," since the result of that treatment "takes away pain."

In the Gospels and Acts, θεραπεύω occurs forty-one times. As I have already mentioned, in thirty-seven instances it can be glossed "to heal, cure," a nonmedical use of the lexeme that assumes the immediate restoration of health without the type of interventions characteristic of ancient medical treatment or nursing (definition 3). A clear example of this meaning occurs in Matt 8:16:

Ὀψίας δὲ γενομένης προσήνεγκαν αὐτῷ δαιμονιζομένους πολλούς·
καὶ ἐξέβαλεν τὰ πνεύματα λόγῳ
καὶ πάντας τοὺς κακῶς ἔχοντας ἐθεράπευσεν.

Now when it was evening, people brought him many who were
demon possessed,
and he expelled the spirits with a word,
and he *healed* all those who were ill.

Here the context makes clear that θεραπεύω may be defined "to cause someone to recover physical health immediately, without medical treatment or nursing," that is, "to cure, heal" (definition 3). Closely similar definitions have been proposed by other scholars: according to H. W. Beyer, "θεραπεύω is used much more often in the sense of 'to heal,' and always in such a way that the reference is not to medical treatment, which might fail, but to real healing."[21] W. Grimm has proposed the meaning "to heal (mi-

21. H. W. Beyer, "θεραπεία, θεραπεύω, θεράπων," *TDNT* 3:129.

raculously)" or "make whole," and Morton Smith has defined this use of Θεραπεύω as to "cure by a miracle,"[22] both similar to my definition 3. Surprisingly, however, this frequent meaning of Θεραπεύω in the Synoptic Gospels finds little support in the Louw-Nida lexicon (L&N), which defines Θεραπεύω as "to cause someone to recover health, often with the implication of having taken care of such a person."[23] The problem with this definition is that the term "often" applies to just three occurrences of Θεραπεύω in the Gospels and Acts (Mark 6:13; Luke 4:23; 8:43),[24] and (perhaps) two further occurrences in the rest of the NT (Rev 13:3, 12); that is, the second part of the definition, which includes the element of care or medical treatment, is only exceptionally the meaning of Θεραπεύω in the NT. This definition would be acceptable were it crafted to describe one of the specific meanings of Θεραπεύω in ancient Greek usage generally, but this is not the intention of the definition, for L&N treats the Greek of the NT as a self-contained linguistic world. The L&N definition of ἰάομαι (and related lexemes), on the other hand, applies equally well to the use of Θεραπεύω: "to cause someone to become well again after having been sick."[25] That Θεραπεύω and ἰάομαι overlap in meaning in the Gospels can be demonstrated from two closely parallel passages in Luke:

καὶ συνήρχοντο ὄχλοι πολλοὶ ἀκούειν καὶ θεραπεύεσθαι ἀπὸ τῶν ἀσθενειῶν αὐτῶν.

And a large crowd gathered to hear and to be *healed* from their ailments. (Luke 5:15)

οἳ ἦλθον ἀκοῦσαι αὐτοῦ καὶ ἰαθῆναι ἀπὸ τῶν νόσων αὐτῶν.

They came to hear him and to be *healed* from their diseases. (Luke 6:18)

The shared meaning of Θεραπεύω and ἰάομαι is also evident in passages of Luke-Acts where these lexemes occur as virtual synonyms (Luke 8:43, 47;

---

22. W. Grimm, "θεραπεύω," *EDNT* 2:143-44; M. Smith, "De tuenda sanitate praecepta (Moralia 122B-137E)," in *Plutarch's Ethical Writings and Early Christian Literature* (ed. H. D. Betz; SCHNT 4; Leiden: Brill, 1978), 35.
23. L&N 1:269.
24. In Acts 17:25 θεραπεύω means "to serve" in the specific sense of "to worship a deity."
25. L&N 1:269.

14:3-4; Acts 28:8-9). This has important implications for the lexical definition of ἰάομαι that we cannot explore at this time.

The foremost Greek-English lexicon of the NT and early Christian literature, BAGD, suggests two main glosses for θεραπεύω: (1) "serve" (the basic meaning of the word) and (2) "care for, wait upon, treat (medically)," including "heal, restore."[26] After "heal, restore," a series of passages are listed that provide examples of that meaning (Athenaeus 522B; *SIG*³ 1004, 21; 1168, 126; 1170, 20; 1171, 7; 1172, 5; Tob 12:3; Sir 38:7). Glosses can be both ambiguous and deceptive, however, for in each of these texts (with the possible exception of *SIG*³ 1004, 21),[27] it is my view that θεραπεύω means "to treat someone medically in such a way that they recover physical health" (definition 2). The literary text cited, Athenaeus *Deipnosophistae* 522B, reads as follows:

θεραπεύσας δ' ὁ Δημοκήδης Ἄτοσσαν τὴν Δαρείου μὲν γυναῖκα, Κύρου δὲ θυγατέρα, τὸν μαστὸν ἀλγήσασαν.

Democedes cured Atossa, the wife of Darius and daughter of Cyrus, who had a painful breast.

Here the aorist form of θεραπεύω could refer to a recovery of physical health without medical therapy were it not for the fact that Democedes has just been identified in the narrative as an ἰατρός, so it is likely that in this context θεραπεύω means "to treat someone medically in such a way that they recover physical health" (definition 2). The majority of the remaining texts cited under meaning (2) in BAGD are from the Synoptic Gospels (Matt 4:24; 8:7, 16; 10:8; Mark 1:34; 3:2, 10; Luke 4:23; etc.). In each of these texts θεραπεύω means "to cause someone to recover physical health immediately without recourse to medical treatment or nursing" (definition 3).

---

26. BAGD 359. The entry in the 6th German edition remained essentially unchanged from the 5th German edition, though a few more texts were referred to in support of meaning (2) in W. Bauer, *Griechisch-deutsches Wörterbuch zu den Schriften des Neuen Testaments und der frühchristlichen Literatur* (ed. K. Aland and B. Aland; 6th ed.; Berlin and New York: de Gruyter, 1988), 729.

27. It it unclear whether this 4th-century-B.C.E. inscription is an exception, for it reads: ἐπαρχὴν δὲ διδοῦν τὸμ μέλλοντα θεραπεύεσθαι ὑπὸ τοῦ θεοῦ μὴ ἔλαττον ἐννεοβόλου δοκίμου ἀργυρίου, "And that the person who will be healed by the god give an offering of not less than nine obols of attested silver." Here θεραπεύεσθαι could mean "to be healed (without recourse to medical treatment)" (definition 3), or (more likely, since it is a present infinitive) "to be cured successfully after a regimen of treatment" (definition 2).

In Frederick Danker's recent translation and revision of the sixth edition by Aland and Aland of the *Griechisch-deutsches Wörterbuch* by Walter Bauer, known by the acronym BDAG, the two basic categories of meaning for θεραπεύω are (1) "**to render service or homage,** *serve* a divinity," and (2) *"heal, restore,"* about which it is said that "a ready transference is made to this mng. from the use of θ. in the var. senses of 'care for, wait upon, treat medically.'"[28] While this new English revision of the Bauer-Aland lexicon makes greater use of definitions of Greek words than any of its predecessors (boldface roman is used for definitions, boldface italics for glosses),[29] in the case of θεραπεύω, the first basic meaning is defined, while the second basic meaning is conveyed through glosses. Further, in the second category of meaning, the clusters of glosses have been placed in reverse order for no apparent reason, when compared with the original German of Bauer-Aland[6] (carried over into BDAG), which uses the following glosses: "**besorgen, ärztlich behandeln,** dann auch **heilen, herstellen.**"[30]

To this point I have focused on the ways in which definition 3 has been treated by lexicographers; there are, however, three healing stories in the Gospels that apparently depict Jesus providing medical treatment to sick people. In the story of the healing of the deaf-mute in Mark 7:31-37, Jesus puts his fingers in the man's ears and spits on his tongue. In the story of the healing of the blind man in Mark 8:22-26, Jesus spits on the man's eyes, while in the healing of the man born blind at Bethsaida, narrated in John 9:1-7, Jesus anoints the man's eyes with a mixture of clay and spit. It is not correct to say that "Heilmittel werden nicht erwähnt"[31] in these narratives, however valid that statement might be for other healing stories. However, in none of these pericopae are the lexemes θεραπεύω or ἰάομαι or their cognates used. Had θεραπεύω been used in any or all of these narratives to describe the healing, it would be a lexical outlier, for it would have to be defined in accordance with definition 2 as "to help someone who is sick recover physical health by providing medical treatment." For whatever rea-

---

28. I am grateful to Professor Danker for providing me with an advance copy of the θεραπεύω entry while I was working on this article.

29. F. W. Danker, *Lexical Evolution and Linguistic Hazard* (Chicago: Univ. of Chicago Press, 2000), 17-18.

30. Bauer, *Griechisch-deutsches Wörterbuch*[6], 729.

31. O. Betz, "Heilung/Heilungen I," in *Theologische Realenzyklopädie*, vol. 14 (ed. G. Krause and G. Müller; Berlin: de Gruyter, 1985), 764.

son, the tradition did not countenance the inclusion of θεραπεύω in any of these three contexts.

There is, however, a text that narrates the preaching and healing ministry of the disciples rather than Jesus in which a particular type of medical therapy is mentioned — anointing with oil (Mark 6:12-13):

καὶ ἐξελθόντες ἐκήρυξαν ἵνα μετανοῶσιν, καὶ δαιμόνια πολλὰ ἐξέβαλλον, καὶ ἤλειφον ἐλαίῳ πολλοὺς ἀρρώστους καὶ ἐθεράπευον.

And after departing, they preached that people should repent, and they cast out many demons, and they were anointing with oil and healing many sick people.

The meaning of this passage is debated, since there is a strong theologically motivated tendency to avoid the obvious implication that the use of oil is medicinal (as many ancient texts confirm; cf. Luke 10:34; Jas 5:14; Josephus *B.J.* 1.657), whatever its supposed symbolic or sacramental significance.[32] That the two imperfect verbs are coordinated with one object, πολλοὺς ἀρρώστους, strongly suggests the medicinal use of oil, so that θεραπεύω here conforms to definition 2, that is, "to help someone who is sick recover physical health by providing medical treatment."

Figurative Extensions of Meaning for Θεραπεύω?

In summarizing her analysis of Greek words for healing in the Synoptic Gospels, Wells claims that "θεραπεύω is primarily a spiritual term, but it can have a holistic effect, affecting the physical, mental, and emotional state of a person, as well as a person's spiritual state."[33] I think that this statement is completely wrong, for θεραπεύω is always used of literal, physical healing in the NT, *never* in a figurative sense.[34] How does Wells ar-

32. Many ancient references are collected in W. K. Hobart, *The Medical Language of St. Luke* (Dublin: Hodges, Figgis; London: Longmans, Green, 1882), 28-29.

33. Wells, *Greek Language of Healing*, 154-55.

34. In Acts 17:25 θεραπεύω is used with the meaning "serve," and so belongs to a different semantic domain. Even in Luke 4:23, where the author has Jesus quote the proverb, "Ἰατρέ, θεράπευσον σεαυτόν," θεραπεύω is used semantically in a literal sense (against Wells, *Greek Language of Healing*, 148-49), though readers are obviously invited to understand the proverb in an analogous figurative sense such as "be consistent," or "do what you

rive at this figurative definition of θεραπεύω? Since her discussion is extensive, I can select only a few examples of the kinds of arguments she advances. In one instance Wells cites a number of passages from Matthew (4:24; 8:16; 12:15; 14:14; 15:30; 19:2; 21:14) and claims that "in every instance this behaviour is accompanied by the activities of preaching and teaching."[35] She then draws a glorious non sequitur: "Since Matthew places all these instances in a teaching context, the inference is that θεραπεύω refers to spiritual, rather than physical, healing."[36] Elsewhere she refers to the cognate noun θεραπεία, which is used with ἰάομαι in Luke 9:11: καὶ ἀποδεξάμενος αὐτοὺς ἐλάλει αὐτοῖς περὶ τῆς βασιλείας τοῦ θεοῦ, καὶ τοὺς χρείαν ἔχοντας θεραπείας ἰᾶτο. Wells integrates this passage into her figurative understanding of θεραπεύω and ἰάομαι by concluding that "in keeping with the verbal use of θεραπεύω in crowd scenes, the therapy appears to be Jesus' message about the kingdom of God."[37] However, just because some of those people who listened to Jesus' message were healed of their diseases does not mean that θεραπεύω should be understood figuratively. The author appears to be guided by the conviction that "the notion of *cure* . . . is completely foreign to θεραπεύω" and that therefore θεραπεύω in the Gospels and Acts must have a spiritual (or figurative) meaning.[38]

Conclusion

In this brief discussion I have argued that unless lexemes such as θεραπεύω are defined, the modern language glosses used as translation equivalents may serve to camouflage rather than reveal their contextual meaning. The distinctive meaning that θεραπεύω has in thirty-seven occurrences in the Synoptic Gospels and Acts becomes obvious only when the word is carefully defined. I have defined this distinctive meaning as "to cause someone

---

tell others to do." Figurative extensions of θεραπεύω referring to spiritual healing occur in 2d- and 3d-century Christian literature (e.g., 2 *Clem.* 9:7; Clement of Alexandria, *Paed.* 1.8; Origen, *Cels.* 8.72). The figurative extension of the medical meaning of θεραπεύω is found earlier in Diodorus Siculus 4.41.3, where the term means "repair, restore," of the parts of a ship that become worn during use.

35. Wells, *Greek Language of Healing,* 138-39.
36. Ibid., 139.
37. Ibid., 153.
38. Ibid., 76.

to recover physical health immediately, without medical treatment or nursing" (definition 3). While I have found no other occurrences of θεραπεύω earlier than the Gospels and Acts that exhibit this contextual meaning, though it occurs in second- and third-century Christian texts,[39] that does not mean that they will not be revealed upon closer investigation. Finally, contrary to the contention of Wells, θεραπεύω is never used in a figurative or spiritual sense in the Gospels and Acts.

39. G. W. H. Lampe, ed., *Patristic Greek Lexicon* (Oxford: Clarendon, 1961), 645.

Exegetical Rigor with Hermeneutical Humility: The Calvinist-Arminian Debate and the New Testament

William W. Klein

The honoree of this *Festschrift,* Professor Jerry Hawthorne, has always been known on the campus of Wheaton College and beyond for his gracious spirit and love for students. Only God knows how many people continue as serious students and scholars of the Bible because they loved to study Greek with Dr. Hawthorne! In many ways he embodies two traits that I would like to pursue in this essay, and which we so desperately need among interpreters today. One is what I will call "hermeneutical humility" (to be explained below). The second is a meticulous concern for the meaning of the text — exegetical rigor. I am personally grateful for Jerry's uncompromising teaching of Greek and his example of exegetical integrity in both his classes at Wheaton and in his scholarly output. May his example provide the model for many to follow, for the sake of Christ and his kingdom.

In a recent conference at Denver Seminary on contextualizing biblical exegesis, I closed my presentation by citing the following experience.

> I remember a chapel speaker here a decade or so ago — Samuel Escobar, a Latin American scholar who was currently teaching in North America. He told us that in his speaking both north and south of the border with Mexico, he would often ask people in his audiences to interpret Jesus' familiar expression, "The poor you always have with you" (John 12:8). The typical North American interpretation was something like, "No matter what efforts are expended to help the poor,

there will always be poor people." Then he recited the explanation of a Mexican woman in an out-of-the-way barrio. She interpreted Jesus' words to mean, "There will always be rich people to exploit us." The two answers say something very different about the contexts of the interpreters.

Of course, anyone who is familiar with teaching the Bible, or engages in formal exegesis of biblical texts, or reads contemporary literature on hermeneutics, has had to contend with this phenomenon. People in different contexts interpret the Bible very differently.[1] On a simple level, many of us have had the experience of listening to a sermon and asking at some point, "I wonder how the preacher got *that* out of the passage? I don't think the author had that in mind at all." Perhaps "that" was not the author's intent, but does that matter? Sometimes what we bring to the text determines what we get out of it. That is precisely the point at issue in this essay.

All who attempt to interpret — whether it be the words of a dear friend, an article in a local newspaper, or any human communication, for that matter — do so on the basis of their "preunderstandings."[2] We all bring to a text our own suppositions and assumptions about the world based on our prior experiences, training, and thinking, and we "interpret our experiences on the basis of these presuppositions,"[3] whether they are true, somewhat true, or false. These beliefs and attitudes constitute our preunderstandings, and they inevitably shape our understanding and perception of reality. "No one is free from them; it is impossible to interpret reality in a 'totally objective' way."[4] There are no neutral observers. If I say "car," you immediately bring to your hearing and interpretation of that

1. For an introduction to the complexities of interpreting cross-culturally, see, inter alia, C. H. Felder, ed., *Stony the Road We Trod: African American Biblical Interpretation* (Minneapolis: Fortress, 1991); D. Smith-Christopher, ed., *Text and Experience: Towards a Cultural Exegesis of the Bible* (Biblical Seminar 35; Sheffield: Sheffield Academic Press, 1995); R. S. Sugirtharajah, *Voices from the Margin: Interpreting the Bible in the Third World* (2d ed.; London: SPCK; Maryknoll, N.Y.: Orbis, 1995); and J. R. Levison and P. Pope-Levison, eds., *Return to Babel: Global Perspectives on the Bible* (Louisville: Westminster John Knox, 1999).

2. For additional perspective on issues concerning interpreters' preunderstandings see W. W. Klein, C. L. Blomberg, and R. L. Hubbard Jr., *Introduction to Biblical Interpretation* (Dallas: Word, 1993), 98-116, 138-51.

3. Ibid., 99.

4. Ibid.

24

word your prior experiences with cars — be they playing with plastic toys, watching a railroad car, or driving an automobile — and if an automobile, whether an orange Volkswagen "Beetle" or a red Cadillac. We cannot help but bring what we have experienced to our interpretation of life. This is beneficial; it helps us make sense out of our world. But it can also be troublesome. So, let me pose a problem.

Two people observe a basket of yellow apples; one person insists they are red and the other that they are green. That would be peculiar, to be sure. Therefore, we would want to assess several factors, including their skills in discerning colors and their personal integrity in reporting what they see. Perhaps one person had never seen a yellow apple. In her experience green apples ripened into red apples, so her answer was an attempt to make sense of her experience. Perhaps her friend was color blind, and he was interpreting the "color" he saw in light of what he understood the colors to mean. If we assume that neither was being dishonest, then other factors accounted for their erroneous analyses. But note the implication in this final sentence: both interpreters were wrong. Objectively and factually, the apples were yellow. In an experiment such as this there can be only four options: she is correct and he is wrong; he is correct and she is wrong; both are correct; and both are wrong. The yellow color of the apples is the criterion of correct interpretation. Is this also true of biblical texts — that there is a factual or objective reality inherent to the text? In Kevin Vanhoozer's words, "Is there something in the text that reflects a reality independent of the reader's interpretive activity, or does the text only reflect the reality of the reader?"[5] Equally important, is uncovering that reality the goal of interpretation?

My contention in this essay is that the prior commitments of so-called Calvinists and Arminians exert far more force than their proponents are willing to admit and strongly influence, if not determine, their exegetical outcomes.[6] Why are interpreters on both sides so passionately convinced they are right, even when they come to seemingly opposite conclusions? When we encounter the theological words "God's sovereignty," what meaning emerges in our consciousness? What about "free will" or

5. K. J. Vanhoozer, *Is There a Meaning in This Text?* (Grand Rapids: Zondervan, 1998), 15.

6. Of course, I am simply highlighting this theological conundrum for the purposes of this essay. The same problems of interpretation surround other theological discussions and biblical exegesis.

"election"?[7] My point is that we adopt an understanding of these terms on the basis of a larger commitment to reality — our preunderstanding. We do not know what these words *mean* in the same sense that an objective or neutral observer *knows* that the apples are yellow. Interpreters define such theological concepts as God's sovereignty not merely on the basis of their unbiased analysis of the relevant biblical texts, but through the grids of their preunderstandings.

To broaden the discussion: Is one's theology in the end completely determined by one's preunderstandings and prior commitments?[8] Does a specific understanding of a text and, hence, one's theology merely grow out of and confirm that one is a Marxist, feminist, or liberation theologian, mainline liberal, evangelical, dispensationalist, Eastern Orthodox, or fundamentalist (to pick a few labels)? Is that all we are doing? Do interpretations say more about the interpreters and their communities than about the texts they are allegedly interpreting? What do the conclusions truly say about the interpreter?

I wish to clarify what I am *not* asserting: I am not leading up to the conclusion that exegesis is impossible. Rather, I wish to assert that matters are not as simple as performing an "inductive" and honest exegesis of texts. Nor am I saying that all interpreters consciously or invariably twist or subvert the meaning of texts to fit their own preconceived ideas. Some do, no doubt, but I wish to consider only those whose intentions are honest.

In one sense this issue raises the question of the goal of exegesis: is the goal to extract or ascertain the meaning inherent *in* the text, or to *make*

---

7. For a survey of some of the philosophical issues surrounding the uses of some of these terms see D. Basinger and R. Basinger, eds., *Predestination and Free Will* (Downers Grove, Ill.: InterVarsity Press, 1986).

8. In Ukraine I have had several opportunities to teach students from many former Soviet countries. Some have come to study in Denver as well. It always startles me how "Arminian" they are, how they intuitively recoil from the Calvinist perspective. At the same time they typically adopt a "pretribulational" view of Christ's rapture of the church. Without presuming to know all the issues, I wonder whether their experiences of persecution — and their witness of former church members who abandoned the faith — lead them to conclude that people can "lose" salvation. Certainly it is psychologically more satisfying to believe that when the going gets really tough, Christ will remove his saints. Historically, it appears that pretribulationalism was the first Western view presented earlier in the 20th century, and it was taught as the only truly orthodox view. Of course, one cannot base theology on experience, but their experiences may affect how they understand certain texts. Indeed, we all do the same kind of things when we do our exegesis.

sense of a text as creative readers?[9] While most evangelicals are uncomfortable adopting a full-blown "reader-response" approach to biblical interpretation, I believe we are doing precisely that when we come to our conclusions on the Calvinist-Arminian debate. Of course, I am no neutral commentator on the dallyings of the combatants; I have my own strong exegetical and theological opinions concerning the debate.[10] I bring my own preunderstandings to this appraisal of the terrain.

On the one hand we must seriously examine our preunderstandings and do all we can to avoid making texts mean what we consciously or unconsciously want them to mean. On the other hand we must accept that preunderstandings profoundly influence human interpretation. We need to be both conscious of our preunderstandings and skilled in the methods of exegesis. But how do the two interact?

The Bible does contain matters that are indeed difficult to understand, even as Peter admitted about some of Paul's writings (2 Pet 3:15-16). No doubt we all struggle with understanding many enigmas in the Bible. Over the years some formerly problematic issues have been solved, at least to the satisfaction of most scholars. But others, like the interpretation of many questions surrounding the large topic of election, still elude any kind of consensus. While no scholars would presume to say they interpret infallibly, some are more "humble" than others in the degree of confidence they claim. Some settle for an interpretive stance that is willing to live with a tension created by what they find to be biblical realities, such as what they see as the Bible's affirmations that God has selected some people to be saved (and not others) and its insistence on human responsibility or culpability for belief in or rejection of the gospel. Others invoke the category of "mystery" when they encounter texts that do not appear to fit their overall framework of interpretation. For a few, matters are perfectly clear, and all texts fit readily.

Let us look at the tensions more closely by assessing the competing alternatives in the debate. First, scholar A concludes that the most adequate system for explaining God's sovereign will for the salvation of humans is to adopt a so-called Calvinist system. Very simplistically, it might

9. This kind of language occurs in E. V. McKnight, *Postmodern Use of the Bible: The Emergence of Reader-Oriented Criticism* (Nashville: Abingdon, 1988), 150. See also R. Crosman, "Do Readers Make Meaning?" in *The Reader in the Text* (ed. S. Suleiman and R. Crosman; Princeton: Princeton Univ. Press, 1980).

10. Some of these opinions are set out in W. W. Klein, *The New Chosen People: A Corporate View of Election* (Grand Rapids: Zondervan, 1990).

proceed along these lines. Since all humans are incorrigible sinners and dead in sin, such spiritual death precludes their doing anything righteous — much less doing anything to accomplish their salvation. They are all doomed. In his love God initiates salvation to be accomplished by the death of his Son for a certain elect group of those doomed sinners. That is, God selects certain ones (thus election is "particular") to be granted the ability to repent and trust in Christ for their salvation. Whom he selects is a matter of his own sovereign, inscrutable, and loving will, for his own purposes, and this choice was made before the foundation of the world — indeed, before people even existed or committed acts of sin. Nothing in any of the elected sinners motivates God's choice of them for salvation. Those to whom he grants the ability to believe do so without exception, and God preserves them as his own until they die and enter his presence.[11]

In a nutshell, all humans are hopeless and helpless; they can do nothing to secure their salvation. But in his sovereign mercy God selected certain ones to rescue, infusing them alone with the ability to apprehend his salvation, and they unfailingly do so. Those not selected go to their justly deserved fate for their sinfulness: eternal damnation.[12]

Scholar B prefers what has come to be called a more Arminian framework. In this scheme of things many affirmations remain the same as for Calvinists, such as the hopeless condition of human sinfulness and the inability to secure salvation. But the Arminian does not understand "dead in sin" to mean "unable to respond to God's offer of salvation." That is, God provided the way of salvation through Christ's death on the cross, and humans have the capacity (free will) to accept or reject God's provision. Those who repent and believe obtain salvation — a salvation, by the way, totally and completely secured by the actions and love of a sovereign God. But election is not particular. That is, God does not make a prior selection of whom to save but makes a provision of salvation available to all and is-

11. A representative though popular explication of Calvinism is C. S. Storms, *Chosen for Life: An Introductory Guide to the Doctrine of Divine Election* (Grand Rapids: Baker, 1987). On a more scholarly level, see the many essays in T. R. Schreiner and B. A. Ware, eds., *The Grace of God: The Bondage of the Will*, 2 vols. (Grand Rapids: Baker, 1995).

12. Among Calvinists there are further delineations and subtleties, of course. Some posit that God selected both those whom he would save and those whom he would damn ("double predestination"; see, e.g., J. Piper, *The Justification of God* [Grand Rapids: Baker, 1983], esp. 136-99), while others simply affirm God's choice of the saved (e.g., G. R. Lewis and B. A. Demarest, *Integrative Theology*, 3 vols. [Grand Rapids: Zondervan, 1994], 3:17-69).

sues a universal invitation: whosoever will may come. Those who reject God's provision spend eternity in hell.[13]

In a nutshell, all humans are hopeless and helpless; they can do nothing to secure their salvation. But in his sovereign mercy God sent Christ to pay the penalty for human sin and invites all to enjoy the blessings of his salvation. Those who repent and accept his offer will enjoy his salvation. Those who reject this sole means of forgiveness go to their justly deserved fate for their sinfulness: eternal damnation.[14]

It turns out that each scholar encounters texts that do not appear to fit so well into the preferred system. Given my admittedly simplistic description of their position above, Calvinists may squirm over some apparently universalist-sounding texts such as:

> For God so loved the world that he gave his only Son, so that everyone who believes in him may not perish but may have eternal life. (John 3:16)[15]

> This is right and is acceptable in the sight of God our Savior, who desires everyone to be saved and to come to the knowledge of the truth. For there is one God; there is also one mediator between God and humankind, Christ Jesus, himself human, who gave himself a ransom for all — this was attested at the right time. (1 Tim 2:3-6)

> The Lord is not slow about his promise, as some think of slowness, but is patient with you, not wanting any to perish, but all to come to repentance. (2 Pet 3:9)

---

13. A series of essays defending an Arminian perspective is found in C. H. Pinnock, ed., *The Grace of God, the Will of Man: A Case for Arminianism* (Grand Rapids: Zondervan, 1989).

14. Of course, there are also variations among those of a more Arminian persuasion. Some, for example, believe that as one has free will to accept God's offer of salvation, one can also subsequently exercise that same will to recant or apostatize (e.g., I. H. Marshall, *Kept by the Power of God: A Study of Perseverance and Falling Away* [London: Epworth, 1969]). Others see God's actions in salvation as securing forever their status as his people. Some understand God's election to follow logically from his foreknowledge of who will believe and persevere. Others view election in corporate terms: God chose the church in Christ (e.g., R. Shank says, "The Biblical doctrine of election does not require such efficient particular foreknowledge, for the election is primarily corporate and objective and only secondarily particular"; *Elect in the Son* [Springfield, Mo.: Westcott, 1970], 155; see also Klein, *New Chosen People*).

15. All quotations are taken from the NRSV unless otherwise noted.

My little children, I am writing these things to you so that you may not sin. But if anyone does sin, we have an advocate with the Father, Jesus Christ the righteous; and he is the atoning sacrifice for our sins, and not for ours only but also for the sins of the whole world. (1 John 2:1-2)

Conversely, Arminians may have some trouble explaining such texts as:

There is no one who is righteous, not even one; there is no one who has understanding, there is no one who seeks God. All have turned aside, together they have become worthless; there is no one who shows kindness, there is not even one. (Rom 3:10-12)

Everything that the Father gives me will come to me, and anyone who comes to me I will never drive away. . . . And this is the will of him who sent me, that I should lose nothing of all that he has given me, but raise it up on the last day. . . . No one can come to me unless drawn by the Father who sent me; and I will raise that person up on the last day. (John 6:37, 39, 44)

When the Gentiles heard this, they were glad and praised the word of the Lord; and as many as had been destined for eternal life became believers. (Acts 13:48)

So then he has mercy on whomever he chooses, and he hardens the heart of whomever he chooses. . . . What if God, desiring to show his wrath and to make known his power, has endured with much patience the objects of wrath that are made for destruction; . . . and what if he has done so in order to make known the riches of his glory for the objects of mercy, which he has prepared beforehand for glory — including us whom he has called, not from the Jews only but also from the Gentiles? (Rom 9:18, 22-24)

Other difficult texts must be explicated, to be sure, but these highlight some of the issues involved.

What is done with problematic texts such as these? A common tactic, obviously, is to attempt to show how the problematic texts really are consistent with the preferred system, despite initial appearances to the contrary. Or at least interpreters try to show that there is some reading of the text that will enable it to fit into the system. They may in humility agree that their interpretations of some texts are more strained than of others, but they insist that the overall picture is clear enough to warrant the system. They minimize the "offending" texts and relegate them to the closets or attics into which they do not frequently go. They will live with the tension of the texts that do not seem to fit well.

If one existed, what might an "objective" observer say about the interpretation of some of the texts? Are the apples yellow, green, or red? What if the proposed interpretations of several of the texts are too strained or unconvincing? What if the objective observer said that the most exegetically defensible interpretations of the texts are inimical to the system? If even one text denies an essential tenet of the system, can the system remain unscathed? Must the flawed system be jettisoned?

This gives rise to a different and popular approach mentioned above — to claim *mystery* — and this is favored by many Calvinists.[16] That is, they apply the truism, "God's ways are above our ways." In other words, they insist, the text may appear to be contrary to the clear system amply taught elsewhere; and, while it remains paradoxical (some might even say contradictory) for our finite minds, in God's overall plan it fits and makes sense, at least to God. After all, it is stressed, why do we imagine we can understand all the ways of God?

These Calvinists may illustrate this point with the example of the Trinity. Who can understand the orthodox conclusions of the ecumenical councils, that God is of one substance but existing in three persons? Or take Christology: How can Jesus be fully God and fully man? Since we cannot explain some such realities, they argue, why do we balk when we cannot explain all the facets of election?

Thus many Calvinists will insist that it is a mystery how the Bible can affirm that God loves all people and wants all to be saved, while at the same time insisting that he selects only some to apprehend salvation. God wishes (wills) to save all; he does not desire any to perish; but he only exercises his elective will to save a remnant. There may be a wideness in God's mercy, but he shows mercy to some and hardens others as he wills. God may so love the world, but he only foreknows with that special determining love those whom he chooses for salvation. You ask, Is God's love or will divided or at odds?[17] It may appear so to us, but it is truly a divine mystery,

16. I believe this is a fair analysis. To the best of my knowledge, Arminians do not typically employ this category.

17. J. Piper attempts to respond to this problem in "Are There Two Wills in God? Di-

they retort. If only those to whom God has given the gift of faith can believe, how can God hold unbelievers responsible for their failure to believe? It may appear that God is requiring and holding people accountable for what they cannot do, but that shows how mysterious and exalted are God's ways above our finite minds.

On the other hand, many Arminians insist confidently that they can explain how these matters work, how God can love all, but how not all will be saved. It is simple: God wants all to be saved, but people of their own free will consent or refuse to repent and believe. God has made the provision for all to be saved; it is up to people to accept or reject the provision. But objectors may ask, Can sinful humans simply decide to believe? Has sin not truncated or even destroyed any human ability to trust God? No, they insist, the Bible assumes people have the capacity to believe. Does not the Bible insist that God is responsible for the salvation of each and every individual? Do humans ultimately have themselves to thank for their salvation, for it was they who decided to trust in God? No, God has offered humans a gift; accepting God's gift does not mean they have earned salvation or are taking anything away from God's sovereignty. Arminian simplicity would be no virtue if in the process Arminians ravaged the biblical portrayal of human depravity or if they exalted the potency of human free will in order to actualize their system. But they insist these are false charges that emerge more out of the Calvinists' presuppositions than the biblical presentation of salvation. Sinners do have the capacity to embrace God's gift, and numerous texts assert their culpability if they do not. The biblical writers assume that sinners have wills and can choose to obey (read the prophets' appeals to the Jews; i.e., Jer 3:12-13; Amos 5:14-15).

I believe we must be extremely careful that we do not embrace contradiction in the guise of appealing to mystery. An interpretation must be logical in the strict sense. D. A. Carson clarifies some meanings for the use of the term "logic."[18] I agree with him that we need to avoid contravening logic in the sense of agreed-upon universals: "the fundamental 'laws' of logic, such as the law of noncontradiction and the law of the excluded middle."[19]

---

vine Election and God's Desire for All to Be Saved," in *Grace of God,* ed. Schreiner and Ware, 1:107-31.

18. D. A. Carson, *Exegetical Fallacies* (2d ed.; Grand Rapids: Baker, 1996), 87-88.
19. Ibid., 89.

The issue of logic, then, naturally leads to a question about some people's understanding of salvation and election: What does it mean to affirm both that God wants all people to be saved and that God selects only some for salvation? Does this contravene "logic" in Carson's sense above (i.e., does it go against the law of noncontradiction)? Or do the tensions these affirmations appear to raise only show that certain elements of God's provision of salvation must be termed a mystery? Calvinists frequently opt for mystery here. Arminians say that no amount of appealing to "mystery" or a to a non-Western type of logic will erase the fallacious reasoning.

Let us take another tenet. Both groups assent to the doctrine of "total depravity." For Calvinists this reality renders any human incapable of exercising saving faith apart from God's prior quickening work. How can dead people respond to the gospel, they ask? Paul affirmed in Rom 3:10-11, "as it is written: 'There is no one who is righteous, not even one; there is no one who has understanding, there is no one who seeks God.'" If Paul is accurately describing the human condition in sin, then how, apart from divine enabling, could a sinner respond to the call to repentance and faith? Besides, Jesus says in John 6:44, "No one can come to me unless drawn [ἕλκω] by the Father who sent me." Does that not settle it? God must take the initiative if any will be saved.

Arminians also affirm that all are sinful and incapable of securing salvation on their own (i.e., totally depraved), but they point to the clear evidence of all kinds of evangelism portrayed in the Gospels and Acts. The texts give no hint of a prior quickening required for any to believe. They appeal to the universality of God's love and grace and the apparent ability of humans to reject or accept God's provisions. They insist that the Bible consistently affirms human responsibility apart from which divine punishment seems arbitrary and unjust. They listen to Jesus' words, "Jerusalem, Jerusalem, the city that kills the prophets and stones those who are sent to it! How often have I desired to gather your children together as a hen gathers her brood under her wings, and *you were not willing!*" (Matt 23:37; italics added). Why would Jesus so lament, they ask, if he knew that apart from divine quickening these recalcitrant Jews were incapable of repenting and trusting in him? In fact, Arminians often point to the universalistic-sounding appeals to faith, as though people are capable of trusting in Christ if they will. In order to complement John 6:44 they quickly point to 12:32, where the same verb, ἕλκω, occurs: "And I, when I am lifted up from the earth, will *draw all people* to myself" (italics added).

True, God must take the initiative, and he has done so by sending Christ to die and become the propitiation for the sins of all people, not merely the elect.

Is one camp right and the other wrong? Are the apples yellow? Or are preunderstandings determining the outcome? I conclude that readers are *making* sense out of the texts; the preunderstandings of the two groups channel and control the kinds of sense they *make*.

There is another question to pose here: Are some texts difficult because we do not yet possess all the information we require to unpack their meaning, or are they puzzling because interpreters are trying to make them fit their own preconceived constraints or preferred system? What does the following sentence mean: "[God] desires [or wills, θέλει] everyone to be saved and to come to the knowledge of the truth" (1 Tim 2:4)? Is this an easy sentence to understand, or is it obscure? Check the standard commentaries and you will be surprised by what you find. Some interpreters opt for what appears to be the face value explanation of these words, something like, "God wills that all people without exception come to know the truth of the gospel and be saved." That is why, in the context, Jesus is termed the mediator between God and people.[20] Other commentators would say, "Not so fast. 'Everyone' (πάντας ἀνθρώπους) does not mean all people without exception, but all kinds of people."[21] So God's will is not that all people be saved, but some people from each kind of group, for example, governors, farmers, soldiers, and housewives.

Is the first interpretation more objective than the second? Has the second more at stake in discovering a less-than-straightforward reading? The reader of 1 Timothy must decide. But the reader must also decide which commentator to trust. How is the reader to assess not only his or her own preunderstandings, but also that of the commentators? We know that

---

20. A few examples include: I. H. Marshall, *A Critical and Exegetical Commentary on the Pastoral Epistles* (ICC; Edinburgh: T&T Clark, 1999); G. F. Fee, *1 and 2 Timothy, Titus* (2d ed.; NIBCNT; Peabody, Mass.: Hendrickson, 1988); and L. T. Johnson, *Letters to Paul's Delegates: 1 Timothy, 2 Timothy, Titus* (Valley Forge, Pa.: Trinity Press International, 1996). Johnson goes so far as to say, "God wills the salvation of all. Nowhere in the NT is there such an inclusive statement of hope concerning all humanity" (*Letters*, 132).

21. For example, on the Calvinist side see G. W. Knight III, *The Pastoral Epistles: A Commentary on the Greek Text* (NIGTC; Grand Rapids: Eerdmans; Carlisle: Paternoster, 1992); and W. Hendriksen, *I & II Timothy & Titus* (New Testament Commentary; Grand Rapids: Baker; Edinburgh: Banner of Truth, 1957).

commentaries in some series will, not surprisingly, discover Calvinist interpretations, while those in other series will discover Arminian senses for the texts. Do we simply buy or consult those that will confirm our biases?

We could perform this same exercise in the commentaries by looking at many disputed texts. Whose reading appears straightforward, and whose looks more strained? Do Calvinists and Arminians have an equal amount of both readings? Would we decide that one of the views is more likely to be true if it had a larger number of "straightforward" interpretations and a fewer number of "strained" ones?

Readers of this essay may have responded differently to the times I have cited Calvinist and Arminian arguments. They may believe I have caricatured one or the other of the views, or not presented its case as strongly as it could be. Or they may think I did not point out more of the weaknesses of one or the other, or what they believe is the Achilles' heal of the argument. No doubt they would be correct on some or all of these assessments. The issues were presented through the grid of *my* preunderstandings. But readers have evaluated what I wrote through the grids of *their* preunderstandings!

It seems to me that the time has come for more hermeneutical humility and rapprochement on this issue (and others over which well-intentioned interpreters wrangle). My point is not to argue that a text can have any meaning a reader wishes it to have.[22] As I have argued elsewhere, I believe the goal of biblical interpreters ought to be textual meaning: "that which the words and grammatical structures of that text disclose about the probable intention of its author/editor and the probable understanding of that text by its intended readers."[23] This implies that we ought to exert every effort and all possible tactics to determine the meaning of the texts before us. The impact of preunderstandings does not excuse us from doing the difficult work of exegesis, of unpacking the sense of the text that the original authors and readers were most likely to have understood. We ought vigorously to present and defend what we believe to be the best interpretations of texts.

For those of us who believe in the revelatory character of the Bible,

---

22. For an extremely insightful discussion of the various kinds of pluralities of meaning readers find in texts see Vanhoozer, *Is There a Meaning*, 416-21. See also Klein et al., *Introduction*, 117-34.

23. Klein et al., *Introduction*, 133.

we are bound to understand as best we can what God has communicated to his people through its pages. No hermeneutical relativism or nihilism will do for evangelicals with a high view of Scripture.[24] But because our preunderstandings (among other things) color how we understand reality in general — and, more specifically, cloud our ability to understand precisely and infallibly the meaning of texts — as brothers and sisters in Christ, we need to admit and accommodate the limits of our understanding. On a personal note, one reviewer of my book on election, *The New Chosen People,* called me a "Judas-goat" and chastised Zondervan for publishing such rubbish. The merits of the book aside, it is just such an attitude of hermeneutical triumphalism that I believe is totally unwarranted, especially among evangelicals (and I assume the reviewer would embrace that description). We need to learn how better to live with and embrace brothers and sisters who adhere to different understandings of texts.

Jesus insisted, "By this everyone will know that you are my disciples, if you have love for one another" (John 13:35). Others will not become convinced we are Jesus' followers when we all agree on whether Calvinism or Arminianism (or some alternative) is the correct grid for understanding God's program of salvation. Unity in interpretation is not the litmus test; in fact, as I have briefly sketched out above, such unity is an impossible goal given our preunderstandings. Alas, in the history of the church such love has also remained an elusive goal. But embracing one another in love is Jesus' criterion of discipleship. As love covers a multitude of sins, it ought also to cover all our inadequacies of interpretation due to our preunderstandings, and the other failings to which we are prone as we do our interpretive work. Too often evangelicals with different interpretations of issues like election have resorted to rock throwing, impugning motives, or cavalierly dismissing their opponents' views, as if one side had a corner on correct methodology or as if preunderstandings adversely affected only the other side. We might learn about the merits of alternative views if we did not see their proponents as completely misguided or lacking in exegetical ability. More important items crowd our agenda as Christians in an unbelieving world than to attack fellow Christians.

---

24. In an article written over twenty-five years ago, C. F. H. Henry answered no to the question, "The Interpretation of the Scriptures: Are We Doomed to Hermeneutical Nihilism?" *RevExp* 71 (1974): 197-215.

Finding the Devil in the Details:
Onomastic Exegesis and the Naming of Evil in the World of the New Testament

Douglas L. Penney

Since we are members of *homo loquens,* our words generally function so well and so easily that contemplating diachronic semantic change requires effort. Humans attribute significance not only to the meaning of a word, but (sometimes wrongly) to the word's origin. The shifting of meanings linked to a seemingly constant symbol produces tensions that are as ancient as the debate regarding the origin of words. In the preface to his *Dictionary of the English Language,* Samuel Johnson observes:

> I am not yet so lost in lexicography, as to forget that words are the daughters of the earth, and that things are the sons of heaven. Language is only the instrument of science, and words are but the signs of ideas: I wish, however, that the instrument might be less apt to decay, and that signs might be permanent, like the things they denote.[1]

Yet even earlier, Plato's dialogue *Cratylus* records Socrates' use of the now famous term *deus ex machina* to describe a less than ideal approach to this very question: Whence come words? He prods Hermogenes, his interlocutor:

> οὐ γὰρ ἔχομεν τούτου βέλτιον, εἰς ὅ τι ἐπανενέγκωμεν περὶ ἀληθείας τῶν πρώτων ὀνομάτων, εἰ μὴ ἄρα βούλει, ὥσπερ οἱ τραγῳδιοποιοὶ

---

1. *Dictionary of the English Language* (ed. S. Johnson; London: W. Strahan, 1755).

ἐπειδάν τι ἀπορῶσιν ἐπὶ τὰς μηχανὰς καταφεύγουσι θεοὺς αἴροντες,
καὶ ἡμεῖς οὕτως εἰπόντες ἀπαλλαγῶμεν, ὅτι τὰ πρῶτα ὀνόματα οἱ θεοὶ
ἔθεσαν καὶ διὰ ταῦτα ὀρθῶς ἔχει. ἆρα καὶ ἡμῖν κράτιστος οὗτος τῶν
λόγων;[2]

Socrates observes that to say the gods are responsible for names is to be
content with no answer as to how they came about.

This linguistic intrigue that motivates the *Cratylus* reappears with regard to the words employed as names and titles of evil in the NT world.
Whence come the names for evil powers in the NT? The following discussion offers examples illustrating the methods by which the creators and us-
ers of Second Temple literature arrived at designations for powers, both
good and evil.

The term *onomastic exegesis* refers to the propensity in Second Temple interpretation of the HB to either regard certain adjectives or nouns as
names, ranks, or titles of angelic and demonic powers or to develop those
terms diachronically into names.[3] The cases of diachronic semantic shift
under discussion here generally fall into several categories that are not mu-
tually exclusive, but descriptive of the process or path that such words
trace. Some terms are candidates for "angelization" because of their appropriate semantics, some because they may be personified in a given context,
and others exhibit angelization in translation (e.g., the LXX may disclose
that the interpreter understood certain terms in the MT to be angels; thus
translation can be a better guide to contemporary meaning and function
than etymology or context in the source language). The following examples, drawn from the HB, a host of Second Temple literature, and the NT itself, illustrate the use of these mechanisms.

2. "For there is no better theory upon which we can base the truth of the earliest
names, unless you think we had better follow the example of the tragic poets, who, when
they are in a dilemma, have recourse to the introduction of gods on machines. So we may get
out of trouble by saying that the gods gave the earliest names, and therefore they are right. Is
that the best theory for us?" Plato, *Crat.* 425 D-E. Translation of H. N. Fowler, *Plato, Cratylus,
Parmenides, Greater Hippias, Lesser Hippias* (LCL; Cambridge: Harvard Univ. Press, 1953).

3. It is common for adjectives and other descriptive terms for evil to develop into
more formal labels and names. See S. I. Johnston, *Restless Dead: Encounters between the Living and the Dead in Ancient Greece* (Berkeley: Univ. of California Press, 1999), 134, 164, 174,
181.

The Case of Satan As an Example
of the Diachronic Emergence of Title and Name

Appropriate semantics probably display most clearly how a generic term for evil may rise to designate a personified evil. As an example, consider what we do and do not know about the derivation of the title "Satan."[4] The Hebrew noun itself is difficult to link convincingly to a verbal root. Most of its occurrences, some would say all, can be read as generic nouns rather than as a proper name, leaving the nature of the adversary in the HB rather nebulous. Even the presence of a definite article does not necessarily mark the word as a proper noun. While the demonstrative or deictic use of the article is well known, it may also serve a generic function and "deemphasize precise identity."[5] In each case one must decide whether the label *satan* refers to a generic adversary (be it human or supernatural, e.g., the role of adversary having been assumed by one of the בני אלהים for the functioning of the divine council) or, as understood in later literature, whether it is a title permanently assigned to a fallen member of the divine council.

Four passages require consideration. The first example I mention in passing: the Balaam cycle describes the angel of Yahweh as (an) adversary, a satan (Num 22:22), sent to oppose the prophet. Second, there is the curious substitution of the Chronicler in which "the anger of the LORD was kindled against Israel, and he incited David against them" (2 Sam 24:1), is replaced by "Satan stood up against Israel, and incited David to number Israel" (1 Chr 21:1). One cannot automatically assume that the alteration stems from a changing theodicy during the interim between Samuel and Chronicles. Indeed, lying spirits sent from the council (2 Chr 18:18-22) suggest that theodicy is not the incentive.[6] Many invoke the absence of an article on the noun שׂטן as evidence of a proper name, but one cannot rule out that the adversary may be a member of the divine council meting out the "wrath of the LORD."

Third, the satan of Job is subservient to God, not the wildcard, evil free agent depicted in later literature. This satan urges God to "stretch out your hand now and touch his bone and his flesh" (2:5), to which the re-

---

4. The case of Satan has been well documented by P. L. Day and C. Breytenbach, "Satan," *DDD²* 726-32. It is summarized here because of its importance as an early and typical example of the processes of onomastic exegesis.

5. Ibid., 728.

6. Ibid., 729-30.

sponse is, "Very well, he is in your power; only spare his life" (2:6). Job's satan is an extension of God's hand/power, unlike the later outlook that appears, for example, in Luke, who makes a sharp distinction by means of a parallel construction between the hand of the devil and that of God — casting out demons either ἐν Βεελζεβούλ or ἐν δακτύλῳ θεοῦ (Luke 11:19-20).

Fourth, even the satan of Zechariah's vision (Zech 3) may be simply an office in the divine council. If the investiture of Joshua indicates the divine acceptance of the Jerusalem community, a pardoning of the people, and if the adversary on the divine council is the permanent enemy of Yahweh's remnant, then the satan of Zechariah 3 is God's permanent opponent, Satan. If, however, Zechariah's vision is intended to unify the schismatic Jerusalem community and galvanize support for Joshua as the divinely appointed king, then the accuser in the divine council may again be a function fulfilled by one of the בני אלהים who is not necessarily an enduring enemy, constantly hostile to God's people.

Having presented these arguments in much greater detail, Peggy Day concludes that "the earliest texts that indisputably contain the proper name Satan date to the second century BCE. (*Ass. Mos.* 10:1; *Jub* 23:29; possibly Sir 21:27)."[7] Her tentative identification of the passage in Sirach illustrates the difficulty of assessing the status of the term in isolated references: ἐν τῷ καταρᾶσθαι ἀσεβῆ τὸν σατανᾶν αὐτὸς καταρᾶται τὴν ἑαυτοῦ ψυχήν, "When an ungodly man curses his adversary, he curses his own soul" (Sir 21:27 RSV; NRSV has "an adversary," with "or Satan" in a note). Once again the issue of whether the article is demonstrative or generic surfaces. But even here the genre and context (advice for harmonious living) hardly call for a supernatural adversary.

In the HB a traditional reading of the nature of Satan appears adequate and secure because the NT and intervening literature more fully develop his role and character that are subsequently, inadvertently, and easily read into the HB usages. Even so, the concept of *satan* in the NT is not so out of touch with its original meaning that it cannot be used of people as slanderers.[8] Still, the overwhelming majority of NT occurrences of σατάν/ σατανᾶς locate the term as a proper noun. However this debate may ultimately (if ever) be decided, its usefulness for our purpose is that one can still see in the history of the noun a diachronic semantic shift from generic

---

7. Ibid., 730.
8. Cf. διάβολος in 2 Tim 3:3 and Titus 2:3.

term to title and ultimately to proper name during the first millennium
B.C.E.

Analogous Examples of Onomastic Exegesis
in Second Temple Judaism

Similar processes and developments lie behind the appearance of aliases
and near synonyms of *satan:* ἀντίδικος, ὁ κατηγορῶν, ὁ κατήγωρ, ὁ ἐχθρός,
ὁ διάβολος, ὁ πονηρός, ὁ πειράζων, βελιάρ (בליעל), and βεελζεβούλ (בעל
דבב). In a way that etymologizing and even context cannot, the translations of these terms testify to the contemporary meaning of *satan* in the
Second Temple period. The importance of recognizing translated aliases
for powers is that in some cases it allows us to reconstruct the thought processes that led Second Temple exegetes to identify certain words in specific
texts as names of those powers.

By what authority does one create names for spirits? The authority or
ability to reinterpret particular passages appears to originate with the ambiguity of the passage in the reader's mind. An illustration from English may
clarify. In my preschool days I sang the hymn "How Great Thou Art" by Stuart K. Hine. I learned the words by heart without ever seeing them written.
Because of my orthographic naiveté I assumed that the phrase "when I look
down from lofty mountain grandeur" mentioned a specific geographic feature named Mt. Grandeur. As I later realized, English maintains the distinction between proper name and generic noun by means of a convention —
capitalization for proper nouns. Hebrew, Greek, and other ancient languages,
rather than employing capital letter forms, relied on context for this distinction, with the result that personification and titularization of attributes and
generic nouns became much easier. The examples below show that instances
of onomastic exegesis were common in the Second Temple period, driven by
a consuming goal to discover deeper, hidden meanings in the sacred text.

Second Temple angelologers identified previously undetected angelic
names and titles hidden in the sacred text, especially in poetic metaphor.[9]

---

9. The term ὄνομα encompasses "title," "rank," and "authority"; BAGD, s.v. ὄνομα.
"Name" and "Power" can be interchangeable; so H. Berkhof, *Christ and the Powers* (trans.
J. H. Yoder; Scottdale, Pa.: Herald, 1962), 34. The NT, like the magical papyri and apocryphal
literature, treats names as important in exorcisms (cf. *Testament of Solomon*). Consider the
importance of names in Mark 5:9; Acts 8:10; 19:13-15; Eph 1:21; and Phil 2:10; and types of

The LXX exhibits this inclination, inserting the word ἄγγελος (although the MT has no מלאך) in Job 40:11. Here the MT's הפץ עברות אפך וראה כל גאה והשפילהו, "Pour forth the overflowings of your anger, and look on everyone that is proud, and abase him," becomes ἀπόστειλον δὲ ἀγγέλους ὀργῇ πᾶν δὲ ὑβριστὴν ταπείνωσον (Job 40:11 LXX).

Yet more examples arise merely by taking metaphors literally, thus personifying terms in these contexts. That God "calls the stars by name" personifies and permits them to be angels.[10] The Lord's command addressed to the snow, rain, and frost (Job 37:4-6) gives rise to the weather angels of *Jub.* 2:2. Ps 104:4 makes messengers (i.e., angels) of winds and fire.[11] Fire, sea, and wind angels appear in Rev 7:1; 8:5, 7-12; 14:18; 16:5. Meteorological angels emerge in *Jubilees* 2, *1 Enoch* 75, and *2 Enoch* 40.[12]

But industrious exegetes overshadowed these trivial examples, uncovering many more obscure angels. Saul Olyan's study of their methods collects angel names from Jewish literature contemporary with Scripture, including many of the following terms.[13]

The label אופנים designates an angelic brigade. Derived from אופן, "wheel," in Ezekiel's vision (1:15; 10:12), these angels appear in 4QShirShabb

---

spirits in Acts 16:16 and 1 John 4:3. See esp. G. H. Twelftree, *Jesus the Exorcist: A Contribution to the Study of the Historical Jesus* (WUNT 2/54; Tübingen: Mohr [Siebeck], 1993).

10. Ps 146:4 (LXX). Revelation presents stars as angels (1:20; 9:1). Mark 13:25 places ἀστέρες parallel to δυνάμεις. Other examples occur outside the canon: δεσμωτήριον τοῦτο ἐγένετο τοῖς ἄστροις καὶ ταῖς δυνάμεσιν τοῦ οὐρανοῦ, *1 En.* 18:14; cf. *1 En.* 88:1-3; the *Testament of Solomon* argues that falling stars are demons (*T. Sol.* 20:16-18; cf. Luke 10:18), as did several Mediterranean mythologies. For Akkadian see *CAD*, s.v. *ṣēru;* for Greek, cf. the fever that accompanies summer meteor showers, *Il.* 22.25-31; for Islamic links between plague, meteors, and demons, see M. W. Dols, *The Black Death in the Middle East* (Princeton: Princeton Univ. Press, 1977), 89 and 116n.34; for Hebrew, see T. H. Gaster, *Myth, Legend, and Custom in the Old Testament* (2 vols.; New York: Harper & Row, 1969), 2:670-71, 764-65, although Gaster stops short of making the arrows of Resheph meteors.

11. Heb 1:7, 14; cf. Ps 78:49.

12. Cf. A. S. Peake's discussion of angelology ("Epistle to the Colossians," in *Expositor's Greek Testament* [ed. W. R. Nicoll; 5 vols.; Grand Rapids: Eerdmans, 1961], 3:478-84).

13. S. M. Olyan, *A Thousand Thousands Served Him: Exegesis and the Naming of Angels in Ancient Judaism* (Texte und Studien zum Antiken Judentum 36; Tübingen: Mohr [Siebeck], 1993). For the sake of clarity and giving credit where it is due, I should note that Olyan's study understands Ophannim, Maasim, Doqiel, Azazel, Mastemah, Mastemot, and Abaddon, as well as Thrones, Penuel, and עברות אפיך, as ἄγγελοι. See his summary (116-20) and the appendix listing angelic titles and their source texts (121-23). Further citations for particular powers appear in the respective articles of *DDD²*.

(4Q403 II, 15; 4Q405 20–21–22 3, 9); *1 En.* 61:10; 71:7; and *2 En.* 20:1. Another angelic brigade from Ezekiel's vision (Ezek 1:16), the מעשים, appears in 4QShirShabb (4Q405 20–21–22 10) parallel to אופנים. The angel name Δοκιηλ occurs in the *Testament of Abraham,* taken from the hapax legomenon דק, "veil," in Isa 40:22, "he . . . stretched out the heavens like a *veil.*"[14]

The same literature contains exegetical demons. The name *'ăzā'zēl* (עזאזל), the "scapegoat" of Leviticus 16, emerges as a demonic figure in *1 En.* 8:1; 10:4; *Apoc. Ab.* 13:6; and 4Q180 I, 7-8. משטמה and משטמות (singular and plural), appearing in *Jubilees,* 1QM, 1QS, CD, 4Q390, and elsewhere, derive from the only two uses of this term, "animosity," in Hebrew Scripture (Hos 9:7, 8).[15] Like Satan, Belial, and Abaddon, the name Mastemah follows the general semantic evolution from sinister concept, to role, to proper name. Let us now turn to the exegetical logic and derivational processes that generated this and other demonic names.

Suggestions of Additional Exegetically Derived Powers and Their Source Texts

The patterns of development sketched by the examples above yield a powerful tool for investigating other powers that may owe their titles to onomastic exegesis. As methodological examples, consider three dilemmas: the perennially problematic etymology of Beelzebub; the rise of Legion as a demonic label; and finally the tendency of scholars to overlook the existence of the "fowler's-net demon" and its relation to the hermeneutical logic behind the derivation of Mastemah. In the last two examples, the use of the source text is reflected in the NT; in the first two examples, the names derived from the source texts appear themselves in the NT.

Beelzebub

As noted above, the practice of translating titles of powers often renders more specific the contemporary meaning of such titles. Consider the "bi-

---

14. Olyan, *Thousand Thousands Served Him,* 117.

15. J. W. van Henten, "*Mastemah,*" *DDD*² 553-54. משטמה (Hos 9:8) is parallel to פח יקוש, itself a demonic evil in Ps 91:3 (see the detailed discussion below).

lingual" demons: ὁ διάβολος, ὁ ἀντίδικος (1 Pet 5:8), ὁ ἐχθρός (Matt 13:39), ὁ κατήγωρ and ὁ κατηγορῶν (Rev 12:10), corresponding to both שׂטן and בעלדבב. These translations rely on adversarial legal terminology. This suggests that the etymology of בעלדבב advanced by Peggy Day should have been sufficient, but new evidence bolsters her derivation of Beelzeboul from Aramaic בעל דבב.[16]

One need not accept Beelzeboul rather than Beeldebab as the starting point, since altered forms reflect the practice of using euphemisms or intentionally mispronouncing demonic names to avoid summoning them.[17] The common English adage "Speak of the devil . . ." is rarely quoted in full, but if continued affirms ". . . and he will appear."[18] The practice of altering names of powers is common across cultures and known from the Middle East.[19]

Satan's role as accuser before the divine council (Job 2:1; Dan 7:10; Zech 3:1; Rev 12:10) dovetails with the other legal terminology employed in naming evil powers. The connection with Akkadian legal terminology is emphasized by the appearance of the same term in an Ugaritic incantation attesting to the antiquity of bʿl dbb (Ras Ibn Hani 78/20).[20] Kaufman's objection that בעל דבבא never had any legal connotation may be moot since בעיל דבבו, "enmity," well attested in Jewish Palestinian Aramaic, points directly to the semantics of Hebrew משטמה, suggesting the titles are synonymous and interchangeable.[21] The underlying judicial outlook implied by terms such as ὁ κατηγορῶν, ὁ διάβολος, and ὁ ἀντίδικος (which correspond to both Hebrew שׂטן and Aramaic בעל דבב) also explains the mo-

---

16. P. L. Day, *An Adversary in Heaven: śāṭān in the Hebrew Bible* (HSM 43; Atlanta: Scholars Press, 1988), 151-59. The competing alternatives discounted by Day nevertheless live on through repetition; see W. Herrmann, "Baal Zebub," *DDD²* 154-56.

17. Day, *Adversary*, 156.

18. See the discussion of *Devil* as a taboo word in I. Opie and M. Tatem, eds., *A Dictionary of Superstitions* (Oxford: Oxford Univ. Press, 1989), 118-19.

19. Cf. the analogous custom in English of altering "Jesus Christ" to "Judas Priest" and "God" to "Gosh," etc. For the Middle East, see M. W. Dols, *Majnun: The Madman in Medieval Islamic Society* (Oxford: Oxford Univ. Press, 1992), 290.

20. D. L. Penney and M. O. Wise, "By the Power of Beelzebub: An Aramaic Incantation Formula from Qumran (4Q560)," *JBL* 113 (1994): 627-50, esp. 633.

21. S. A. Kaufman, *The Akkadian Influences on Aramaic* (AS 19; Chicago: Univ. of Chicago Press, 1974), 42; Day, *Adversary*, 158n.31; M. Sokoloff, *A Dictionary of Jewish Palestinian Aramaic of the Byzantine Period* (Dictionaries of Talmud, Midrash and Targum 2; Ramat-Gan: Bar Ilan Univ. Press, 1990), s.v. בעיל דבב.

tivation for the use of the legal term ὁ παράκλητος (1 John 2:1; John 14:16). The words are antonyms, as are Χριστός and Βελιάρ (2 Cor 6:15).

Legion

The next two cases illustrate how a special interpretation of a particular passage may be essential to understanding how names are drawn from it. The first passage in question, Psalm 91, is most amenable to onomastic exegesis because of its long tradition of employment against spiritual evils. An unbroken chain of apotropaic amulets containing portions of this psalm stretches from the twentieth century back to the time of Christ.[22] Magic bowls and amulets frequently quote portions of Psalm 91.[23]

The *Songs of the Sage* (4Q511 VIII, 6) from Qumran quotes the incipit of Psalm 91.[24] The Psalms scroll from Cave 11 (11QPsᵃ XXVII, 10) mentions four Davidic compositions it calls "songs for making music over the stricken," one of which seems to be Psalm 91.[25] The Talmud corroborates

22. T. Schrire, *Hebrew Amulets: Their Decipherment and Interpretation* (London: Routledge & Kegan Paul, 1966).

23. It is rivaled only by Ps 121, Num 6:24, or Zech 3:2. The Zechariah text is clearly in exorcistic use at the writing of Jude 9. The high-priestly blessing occurs in an amulet from the 6th or 5th century B.C.E.; see A. Yardeni, "Remarks on the Priestly Blessing on Two Ancient Amulets from Jerusalem," *VT* 41 (1991): 176-85. For the use of psalms in amulets, see E. Davis, "The Psalms in Hebrew Medical Amulets," *VT* 42 (1992): 173-78. Examples of Ps 91 appear in: J. Naveh and S. Shaked, *Magic Spells and Formulae: Aramaic Incantations of Late Antiquity* (Jerusalem: Magnes, 1993), 24; J. Naveh and S. Shaked, *Amulets and Magic Bowls: Aramaic Incantations of Late Antiquity* (2d ed.; Jerusalem: Magnes; Leiden: Brill, 1987), 184-87 (and pl. 27), 237-38 (and pl. 39); C. D. Isbell, *Corpus of the Aramaic Incantation Bowls* (SBLDS 17; Missoula, Mont.: Scholars Press, 1975), 118-19 (text 52.9). For a striking example of an amulet based on Ps 91, see C. Bonner, *Studies in Magical Amulets, Chiefly Graeco-Egyptian* (Ann Arbor: Univ. of Michigan Press, 1950), no. 324. For this amulet in greater detail and color, see http://www.lib.umich.edu/pap/magic/defi.display.html.

24. M. Baillet, "Cantiques du Sage," [4Q510-511] in *Qumrân Grotte 4.III: (4Q482-4Q520)* (DJD 7; Oxford: Clarendon, 1982), 215-62 (see pl. 59); B. Nitzan, "Hymns from Qumran — 4Q510-4Q511," in *The Dead Sea Scrolls: Forty Years of Research* (ed. D. Dimant and U. Rappaport; STDJ 10; Leiden: Brill, 1992), 53-63; and B. Nitzan, *Qumran Prayer and Religious Poetry* (trans. J. Chipman; STDJ 12; Leiden: Brill, 1994), 227-72, esp. 242.

25. שיר לנגן על הפגועים ערבה. See J. A. Sanders, *The Psalms Scroll of Qumrân Cave 11 (11QPsᵃ)* (DJD 4; Oxford: Clarendon, 1965), 91-93 (and pl. 16). These four psalms may be those preserved in 11QPsApᵃ, as argued by É. Puech, "*11QPsApᵃ*: Un rituel d'exorcismes: Essai de reconstruction," *RevQ* 14 (1989): 377-408 (see esp. 402).

this custom, recording opinions on whether this psalm should be used for protective purposes on the Sabbath.[26]

The NT hints at demonic associations in its use of Psalm 91. In the temptation narratives, the devil cites the angelic intervention promised in Ps 91:11-12.[27] Further, Jesus tells his seventy jubilant exorcists, "I saw Satan fall from heaven. . . . I have given you authority to tread on serpents and scorpions" (Luke 10:18-19), in wording that reflects Ps 91:13. Thus the people of the Second Temple period employed this psalm for healing and protection against the evils and were accustomed to seeing the devil and his minions in its words.

Internal evidence from Psalm 91 suggests that its magical use need not be new or innovative. Almost a century ago, Oesterley showed that the psalmist's choice of vocabulary suggested that he consciously composed a psalm to protect against otherworldly evils.[28] Although his work received little notice, my research has not only confirmed Oesterley's finding but shown that he underestimated the number of evils. Some that he could not explain he emended away, but now (in the light of subsequent discoveries) these can be shown to designate additional demons, thus bolstering his findings.[29] Psalm 91 was intended as assurance of protection or as protection itself against evil spirits.

The exorcistic uses of this psalm at the time of Jesus, far from being new and novel, show instead that the Jews had not forgotten the author's purpose. They saw in its terminology mentions of powers, good and evil. In addition to words for evils that are easily personified (Destruction, Pestilence, Terror, Noon-Day Demon [δαιμονίου μεσημβρινοῦ, Ps 90:6 LXX]), other terms contributed to the list of evils in less obvious ways. In the midrash on Ps 91:4, several rabbis argue that there are "one thousand demons on the left and ten thousand on the right," clearly viewing the numbers as military units in the spiritual battle.[30] The μυριάς of v. 7 (LXX) commonly

26. Cf. *y. Šabb.* 6:2 and *b. Šebu.* 15b.

27. Matt 4:6; Luke 4:10-11. In spite of the brevity of Mark's temptation, the beasts and angels of Mark 1:13 still allude to Ps 91:11 and 13.

28. W. O. E. Oesterley, "The Demonology of the Old Testament, Illustrated by Psalm XCI," *The Expositor* ser. 7, vol. 4 (1907): 132-51.

29. D. L. Penney, "'This World with Devils Filled': Apotropaic Vocabulary in Psalm 91" (paper presented at the annual national meeting of the SBL, Philadelphia, Nov. 18, 1995).

30. The rabbis agreed that the one thousand were demons, but debated the ten thousand. Some argued that they were angels because they were "on the right." Others argued

refers to divisions of celestial armies (both angelic [cf. Heb 12:22; Jude 14; Rev 5:11] and demonic [cf. Rev 9:16]). After being updated (as we have seen with the names and titles of other powers) from Greek to the corresponding Latin, this term became the "legions of angels" (Matt 26:53) or demonic Legion (Mark 5:9; Luke 8:30) of the NT.[31] Each step required by this proposed derivation of Legion follows secure precedents established by the examples of names of other powers presented above.

The Fowler's-Net Demon and Mastemah

One more term from Psalm 91 may shelter an evil that the ancients recognized. Several have argued that the "fowler's snare" (פח יקוש, v. 3) represents figuratively the machinations of evildoers and therefore cannot possibly be demonic. It demonstrates, they claim, the metaphorical, and therefore nonsupernatural, nature of the other evils in this psalm. Likewise, while Oesterley recognized and liked the magical associations of "snare," he thought the apparently pedestrian semantics of the "fowler" out of place — for him it was a metaphor of a human menace in a sequence of otherwise clearly demonic perils.[32] In his commentary Oesterley emends the text.[33] Dahood, like Oesterley, retains פח, but removes יקוש, citing metrical reasons.[34]

But are these changes warranted? Not at all. The imagery of nets and net demons in Akkadian magical literature makes such emendation unjustified. Oesterley's proposed emendation would ruin the author's carefully

---

that the phrase "shall fall" (rather than "shall be assigned to thee") applies to both numbers, making both demons. See W. G. Braude, *The Midrash on Psalms* (2 vols.; Yale Judaica Series; New Haven: Yale Univ. Press, 1959), 2:103.

31. D. L. Penney, "My Name Is Legion for We Are Myriad (Mark 5:9 and Ps 91:7)" (paper presented at the annual meeting of the Midwest region of the SBL, Wheaton, Ill., Feb. 17, 1997).

32. He cites the Briggses, who remove the phrase "of the fowler" because it "destroys the measure" (C. A. and E. G. Briggs, *A Critical and Exegetical Commentary on the Book of Psalms* [ICC; 2 vols.; Edinburgh: T&T Clark, 1906-7], 2:280). See Oesterley, "Demonology of the OT," 137-38.

33. "In these verses there is nothing to show that the evils . . . have anything to do with the works of evil-disposed men; so that the mention of 'the fowler' is out of place, and may well have been introduced by a copyist influenced by Ps. 124⁷, Hos 9⁸" (W. O. E. Oesterley, *The Psalms: Translated with Text-Critical and Exegetical Notes* [London: SPCK, 1962], 409).

34. M. Dahood, *Psalms 51–100* (AB 17; Garden City, N.Y.: Doubleday, 1968), 330.

selected image and destroy the very evidence that Oesterley himself sought. The phrase "snare of the fowler," although admittedly cumbersome in the Hebrew poetry (as Dahood observes), nevertheless reflects a well-attested Mesopotamian belief in net demons. Human use of nets goes back tens of thousands of years.[35] In the ancient Near East, nets were the weapon of choice in both warfare and hunting. Gods, demons, and people all used nets against one another.[36] Incantations and spells, diseases and nightmares all figured as nets.[37] Numerous Akkadian deities wield nets. Nisaba uses a *saparru*-net.[38] Marduk wields an *azamillu*-net.[39] Shamash carries a *šētu*-net (a fowler's net).[40] Lamaštu's hand "is an *alluḫappu*-net."[41]

Several demons become so closely associated with the weapon they carry that the word for net becomes the demon's name. The aforementioned *alluḫappu*-demon is one, but there are others. The evil *alû*-demon "claps down on a man like a *kātimtu*-net," yet another fowler's net.[42] Therefore, far from requiring emendation, the פח יקוש of Psalm 91 is an ancient, vividly literal Hebrew translation of the Akkadian "fowler's-net demon," a demon that no one should exorcise from the text.[43]

35. Impressions of a net have survived in clay from 26,000 B.C.E.; see R. Gore, "People Like Us," *National Geographic* 198, no. 1 (July 2000): 90-117 (esp. 98-99).

36. See the incantation adjuring seven different net-wielding demons in R. C. Thompson, *The Devils and Evil Spirits of Babylonia* (Luzac's Semitic Text and Translation Series 14-15; 2 vols.; 1903-4; repr. New York: AMS Press, 1976), 2:59; and *ANET*, 540, §101(649), "May Shamash clamp his bronze trap over you."

37. Akkadian spells and incantations are nets cast by the magic's practitioner (*CAD*, s.v. *saparru* A). The magical worldview typically sees spiritual warfare as a two-way street. The spirit and the exorcist use the same weapons and words against each other. The magician uses magic nets, often represented by flour or rope circles on the ground, to counteract the demon's invisible net. No doubt this accounts for the epithet of the late-first-century-C.E. healer Honi the Circle-Drawer (G. Vermes, *Jesus the Jew: A Historian's Reading of the Gospels* [London: Collins, 1973; New York: Macmillan, 1974], 69-72). The demon can likewise adjure the exorcist just as the exorcist normally adjures the demon (Mark 5:7). The demons may be interested in the exorcist's name (Acts 19:15) and vice versa (Mark 5:9).

38. *CAD*, s.v. *saparru* A.

39. *CAD*, s.v. *azamillu*.

40. *CAD*, s.v. *šētu* A.

41. *CAD*, s.v. *alluḫappu*. The *alluḫappu*-demon, the one called "net," is lion-headed with human hands and feet.

42. *CAD*, s.v. *kātimtu*.

43. The absence of an article devoted to the fowler's-snare demon in *DDD*² will surely need to be rectified.

The fowler's snare also occurs in Hos 9:7-8, a passage containing the only two occurrences of the word מַשְׂטֵמָה. Originally an abstract noun meaning "animosity, enmity, hatred," מַשְׂטֵמָה seems to have followed a semantic development or extension similar to שָׂטָן, expanding to become a proper noun designating the epitome of evil. Once again, the use and meaning attested in the Qumran documents and other noncanonical Jewish writings, in keeping with the practice of deriving names from the canonical text, appears to emanate from these very verses. In coincidence with the rather negative views expressed in the Qumran documents with regard to the current activities in the temple, a verse stating "Hatred (מַשְׂטֵמָה) is in the house of his God" (Hos 9:8) might have suggested that an evil spirit named Hatred had taken up residence in the temple.[44] If, as seems likely, this Qumranic term for Satan derives from these verses, what (other than the meaning) might have prompted such a reading? Consider the term parallel to מַשְׂטֵמָה in v. 8, the "fowler's snare." Did an awareness that the term "fowler's snare" potentially designated a demon also suggest to ancient interpreters a parallel demonic meaning for מַשְׂטֵמָה?

The words, phrases, and images employed in the magical literature are very long-lived. In spite of the dearth of Semitic magical texts from the Roman period and especially from Second Temple Palestine, many words, phrases, and motifs appear in Aramaic magical texts from the Islamic period almost unchanged from their antecedents in the Akkadian texts. This longevity points to a continuous surviving tradition of magical texts in spite of the paucity of archaeological finds.[45] The concept of nets and net demons also follows this pattern. Later Aramaic and Greek magical texts continue the tradition, speaking of nets as demonic weapons.[46] The same concept lies behind the NT metaphor "snare of the devil."[47] The invisible demonic nets may cause physical or intellectual stumbling.[48] Even in rela-

---

44. Cf. other verses with similar messages, e.g., Hos 4:19, "A(n evil) spirit oppresses them with its wings."

45. Penney and Wise, "By the Power of Beelzebub," 629-30.

46. An unpublished magic bowl in the collection of the Oriental Institute (no. A33981) contains not the expected circular text but the drawing of a net, presumably to trap the demon. A fourth-century church father argues that πονηρὸς δαίμων of the disease strangles his victim with a βρόχος, "a snare for birds" (Himerius, *Declamationes et orationes*, 8.13; cited in BAGD s.v. δαίμων; for text see *TLG*). Cf. also Naveh and Shaked, *Amulets and Magic Bowls*, 127; and E. S. Drower and R. Macuch, *A Mandaic Dictionary* (Oxford: Clarendon, 1963), s.v. *liha*.

47. 1 Tim 3:7; 2 Tim 2:26.

48. Note the parallel of snare and stumbling in Rom 11:9, quoted from Ps 69:22-23.

tively recent times the net as a metaphor for the devil's tool or agent continues.[49] The concept of snare as the devil's agent, the existence of net demons, and the semantics of "enmity" have all combined to make Hos 9:8 an excellent source text for Mastemah.

Examples of Onomastic Exegesis in the New Testament

The NT writers avail themselves of several designations from Jewish angelology and demonology. There are many examples of this in addition to those already mentioned above. The empty thrones of Dan 7:9 emerge as Angelic Thrones in the *Testament of Levi*, *2 Enoch*, and many other books.[50] This concept also appears in Col 1:16: θρόνοι . . . κυριότητες . . . ἀρχαί . . . ἐξουσίαι, "thrones . . . dominions . . . rulers . . . authorities."

Thunder angels serving as the oracular voice of God in various psalms reappear in *3 Enoch*, *Jubilees*, and the *Testament of Adam*.[51] The Qumran *Brontologion* (4Q318), a thunder diviner's handbook, provides another contemporary witness to thunder as message and messenger.[52] Similarly, the Gospel of John (12:29) records ὁ οὖν ὄχλος . . . ἔλεγεν βροντὴν γεγονέναι, ἄλλοι ἔλεγον· ἄγγελος αὐτῷ λελάληκεν and interprets the thunder oracle. In the Apocalypse, ἃ ἐλάλησαν αἱ ἑπτὰ βρονταί cannot be transcribed (Rev 10:3-4).[53]

---

49. "The webs on the brambles were white; the devil throws his net over the blackberries as soon as September's back is turned" (D. H. Lawrence, *White Peacock* VI [1911], cited in Opie and Tatem, *Dictionary of Superstitions*, 29).

50. *T. Levi* 3:8, "thrones and authorities" (*OTP* 1:789); *Apoc. El. (C)* 1:10, "nor will the thrones hinder them" (*OTP* 1:737); *Apoc. El. (C)* 4:10, "you have been hostile to the thrones, you have acted against the angels" (*OTP* 1:747); *2 En.* 20:1, "archangels . . . dominions . . . cherubim . . . seraphim and the many-eyed thrones" (*OTP* 1:134); and the scene from the *Apocalypse of Zephaniah* quoted in Clement of Alexandria, *Strom.* 5.11.77 (*OTP* 1:508); see also *Sepher HaRazim* 3:2-3; *T. Adam* 4:8 (*OTP* 1:995); and M. de Jonge, "Thrones," *DDD²* 864-66.

51. Ps 77:18; 104:7 (cf. 1 Sam 7:10; 12:17); *3 En.* 14:4, "Ra'ami'el, who is in charge of thunder" (*OTP* 1:267); *Jub.* 2:2, "angels of resoundings and thunder and lightning" (*OTP* 2:55); *T. Adam* 4:3 (*OTP* 1:995).

52. M. O. Wise, "Thunder in Gemini: An Aramaic Brontologion (4Q318) from Qumran," in *Thunder in Gemini: And Other Essays on the History, Language and Literature of Second Temple Palestine* (JSPSup 15; Sheffield: JSOT Press, 1994), 13-50.

53. Cf. Rev 16:17-18. Other thunders are intelligible: Rev 14:2; 19:6.

As was the case with angel names, the NT also utilizes "discovered" demon names. The מַשְׁחִית, "Destroyer," of Exod 12:23 also appears in 2 Sam 24:16 and Ezekiel 9 (cf. 2 Kgs 19:35).[54] Plague and destroying angels are further elaborated in *1 En.* 53:3; 56:1; 66:1; and 1QS IV, 12. The Destroyer (ὀλοθρεύων/ὀλοθρευτής) resurfaces in Heb 11:28 and 1 Cor 10:10 through the LXX's translation of מַשְׁחִית.[55]

Just as in CD V, 17 and 11Q13 II, 13, the בְּלִיַּעַל, "wickedness," of Hebrew Scripture becomes a personified synonym for Satan (2 Cor 6:14-15).[56] Similarly, the spirit named Μεγάλη (Acts 8:10) may derive from Ps 146:5 (LXX).[57] The four furies of Ps 78:49, חֲרוֹן אַפּוֹ עֶבְרָה וָזַעַם וְצָרָה, "anger, wrath, indignation, distress," called "a company of destroying angels," perhaps reappear as four bound angels leading the plague-inflicting army of two myriad myriad in Rev 9:15-16.[58] The angel Ἀπολλύων (Rev 9:11) owns a textual pedigree drawn from Hebrew poetry, where אֲבַדּוֹן, "perdition," parallels other personified enemies of God.[59] Therefore, numerous examples of onomastic exegesis occur throughout the NT.

Conclusion

The samples offered above, limited to terms relevant to NT study, display the method and logic of the techniques employed to discover names for powers as practiced in the Second Temple period. Growing out of a history of semantic reflection, personification, and translation, this was a fruitful

54. 1 Chr 21:1 equates "Satan" with "the anger of the LORD" (2 Sam 24:1), thereby personifying Wrath, as in Num 16:46 (MT 17:11), "wrath has gone forth from the LORD; the plague has begun." Similarly, *Jubilees* treats the situation in Exod 4:24, when "the LORD met him [Moses] and tried to kill him," as an encounter with Mastemah (*Jub.* 48:2).

55. S. A. Meier, "Destroyer," *DDD²* 240-44.

56. S. D. Sperling, "Belial," *DDD²* 169-71.

57. In the context of God calling the stars by their angelic names, the phrase μέγας ὁ κύριος ἡμῶν, καὶ μεγάλη ἡ ἰσχὺς αὐτοῦ from Ps 146:5 may represent the exegetical source for the spirit named in Acts 8:10 — ἡ δύναμις τοῦ θεοῦ ἡ καλουμένη Μεγάλη.

58. Similar LXX exegesis renders עֶבְרוֹת, "furies," of Job 40:11 by ἄγγελοι. Cf. the seven plague angels (Rev 15:1), the seven demons of the Pazuzu plague (*ANEP* no. 658) and Lamaštu amulet (*ANEP* no. 660), or the seven Apkallu (J. C. Greenfield, "Apkallu," *DDD²* 72-74). Cf. Matt 12:45; Luke 8:2.

59. Prov 15:11 and Job 26:6 (par. Sheol); Job 28:22 (par. Death); Job 31:12; Ps 88:11 (par. Grave).

method, providing much of the vocabulary for evil used in the NT and its contemporary literature. The literalization of metaphor, orthographic ambiguity, and the belief that canonical texts hold mysteries open to those who search the Scriptures diligently all combined to make the Second Temple period the golden age for the emergence of the vocabulary of evil through onomastic exegesis.

Part II

GOSPELS AND ACTS

The Spirit in the Gospels:
Breaking the Impasse of Early-Twentieth-Century German Scholarship

John R. Levison

Introduction

While in his professorial life Gerald F. Hawthorne instilled in a generation of college students a love for the intricacies of Greek grammar and syntax, in his private and professional lives he mused considerably on the implications of early Christian pneumatology. In keeping with Gerald Hawthorne's preoccupation with pneumatology — which generated initially a master's thesis presented to Wheaton College in 1954 and ultimately, nine college generations later, *The Presence and the Power* — I shall also reflect on the topic of pneumatology.[1]

The particular prism of this brief study is somewhat peculiar. I intend to devote the first portion of my analysis to three early-twentieth-century German studies of early Jewish and Christian pneumatology, all of which were published by 1926, within a year of Hawthorne's birth. These studies belong to a period of extraordinary fecundity that followed on the heels of Hermann Gunkel's influential *Die Wirkungen des heiligen Geistes*.[2]

---

1. G. F. Hawthorne, "The Significance of the Holy Spirit in the Life of Christ" (M.A. thesis, Wheaton College Graduate School, 1954); idem, *The Presence and the Power* (Dallas: Word, 1991). I am grateful to Karen Carroll, copy editor at the National Humanities Center, for proofreading the manuscript of my article, much of which I composed in the solitude of the Center.

2. H. Gunkel, *Die Wirkungen des heiligen Geistes nach der populären Anschauung der*

In 1899, in the preface to a second edition, Gunkel issued the challenge that monographs be written on various aspects of early Christian pneumatology. Hans Leisegang, Friedrich Büchsel, and Heinrich von Baer, among others, adopted vastly differing approaches and explored diverse literary corpora in their effort to trace the contours of the spirit that lay at the base of nascent Christianity.[3] I limit myself in this article principally to one aspect of their method that has a direct impact on our assessment of the significance of the holy spirit in the life of Jesus: the conceptual foreground of the holy spirit.[4]

The purpose of this initial analysis of the works of Leisegang, Büchsel, and von Baer is to differentiate their fundamental assumptions and method in order to explore the impasse to which their studies led them — an impasse that has been resurrected in more recent assessments of the significance of the spirit in the life of Jesus. In the second part of this study I shall suggest a way to break this impasse by analyzing the significance of the spirit in one section of an early Jewish text, the *Liber antiquitatum biblicarum*. The purpose of this study, therefore, is twofold: to wrest from relative obscurity three important German studies of early Christian pneumatology, and to press for a fresh paradigm that is adequate to the task of embracing the rich foreground of early Christian pneumatology.

The Foreground of the Spirit: Early-Twentieth-Century German Contributions

Hawthorne began his study with the assertion that what "is known and understood and taught about the Spirit in the New Testament is directly related to what was known and understood and written about the Spirit in

---

apostolischen Zeit und nach der Lehre des Apostels Paulus (Göttingen: Vandenhoeck & Ruprecht, 1888).

3. I am reluctant to omit the masterful monograph by P. Volz, *Der Geist Gottes und die verwandten Erscheinungen im Alten Testament und im anschließenden Judentum* (Tübingen: Mohr, 1910). Volz analyzed with extraordinary acuity the development of perceptions of the spirit in Israelite and early Jewish literature. The second part of the book, in which he analyzed "Pneumatische Personen" and "Die Geisthypostase," is extremely interesting. Unfortunately, Volz devoted but a few concluding pages to early Christian literature; his monograph does not, therefore, suit the parameters of this article.

4. Throughout this article, "spirit" and "holy spirit" are not capitalized since the time in question predates the advent of trinitarian theology.

the Old Testament and intertestamental literature."[5] In practice, Hawthorne turned principally to the Old Testament and only infrequently to early Judaism, which, he contended, "contains many of these same ideas about the Spirit of God," but which, on the other hand, is characterized less by the present experience of the spirit than by the expectation that the messiah would inaugurate an age of the spirit in the future.[6] Hellenistic Jewish authors, such as Philo Judaeus and Flavius Josephus, as well as Greco-Roman authors, such as Cicero and Plutarch, play virtually no role in Hawthorne's analysis of the significance of the spirit in the life of Jesus.

Precisely this question of the foreground of early Christian pneumatology proved riveting to early-twentieth-century German scholars and led to wildly divergent assessments of the influence of the Old Testament, Palestinian Judaism, Diaspora Judaism, and Greco-Roman beliefs on early Christianity. The poles of this debate are represented by Hans Leisegang, an avid proponent of the *religionsgeschichtliche Schule,* who attributed the development of early Christian pneumatology to Greco-Roman influence, over against Friedrich Büchsel and Heinrich von Baer, who anticipated Hawthorne's position by arguing that the Old Testament and its postbiblical interpreters exercised a singular influence on early Christian beliefs about the significance of the holy spirit in the life of Jesus.

Hans Leisegang

In 1919 Hans Leisegang devoted an entire volume to the question, "Ist die Lehre vom Heiligen Geiste griechischen oder orientalischen Ursprungs?"[7] This terse query led Leisegang to ponder whether

5. Hawthorne, *Presence and Power,* 2.

6. Ibid., 22-23 (see also idem, "Holy Spirit," *DLNT* 490, 492). Hawthorne (*Presence and Power,* 90n.1) conceded that the Jews whose beliefs are represented in the Dead Sea Scrolls believed in the persistence of the spirit. I have attempted to refute the notion that first-century Jews saw themselves bereft of the spirit in "Did the Spirit Withdraw from Israel? An Evaluation of the Earliest Jewish Data," *NTS* 43 (1997): 35-57.

7. H. Leisegang, *Der Heilige Geist: Das Wesen und Werden der mystisch-intuitiven Erkenntnis in der Philosophie und Religion der Griechen* (Leipzig: Teubner, 1919), 4. For critical discussions of Leisegang, see I. Heinemann, "Philons Lehre vom Heiligen Geist und der intuitiven Erkenntnis," *MGWJ* 64 (1920): 8-29, 100-122; "Die Lehre vom Heiligen Geist im Judentum und in den Evangelien," *MGWJ* 66 (1922): 169-80, 268-79; C. K. Barrett, *The Holy Spirit and the Gospel Tradition* (London: SPCK, 1947), 10-14, 36, 132, 134; Max Turner, *Power*

vielleicht auch der Teil der christlichen Lehre, der sich um den Begriff des πνεῦμα ἅγιον gruppiert und den man von theologischer Seite nicht anders als aus dem Alten Testamente, besonders den Propheten verstehen zu können meinte, aus dem hellenistischen Geistesleben entsprungen sein könnte, ja daß vielleicht sogar die Theologen und Gelehrten der hellenistischen Zeit mit einem im Griechentum bereits völlig ausgebildeten Begriffe vom Heiligen Geiste an das Alte Testament herantraten und ihn in dem πνεῦμα ἅγιον der Septuaginta wiederzufinden glaubten.[8]

Leisegang recognized the difficulty such a hypothesis posed. How could he reconstruct Greek conceptions of pneumatology when no pre-Christian author exhibits a pneumatology nearly so developed as the NT, and the earliest authors with comparably developed pneumatologies arise after the first century and are likely influenced by Christianity?

To avoid throwing himself helplessly upon the horns of this dilemma, Leisegang identified Philo Judaeus as the single most significant figure of antiquity for grasping the historical emergence of the concept of πνεῦμα ἅγιον. Philo lived "in der Mitte" of the "problematische Zeitalter der Geistesgeschichte des Abendlandes" — a period characterized by the masses' waxing mistrust of philosophy before the ascendancy of religion. Philo lived also "in der Mitte" of Greek culture, Judaism, and Christianity.[9] He provided Leisegang, therefore, with the perfect building block for his project: here was a literary figure who referred often and creatively to the divine spirit, whose commentaries on the Bible can unequivocally be considered religio-philosophical, and whose interpretations encapsulated popular mystical conceptions of the spirit that embodied a marvelous coalescence of Jewish and Greek conceptions.

Leisegang felt confident that he was capable of distilling the Greco-Roman conceptions from the Jewish veneer that Philo, in Leisegang's opinion, had spread over them. Philo could provide, therefore, a window into popular Greco-Roman religiosity: "Philons Anschauungen zwar tief im griechischen Volksglauben wurzelten, daß er aber die Volksvorstellungen bereits durchtränkt mit griechischer Philosophie übernahm . . . sich der

---

from on High: The Spirit in Israel's Restoration and Witness in Luke-Acts (JPTSup 9; Sheffield: Sheffield Academic Press, 1996), 26-29.

8. Leisegang, *Der Heilige Geist,* 4.

9. Ibid., 14.

Volksglaube unter seinen Händen zu einer philosophischen Religion der Gelehrten umgestaltete."[10]

Having reconstructed, in accordance with the subtitle of his first volume, "the essence and being of mystical-intuitive knowledge in the philosophy and religion of the Greeks," Leisegang turned in his second volume to early Christianity. The nature of the Gospels required of Leisegang a refinement of his method, which would consist essentially of two related components: *Religionsgeschichte* and *Traditionsgeschichte*.

The *religionsgeschichtlich* component of Leisegang's study lies along the continuum of his prior volume, for he was once again intent on determining whether the teaching on the holy spirit was of Jewish or Greek origin. This task does not consist merely of identifying discrete elements and classifying them as Jewish or Greek. Leisegang decried such a simplistic taxonomy and starkly pointed out that he was not undertaking a typical "Zusammenstellung einzelner . . . herausgerissener Sätze, die eine gegenseitige Abhängigkeit und Entlehnung von einer Religion zur anderen."[11] Rather,

> Für die Beurteilung des Ganzen möchte ich hier ausdrücklich darauf hinweisen, daß es mir durchaus fern liegt, die jüdischen und sonstigen orientalischen Einflüsse auf die synoptische Tradition durch einseitige Betonung der griechischen Motive in den Hintergrund zu stellen. . . . Es ist dabei immer zu beachten, daß meine Fragestellung nicht lautet: Welche Worte, Begriffe und Vorstellungen in den Evangelien sind ihrem letzten Ursprung nach griechisch oder semitisch? Ich frage vielmehr: Was mußte sich der Grieche unter den Worten, Begriffen und Vorstellungen denken, die er in der evangelischen Überlieferung fand, und was hat er sich tatsächlich unter ihnen gedacht? Was hat er aus der Tradition gemacht? Was hat er in sie hineingedeutet?[12]

The ability to answer this question hinges, of course, upon a related task, namely the identification of the sort of Greek milieu from which this hypothetical Greek reader would have emerged.

Consequently, Leisegang sought to demonstrate that the sort of

---

10. Ibid., 240.

11. H. Leisegang, *Pneuma Hagion: Der Ursprung des Geistbegriffs der synoptischen Evangelien aus der griechischen Mystik* (Leipzig: Hinrichs, 1922), 3.

12. Ibid., iii-iv.

Greek sensibilities reflected in the Synoptic Gospels are *popular* rather than sophisticated, "primitiven Volksglauben" rather than "gelehrte Spekulation."[13] Here we are led back to Leisegang's first volume, in which he had contended that the influence of learned philosophies waned in the presence of popular religious vitality.

According to Leisegang, those Greek conceptions that illuminate early Christian pneumatology are not only popular, they are also *mystical*. Christianity lay within a popular culture that was characterized by a re- newed interest in matters of the spirit. Christianity and Hellenism were "beide als Kinder eines Geistes . . . des heiligen Geistes der Mystik, der von unten, aus der Masse des Volkes nach oben stieg und Wissenschaft und Philosophie über den Haufen warf."[14]

Leisegang drew a *traditionsgeschichtlich* inference from this *religions-geschichtlich* distinction between Jewish and Hellenistic conceptions. In his opinion, the Hellenistic character of spirit material in the Gospels points to its being demonstrably later:

> alle Stellen, an denen in den synoptischen Evangelien vom heiligen Geiste als eines das Leben und die Lehre Jesu tragenden Faktors die Rede ist, gar nicht zum ursprünglichen, auf palästinensischem Boden erwachsenen Evangelium von Jesus gehörten, sondern später in Rück- sicht auf das Heidentum und aus seinem Geist heraus entstanden sind und sich als Zusätze oder Abänderungen der ältesten Bestandteile evangelischer Überlieferung erkennen lassen.[15]

To corroborate these data, Leisegang posed the question of why the spirit virtually disappears during the life of Jesus: "Wo bleibt die Ausnutzung des Motivs der pneumatischen Empfängnis der Maria und der auf diesem Vorgang beruhenden Gottessohnschaft als wirksamster Beweis für die wunderbare, übernatürliche Kraft des Heilands und Todüberwinders?" Further, those references to the spirit that do occur in the Gospels, follow- ing the birth narratives, point to "keinem organischen Zusammenhange" with the overall context of the Gospels.[16]

Leisegang promised *religionsgeschichtlich* sophistication rather than

13. Ibid., 3.
14. Ibid., 4.
15. Ibid., 5.
16. Ibid., 12-13.

naiveté, and the character of that sophistication is no more evident than in his lengthy analysis of Luke's birth narratives. Leisegang observed that the vocabulary associated with the spirit, particularly the verb ἐπισκιάζω ("to overshadow") in Luke 1:35, reflects Greek conceptions of mantic prophecy, such as can be found in Philo's writings, according to which the mind is overshadowed by the spirit.[17] Prophetic inspiration, however, is hardly tantamount to actual impregnation, so Leisegang was compelled to garner data from farther afield to associate prophetic inspiration with Mary's pregnancy. Such data included: the commonplace belief that the Delphic priestess received the inspiring πνεῦμα through her genitalia; more generally, the belief that inspiration could develop within the womb of the prophet; the association of μανία in medical literature, such as Galen's writings, with the womb; myths of the birth of gods, such as Dionysius and Branchus, that associate divine birth with prophetic gifts; the Greco-Roman association of divine begetting with virginity that Leisegang discerned in Philo's allegories, according to which four virgins, who symbolize the virtues, are made pregnant by God and bear children; and the use of the word ψυχή ("soul") as a euphemism for the womb in folk religion, as it is reflected in the magical papyri.[18]

Leisegang gathered these data because he believed them to be various manifestations of a taut association among prophetic inspiration, divine begetting, and virginity — such as is reflected in the spirit's overshadowing of a virgin, Mary, to bear a prophetically endowed child and to break out herself in prophetic utterance. The stunningly divergent genres of literature represented here — popular conceptions of Delphic inspiration, of so-called ventriloquists, of "soul" as a euphemism for "womb"; medical analyses of μανία and the womb; myths in narrative form associated with Apollos and Branchus; and religio-philosophical allegorical interpretations of virginity — serve for Leisegang to demonstrate how widespread the association of divine begetting, virginity, and prophecy was in the Greco-Roman world.

Having established this association with respect to the inspiration of human beings, Leisegang turned to another indication of this pattern: the divine or heavenly world, in which God the Father is said to impregnate Wisdom, who bears the Logos, according to Philo's allegorical interpreta-

17. Ibid., 25-27.
18. Ibid., 31-48.

tion.[19] This in turn led Leisegang to a lengthy discussion of various other corpora. In the *Protoevangelium of James,* for example, the pregnancy of Mary is attributed variously to an array of divine entities, including λόγος, δύναμις, πνεῦμα, and ἄγγελος.[20]

Leisegang's discussion, which encompasses vast corpora of literature — from popular to medical to philosophical — is certainly sophisticated, particularly if his point be taken that the variety of these genres is evidence of a tenacious pattern in the Greco-Roman world in which prophetic utterance, virginity, and divine begetting were associated with one another. On the other hand, the prolixity and complexity of Leisegang's discussion of the foreground to Luke's birth narratives also provided fodder for the less generous assessment of his critic, Heinrich von Baer, to whom Leisegang's proposal appeared less as a compelling display of erudition than as an "überaus komplizierten Irrwegen . . . sein ganzes Labyrinth."[21]

Friedrich Büchsel

While Friedrich Büchsel's encyclopedic examination of the spirit does not contain an attack of Leisegang's approach to the foreground of early Christian pneumatology, many particular criticisms of Leisegang's interpretations appear in brief discussions and lengthy notes.[22] It is Büchsel's approach more generally, however, that accentuates the contrast between his work and Leisegang's. Leisegang had interpreted each reference to the spirit discretely because he did not deem them to be the product of a single mind or tradition. Consequently, references to the spirit could be interpreted somewhat independently from one another although all reflect the milieu of popular Greco-Roman mysticism. Büchsel was critical of this approach in part because he took more seriously than Leisegang the narrative and theological context of the Gospels.

19. Ibid., 50-55.

20. Ibid., 55-67. Leisegang also observed (67-69) that the first storm of mystical experience and enthusiasm came upon women; hence the relevance of these data for understanding Luke's portrayal of Mary's experience.

21. H. von Baer, *Der Heilige Geist in den Lukasschriften* (Stuttgart: Kohlhammer, 1926), 123.

22. F. Büchsel, *Der Geist Gottes im Neuen Testament* (Gütersloh: Bertelsmann, 1926), e.g., 143n.2, 162n.1, 169n.1, 179n.6, 186n.1, 193, 197, 198n.4, 199n.2, 200n.1.

The theological crux of the Gospel narratives is that Jesus is a *Pneumatiker*. His whole life flows from this center: his prophetic authority; his ascetic bent, as during his fast in the desert, as well as in his sayings that repudiate the family; and his visionary experiences. All of these flow from his experience of the spirit. Central to Jesus' life as a *Pneumatiker* was his visionary experience at the Jordan River, in which Jesus came to understand that the center of his life was the love of God, to which he as God's son could lay claim: "erst ist Jesus Gottes Sohn wie ein Kind, dann wie ein frommer Israelit und seit der Taufe als der, der in dem vollen unmittelbaren Besitz der Liebe Gottes steht, der in einzigartiger Weise Gottes Sohn durch den heiligen Geist ist."[23]

Büchsel contended that Leisegang's mythic and popular interpretation of the spirit that he had culled from Greco-Roman sources is simply incompatible with the portrait of Jesus as *Pneumatiker*. The significance of the spirit in the Gospels, particularly its relation to the love of God, does not originate in the Greco-Roman world or the Hellenistic Christian community; its foreground is ultimately the Old Testament.

This distinction is particularly evident in Büchsel's interpretation of the Lukan birth narratives. There are no traces, Büchsel contended, of the inspiration of a Greek prophetess — an element that plays a principal role in Leisegang's reconstruction of Luke's milieu. According to Büchsel, "zwischen der 'pneumatischen' Empfängnis der griechischen Prophetinnen und der der Maria besteht ein tiefgreifender Unterschied."[24] In fact, the worlds Leisegang had attempted to associate exhibit characteristics that serve only to separate them from one another. "Die Erotik des Mythus, der Polytheismus des Mythus sind diesem wesentlich, und andererseits, die christliche Frömmigkeit ist der Lukaserzählung wesentlich — die große Frage der Erzählung ist: wird Maria glauben, wenn der Engel zu ihr redet, oder durch Unglauben Gottes Werk, die Sendung des Messias, stören . . . deshalb ist ein kausaler Zusammenhang zwischen beiden Erzählungen nicht vorstellbar."[25]

Therefore, the clearest and most plausible foreground of Luke's birth narratives — and the Gospels in their entirety — is "nicht hellenistische Mythenvorstellungen, sondern der jüdische Gedanke, daß Gott durch

---

23. Ibid., 167.
24. Ibid., 200n.1.
25. Ibid., 198n.4.

seinen Geist schafft."[26] The "alttestamentlich-jüdisch" character permeates the Lukan birth narratives: references to the salvation of Israel, expectations of the Messiah, and multiple allusions to the Psalms. "Die Wirkungen des Geistes, die sich bei den Propheten zeigen, sind durchaus die, die man bei den alttestamentlichen und jüdischen Propheten gewohnt ist. Auf den griechischen Volksglauben weist nichts an diesen Propheten und Prophetinnen."[27]

Heinrich von Baer

Nearly half of Heinrich von Baer's *Der Heilige Geist in den Lukasschriften* is devoted to an explicit critique of Leisegang. Significantly, it is the second half of the book — not the first — that contains the critique, for von Baer's work does not rise and fall on the validity of Leisegang's proposal but on von Baer's own interpretation of early Christian pneumatology, which he elaborated in the first part of the book. Like Büchsel, von Baer contended that the overall perspective — the *Gesamtbild* — of early Christian pneumatology can have nothing to do with the alien Greco-Roman world Leisegang had proposed as its source. Von Baer dismissed the *religionsgeschichtliche Schule,* of which Leisegang was a proponent, for its indiscriminate use of parallels: "Es werden oft Parallelen herangezogen, die, äußerlich betrachtet, gewisse Analogien zu Aussagen neutestamentlicher Schriftsteller über den Heiligen Geist aufweisen, die aber in Wirklichkeit einer anderen religiösen Welt entstammen, da das Verhältnis von Gott und Mensch, das hinter diesen Geistesaussagen steht, keineswegs dem Glaubensverhältnis des Christen zur Gottheit entspricht."[28]

According to von Baer, the Christian world — the world evinced by Luke-Acts — regards the spirit as the means of God's activity in the world. The spirit has not been *uniformly* active, however, because history is divided by Luke into three distinct *heilsgeschichtlich* epochs, each of which requires slightly different activities of the spirit: "Es sind verschiedene Heilsepochen, in denen, dem Willen Gottes entsprechend, der Geist sich in

26. Ibid., 200.
27. Ibid., 200-201.
28. Von Baer, *Lukasschriften,* 13-14; see 16, 20, 28-33.

verschiedener Weise den Menschen offenbarte."[29] The first epoch encompasses the prophetic age, including John the Baptist, who by means of the spirit of prophecy announces the coming of the Messiah. The second epoch is inaugurated by the conception and birth of the earthly Jesus, who is empowered by the spirit to bring about God's reign. The third, inaugurated by Pentecost, is characterized by the endowment of the spirit of the risen Lord Jesus upon his followers, who proclaim the good news.

Behind all of these epochs stands a single God whom the Gospel authors know from Old Testament *Heilsgeschichte.* Since the spirit is the driving force of God's *heilsgeschichtlich* activity, it too is inextricably bound to the Old Testament. Unthinkable, therefore, is Leisegang's thesis that early Christian pneumatology can be interpreted aright apart from its Old Testament character, detached from the *heilsgeschichtlich* purpose that lies at its core. The thrust of von Baer's critique, then, is the implausibility of Leisegang's contention that early Christian pneumatology arose independently of Old Testament and Jewish influence. None of the alleged sources Leisegang adduced can, according to von Baer, traverse the impassable gulf that separates Israelite *Heilsgeschichte,* in which God acts through the spirit, from Greco-Roman conceptions of the spirit.

In part two of his study, von Baer presupposed this Old Testament and Jewish fulcrum for Lukan pneumatology as he turned his attention to the *religionsgeschichtlich* foreground of specific references to the spirit in Luke-Acts. His approach can be illustrated, as were those of Leisegang and Büchsel, by his interpretation of the Lukan birth narratives.

Von Baer conceded that a Greek reader might have understood a phrase such as "Son of God" as an indication of the physical begetting of Jesus.[30] For Jews, however, such a physical origin for Jesus would have been abhorrent — "eine Gotteslästerung und ein Greuel" — because of its association with uncleanness according to cultic Israelite precepts.[31] Therefore, for Luke and his Jewish readers, the name "Son of God" would indicate divine origin rather than earthly birth. Further, other words with which this designation is associated, such as "most high" and "power," recollect the conceptual world of the LXX; these conceptions ought "in erster Linie auf

---

29. Ibid., 111.

30. This would have been understood in such a way, according to von Baer (ibid., 125-26), along the lines of primitive mythological conceptions but not in accordance with the philosophical and dualistic precepts of Platonism.

31. Ibid., 125.

die Begriffswelt des griechischen A.T. zurückgreifen müssen."[32] For this reason, von Baer criticized Leisegang for his effort to understand the verb ἐπέρχομαι ("come upon") in Luke 1:35 in Greek terms as the physical approach of the spirit. It reflects rather Exod 40:35 LXX, in which the cloud overshadows and fills Israel with divine glory.

The vocabulary associated with the spirit in Luke 1–2, then, has nothing to do with Jesus' physical birth but everything to do with his status as God's Son. The designation Son of God "ist in dieser überaus zarten Schilderung des Geschehens absolut nichts Konkretes über den Vorgang der Empfängnis des Jesuskindes gesagt, das auf eine physische Beteiligung des Heiligen Geistes hinweist. Das Pneuma Hagion ist auch hier wie bei Matthäus die Bezeichnung der wunderbaren Gotteskraft, durch die das außerordentliche Geschehen auf hyperphysische Art bewirkt ist."[33]

Von Baer's critique of Leisegang results in a concluding word about the birth narratives that expresses more generally the fundamental difference between them vis-à-vis the foreground of the holy spirit in the Gospels:

> Es rächt sich bei Leisegang, daß er in seiner Erklärung ganz einseitig von griechisch-hellenistischen Prämissen ausgeht und die natürlichen Zusammenhänge, die sich aus der Vorstellungswelt des A.T. ergeben, außer acht läßt. Es ist doch erstaunlich, daß er in der Aufzählung der griechischen Vorstellungen von einem lebenspendenden Pneuma solche biblische Anschauungen, wie sie z. B. Ez. 37 vorliegen . . . übersieht.[34]

We may recall at this point that Leisegang had assiduously gathered references to the spirit in several genres of Greco-Roman literature in order to establish a pattern that associates prophecy, virginity, and divine begetting. In the eyes of von Baer, Leisegang's collection is nothing more than a "verwickelte These" that was formed "durch eine künstlich zusammengefügte Kette."[35]

---

32. Ibid., 127.
33. Ibid., 129.
34. Ibid., 131.
35. Ibid., 131.

Toward a Fresh Paradigm for
Understanding the Foreground of the Spirit

Contemporary scholars appear to have been convinced less by the position of Leisegang than by the perspectives of von Baer and Büchsel. Hawthorne appealed with notable frequency to the Old Testament, both Hebrew and Greek, and occasionally to early Jewish literature; he never called on Greco-Roman literature to explain the significance of the spirit in the life of Jesus. Hawthorne is not alone in locating the foreground of early Christianity in Jewish rather than Greco-Roman literature. Robert Menzies commended von Baer for having "argued persuasively against Leisegang for the Jewish origin of Luke's pneumatology."[36] Max Turner, whose discussions of Lukan pneumatology are both equitable and well informed, wrote: "Leisegang's second monograph had relatively little of permanent value to offer. History may well claim its most vital contribution was to stimulate the works largely written to refute him. Nevertheless, this work . . . sharply posed (though it did not satisfactorily answer) the *religionsgeschichtlich* question of the vital background to this concept."[37]

No doubt some of the blame for Turner's evaluation and for the subsequent tendency to opt for the alleged Jewish rather than Greco-Roman foreground of early Christianity lies at Leisegang's feet. His effort, for example, to interpret Jesus' baptism, including the descent of the dove, through the lens of Greco-Roman mystical experiences of rebirth may deserve C. K. Barrett's evaluation: "On one side, [his views] are valuable and true; on another they are impossible and misleading. The connection which is made between the birth, the baptism and the resurrection, by the stress laid, on each of these occasions, on the Sonship of Jesus, is important. But to find in these events, or in the first two of them, a mythological sexual act, which links them with Hellenistic ideas, is to go further than the evidence warrants."[38]

However, to opt in principle for the position of von Baer and Büchsel over against Leisegang is not an altogether satisfactory solution to the *religionsgeschichtlich* question, for it presupposes the existence of a dichotomy between Hellenism and Judaism that simply does not characterize

---

36. R. P. Menzies, *Empowered for Witness: The Spirit in Luke-Acts* (JPTSup 6; Sheffield: Sheffield Academic Press, 1994), 35.

37. Turner, *Power from on High*, 29.

38. Barrett, *Gospel Tradition*, 37.

early Jewish and Christian literature.[39] Barrett himself, while rejecting many of Leisegang's interpretations, recognized that Luke's birth narrative contains a coalescence of Greek and Jewish elements. The picture of the holy spirit as not merely one of producing physical effects (e.g., the miraculous feats of the judges [Judg 3:7-11; 6; 13–16]), but of generating or producing something physical, has a direct parallel in neither of the Testaments. Moreover, Luke combines this unique conception of the spirit with "the notion of divine begetting, which . . . is one that flourishes on pagan rather than Jewish soil" and with "the non-Jewish emphasis upon virginity." This coalescence, remarkably, occurs within a narrative whose language is Septuagintal. Thus, concluded Barrett, "the infancy narratives produce a contradictory impression, since they seem at once Jewish and Hellenistic."[40]

A satisfactory approach to the *religionsgeschichtlich* issue, therefore, ought to recognize that early Jewish and Christian literature may be "at once Jewish and Hellenistic." More to the point, it must address the question raised by von Baer and Büchsel: not just whether Jewish and Greco-Roman elements coexist within a literary text, but whether Greco-Roman elements are incorporated into a context that is clearly forged on the anvil of the Old Testament. In other words, are von Baer and Büchsel correct in their contention that it is inconceivable that early Jewish or Christian authors committed to *Heilsgeschichte* would incorporate alien conceptions of the spirit from their Greco-Roman environment?

A piece of literature that is relevant for answering this question and for breaking the impasse created by the position of Leisegang on the one hand, and von Baer and Büchsel on the other, is the *Liber antiquitatum biblicarum* (or Pseudo-Philo), a narrative retelling of the Bible from creation to the death of Saul, possibly written in Hebrew as early as the first or second century C.E.[41] This postbiblical narrative exhibits extensive incorporation of Greco-Roman elements concerning the spirit within a *heilsgeschichtlich* framework.

Pseudo-Philo's commitment to *Heilsgeschichte* is evident throughout this narrative. The Deuteronomic pattern in the biblical book of Judges of

39. In this regard see the formidable and pioneering work of M. Hengel, *Judaism and Hellenism: Studies in Their Encounter in Palestine during the Early Hellenistic Period* (trans. J. Bowden; 2 vols.; Minneapolis: Fortress, 1974).

40. Barrett, *Gospel Tradition*, 17-18. The solution for Barrett (21-24) lies in Hellenistic rather than Palestinian Judaism, in literary texts such as *Poimandres* in the Hermetic Corpus.

41. See the translation by D. J. Harrington, "Pseudo-Philo," *OTP*, 2:297-377.

sin-punishment-salvation occurs repeatedly, often in speeches that are inserted into the biblical narrative in order to express the book's thesis clearly (e.g., *LAB* 3:9-10; 12:4; 13:10; and 19:2-5). The root of sin — idolatry — which goes to the heart of biblical *Heilsgeschichte,* plays a prominent role in Pseudo-Philo. For example, when Kenaz probes the sins of various tribes, the first three non-Levitical tribes admit to various forms of idolatry (25:9). Gideon's ephod is interpreted as an idol (36:3). In the second version of the Decalogue, all sins are in some way an abuse of idolatry. For instance, the Israelites take God's name in vain by giving God's name to graven images (44:6-7).

In this narrative, which is steeped in *Heilsgeschichte,* the spirit plays an occasional but significant role.[42] Of particular relevance is *LAB* 28:6-10, which transpires as the judge Kenaz (biblical Othniel in Judg 3:9-11) is about to die: "And when they [the prophets and elders of Israel] had sat down, a holy spirit came upon Kenaz and dwelled in him and put him in ecstasy [elevated his mind], and he began to prophesy, saying . . . 'Behold, now I see what I had not hoped for, and I perceive that I did not understand'" (28:6).[43] Kenaz then recounts a vision of cosmic proportions that spans several millennia, from creation to judgment. This remarkable vision concludes:

> And when Kenaz had spoken these words, he was awakened, and his senses came back to him. But he did not know what he had said or what he had seen. But this alone he said to the people: "If the repose of the just after they have died is like this, we must die to the corruptible world so as not to see sins." And when he had said these words, Kenaz died and slept with his fathers. And the people mourned for him thirty days. (28:10)

This depiction of Kenaz's reception of the spirit contains a great deal that does not arise from its biblical source, Judg 3:9-11. The scene in *LAB* begins, first of all, with the observation that the spirit both sprang upon Kenaz and inhabited him. Neither conception, taken independently, is unbiblical. The verb "leapt," *insilire,* echoes 1 Samuel 10–11 rather than Judges 3; in the Vulgate of 1 Sam 10:6, 10, and 11:6, the verb *insilire* depicts

---

42. See my "Prophetic Inspiration in Pseudo-Philo's *Liber Antiquitatum Biblicarum,*" *JQR* 85 (1995): 297-329.

43. The Latin of the narrative portion reads, "et dum sederent, insiluit spiritus sanctus habitans in Cenez, et extulit sensum eius, et cepit prophetare dicens."

the powerful presence of the spirit when it overcomes Saul, causing him to prophesy or to gather his people for war by cutting a yoke of oxen in several pieces. The notion of a spirit that indwells an individual is also at home in numerous texts that speak of wisdom, such as Gen 41:38; Exod 31:3; Num 27:18-20; Deut 34:9; Job 27:3; 32:7-8, 18; Dan 4:5-6, 15; 5:11-14 MT. However, what distinguishes Kenaz's experience from these biblical texts is the juxtaposition of these two very different conceptions of the spirit's advent: the spirit both sprang upon Kenaz *and* indwelt him.

Pseudo-Philo describes, in addition to the mode of the spirit's presence, the effect of the spirit on Kenaz: ecstasy occurred when the spirit incited Kenaz's mind to ascend. The end of Kenaz's ecstatic experience transpired when "he was awakened, and his senses came back to him." Kenaz was in a trancelike state from which it was necessary to awaken him. The ecstatic character of Kenaz's vision is evident as well in its conclusion: "But he did not know what he had said or what he had seen" (28:10).

A rich coalescence of nonbiblical details, therefore, underscores the ecstatic nature of Kenaz's experience. The contours of the holy spirit's effect on Kenaz are clear and well conceived, and they are most decidedly *not* the contours supplied by the *heilsgeschichtlich* narrative he purports to retell. Such extrabiblical elements correspond rather to popular Greco-Roman conceptions of the ascent of the soul as they are detailed by Cicero, in his *De divinatione,* which he composed during the first century B.C.E. In a description of the inspired prophetic ascent of the soul, Quintus, Cicero's brother and a chief proponent of the Stoic view of inspiration, says:

> When, therefore, the soul has been withdrawn by sleep from contact with sensual ties, then does it recall the past, comprehend the present, and foresee the future. For though the sleeping body then lies as if it were dead, yet the soul is alive and strong, and will be much more so after death when it is wholly free of the body. Hence its power to divine is much enhanced by the approach of death. For example, those in the grasp of a serious and fatal sickness realize the fact that death impends; and so, visions of dead people generally appear to them and then their desire for fame is strongest; while those who have lived otherwise than as they should, feel, at such a time, the keenest sorrow for their sins.[44]

---

44. Cicero, *De divinatione* 1.63. Translation of W. A. Falconer, *Cicero,* vol. 20 (LCL; 1923; repr. Cambridge: Harvard Univ. Press, 1996).

Following this summary, Quintus provides an example from Posidonius "of the power of dying people to prophesy" (*Div.* 1.64). Pseudo-Philo's Kenaz could provide another example of such an inspired figure. Just prior to his death, Kenaz's *sensus* is elevated in a vision while he is in a state akin to sleep, from which he must be awakened.

Plutarch, from the late first century C.E., proffers a similar description of inspired ascent before death when, in his interpretation of Plato's *Timaeus* 71E, he states that souls exercise their innate capacity "in dreams, and some in the hour of death, when the body becomes cleansed of all impurities and attains a temperament adapted to this end, a temperament through which the reasoning and thinking faculty of the souls is relaxed and released from their present state as they range amid the irrational and imaginative realms of the future."[45]

The presence of these conceptions of inspiration suggests that the narrative of Kenaz's vision was shaped in a Jewish milieu that incorporated, consciously or inadvertently, fundamental elements of popular Greco-Roman views on the ascent of the soul. That Pseudo-Philo's portrait reflects popular rather than esoteric thinking on the subject is evident in a detail such as the need for Kenaz to be awakened. One of the interlocutors in Plutarch's *De genio Socratis*, Simmias, observes with disdain: "In popular belief, on the other hand, it is only in sleep that people receive inspiration from on high; and the notion that they are so influenced when awake and in full possession of their faculties is accounted strange and incredible."[46]

These observations, illuminating though they may be, do not adequately explain the totality of Pseudo-Philo's additions to Judg 3:9-11. The initiation of Kenaz's vision by a divine spirit also has strong associations in the Greco-Roman world. Once again, Quintus describes the inspiration of Cassandra, "who prophesied . . . under a heaven-inspired excitement and exaltation of soul" (*Div.* 1.89). This laconic description of Cassandra's abilities presupposes a lengthier description in which she illustrates how the human soul's ability to foreknow the future can be abnormally developed: "Therefore the human soul has an inherent power of presaging or of foreknowing infused into it from without, and made a part of it by the will

---

45. Plutarch, *De defectu oraculorum* 432C. Translation of F. C. Babbitt, *Plutarch's Moralia*, vol. 5 (LCL; Cambridge: Harvard Univ. Press, 1936).

46. Plutarch, *De genio Socratis* 589D. Translation of P. H. De Lacy and B. Einarson, *Plutarch's Moralia*, vol. 7 (LCL; Cambridge: Harvard Univ. Press, 1959).

of God. If that power is abnormally developed, it is called 'frenzy' or 'inspiration,' which occurs when the soul withdraws itself from the body and is violently stimulated by a divine impulse" (*Div.* 1.66).

In a later discussion of prophetic ecstasy, Quintus develops, on the basis of *Phaedrus* 246A-47E, the Platonic image of the ascent of the soul:

> Those then, whose souls, spurning their bodies, take wings and fly abroad — inflamed and aroused by a sort of passion — these . . . I say, certainly see the things which they foretell in their prophecies. Such souls do not cling to the body and are kindled by many different influences. For example, some are aroused by certain vocal tones, as by Phrygian songs, many by groves and forests, and many others by rivers and seas. I believe, too, that there were certain subterranean vapours which had the effect of inspiring persons to utter oracles. (*Div.* 1.114)

Of this form of inspiration, the signal example is again Cassandra, who illustrates the principle that "the frenzied soul sees the future long in advance" (*Div.* 1.114).

Characteristic features of the prophetic experience can be garnered from Quintus's accounts of Cassandra: the ascent of the soul apart from the body; a frenzied condition of inflammation and excitement; the impetus of external arousal by a divine impulse; and revealed knowledge of the future.

These features reappear in less anecdotal and more philosophical form in Plutarch's *De defectu oraculorum,* in which Lamprias, another ardent proponent of Stoicism, explains Delphic inspiration in similar terms. Like Quintus in Cicero's *De divinatione,* Lamprias shares the conviction that the condition of enthusiasm requires release from intellectual effort and the stimulation of an external catalyst:

> But that which foretells the future, like a tablet without writing, is both irrational and indeterminate in itself, but receptive of impressions and presentiments through what may be done to it, and inconsequently grasps at the future when it is farthest withdrawn from the present. Its withdrawal is brought about by a temperament and disposition of the body as it is subjected to a change which we call inspiration. (*Def. orac.* 432C-D)

Lamprias continues by giving examples of the catalysts that bring about this change in condition, opting himself for the final example:

Often the body of itself alone attains this disposition. Moreover the earth sends forth for men streams of many other potencies, some of them producing derangements, diseases, or deaths; others helpful, benignant, and beneficial, as is plain from the experience of persons who have come upon them. But the prophetic current and breath is most divine and holy, whether it issue by itself through the air or come in the company of running waters; for when it is instilled into the body, it creates in souls an unaccustomed and unusual temperament, the peculiarity of which it is hard to describe with exactness. (*Def. orac.* 432D-E)[47]

What is indeed striking about Plutarch's explanations is that, though they rely far more on philosophical conceptions — Cicero's rely on illustrations — they follow the same contours as Cicero's in their effort to explain the prophetic experience. In light of the different approaches employed by Cicero and Plutarch, the similarities between their discussions are astonishing, particularly because they span the period from about 50 B.C.E. to 100 C.E., during which time Pseudo-Philo probably composed *LAB*. Each of these elements of popular Greco-Roman culture informs the depiction of Kenaz in *LAB:* just prior to his death, Kenaz's mind *(sensus)* ascends to range the realms of the future when it is leapt upon and indwelt by the holy spirit. The incorporation of these popular elements into Pseudo-Philo's *heilsgeschichtlich* narrative is hardly surprising, in light of the ascendancy of Stoicism during the first century and the singular fame of Delphi.

Even the conclusion to Kenaz's experience exhibits taut affinities with Pseudo-Philo's Greco-Roman milieu: "But he did not know what he had said or what he had seen." This inability to remember reflects a view of inspiration that characterized accounts of oracular ecstasy during the Greco-Roman era and later.

The headwaters of this interpretation are Plato's *Apology* 22C and *Meno* 99C, in which Plato contends that inspired poets do not know what they are saying. This view spawned interpretations in which the inability to recall what was experienced during a period without mental control underlines the authenticity of the prophetic condition. Already during the late first or early second century C.E., the pseudonymous Jewish author of *4 Ezra* reveals an awareness of this interpretation in a description of an inspired experience in which Ezra allegedly dictated ninety-four books. Dur-

---

47. See also Plutarch, *Amatorius* 758E.

ing this period, Ezra's heart poured forth understanding, and wisdom increased in his breast *because* his own spirit retained its memory. The need to explain that Ezra retained his memory suggests that the author is aware of a form of inspiration that entails the loss of memory (*4 Ezra* 14:40).[48] The conviction that inspiration may bring a loss of recollection persists among a wide array of later authors. The second-century-C.E. public speaker and man of letters, Aelius Aristides, discusses the inspiration of the priestesses of Zeus in Dodona, who "know as much as the god approves, and for as long as he approves . . . nor afterwards do they know anything which they have said, but all inquirers understand it better than they" (*In Defense of Oratory* 42-43).[49] The second- or third-century Christian Pseudo-Justinus, in his *Cohortatio ad Graecos,* discusses Plato's admiration for the Sibyl because her prophecies came to pass. She "was filled indeed with prophecy at the time of the inspiration, but as soon as the inspiration ceased, there ceased also the remembrance of all she had said" (37.2). Again, the prophetess had "no remembrance of what she had said, after the possession and inspiration ceased" (37.3).[50] John Cassian, of the late fourth and early fifth centuries, understands demon possession analogously; some of those possessed "are affected by them [demons] in such a way as to have not the slightest conception of what they do and say, while others know and afterwards recollect it" (*Collationes* 12).[51] The Christian prologue to the *Sibylline Oracles,* which was composed no earlier than the end of the fifth century, attributes to the Christian apologist Lactantius the view that, following the inspiration of the Sibyl, "the memory of what had been said ceased with the inspiration. With regard to this even Plato said that they describe many great things accurately while knowing nothing of what they say" (*Sib. Or.* Prologue, 82-91).[52] The diversity of these witnesses to a shared view of inspiration indi-

48. M. E. Stone (*Fourth Ezra: A Commentary on the Book of Fourth Ezra* [Hermeneia; Minneapolis: Fortress, 1990], 120) argues that the retention of memory constitutes a "deliberate" reversal of this topos, i.e., the loss of memory.

49. Translated by C. A. Behr, "To Plato: In Defense of Oratory," in *P. Aelius Aristides: The Complete Works* (2 vols.; Leiden: Brill, 1986) 1:84.

50. Translated by M. Dods, "The Discourse to the Greeks," in *The Ante-Nicene Fathers* (ed. A. Roberts and J. Donaldson; 10 vols.; repr. Grand Rapids: Eerdmans, 1952), 1:289.

51. Translated by E. C. S. Gibson, "Cassian's Conferences," in *The Nicene and Post-Nicene Fathers* (ed. P. Schaff and H. Wace; second series; 14 vols.; repr. Grand Rapids: Eerdmans, 1956), 11:366.

52. Lactantius is also referred to as Firmianus, who probably lived ca. 240-320 C.E. Translated by J. J. Collins, "Sibylline Oracles," *OTP* 1:328.

cates how popular this view remained during the Greco-Roman era, during which period *LAB* was composed. Moreover, the attribution of this interpretation to Plato indicates an awareness that this belief about prophetic inspiration lay along a Greco-Roman trajectory.

This portrait of Kenaz's final vision in *LAB* clearly contains elements related to the spirit that originate within a Greco-Roman milieu. These elements — the proximity of death, the approach and indwelling of an inspiring impulse, the ascent of the mind, a vision of the future, and the inability to remember the inspired experience — are incorporated into a narrative whose focus is *Heilsgeschichte*.

Conclusion

Early-twentieth-century German studies of pneumatology, including the significance of the spirit in the Gospels, were possessed of an extraordinary knowledge of the environment of early Christianity. They differed substantially, however, in their assessments of the relevance of the Greco-Roman environment. Hans Leisegang located the origin of spirit references in the Greco-Roman world, while Friedrich Büchsel and Heinrich von Baer located their origin along an Old Testament and Palestinian Jewish axis. What emerged from their erudition was an impasse concerning the foreground of early Christian pneumatology. The fundamental contention of Büchsel and von Baer is that the Greco-Roman and early Christian conceptions of the spirit are entirely at odds with one another and that, therefore, it is unthinkable for an author such as Luke to have incorporated Greco-Roman characterizations of inspiration in narratives that are grounded in the Old Testament.

It would not have been adequate for me to question that distinction by citing examples of Hellenizations in the writings of authors such as Philo or Josephus, which are replete with Greco-Roman characterizations of the spirit. These authors simply do not have the level of commitment to *Heilsgeschichte* that characterizes Luke-Acts, according to von Baer's interpretation.[53] I have instead analyzed a single early Jewish reference to the spirit in *LAB* with the intent of demonstrating that it is not entirely satis-

---

53. I have analyzed these in detail in *The Spirit in First Century Judaism* (AGJU 29; Leiden: Brill, 1997).

factory to opt for the position of Büchsel and von Baer over against that of Leisegang.

LAB is the work of an author who readily incorporates Greco-Roman conceptions of the spirit within a theological perspective that is firmly rooted in *Heilsgeschichte*. It appears to be of no concern to Pseudo-Philo that the popular interpretations of the spirit he adopts have to do with pagan prophets such as Cassandra and the invasive god, Apollo, before whom she cowered. Büchsel's unequivocal assertion that "zwischen der 'pneumatischen' Empfängnis der griechischen Prophetinnen und der der Maria besteht ein tiefgreifender Unterschied," may therefore be misguided.[54] Indeed, Pseudo-Philo is an excellent example of an ancient Jewish author, a strong proponent of biblical *Heilsgeschichte,* who does not regard the alleged gulf between Jew and pagan as a barrier to the incorporation of Greco-Roman conceptions of the spirit.[55]

This study has demonstrated, then, that the current paradigm is unable to account for the rich cultural diversity reflected in ancient texts such as *LAB* and Luke-Acts. The character of literary texts such as these suggests the need for a fresh paradigm for studying the significance of the spirit in the Gospels that — once again in the words of C. K. Barrett — "produce[s] a contradictory impression, since they seem at once Jewish and Hellenistic."[56]

---

54. Büchsel, *Der Geist Gottes im Neuen Testament,* 200n.1.

55. For other examples of this phenomenon in *LAB,* see my *Spirit in First Century Judaism,* 99-130.

56. Barrett, *Gospel Tradition,* 18.

A Leper in the Hands of an Angry Jesus

Bart D. Ehrman

I am very pleased to dedicate this article to my mentor and friend, Jerry Hawthorne. He first taught me Greek — more than twenty years ago now — and then exegesis. Even though, with characteristic modesty, he occasionally slights his expertise in the field, he also introduced me to the rigors and joys of textual criticism and the study of Greek MSS. No one was ever more patient with a more hardheaded student; and though he probably did not know it at the time, his commitment both to questioning what he thought and to remaining committed to what he believed has been an inspiration for a lifetime.

In those days — and still, I believe — Jerry was particularly interested in the human life of Jesus, when most of his students were far more interested in his divinity. But for Jerry, Jesus was human in every way (though, of course, also divine) — he participated in the human condition in all its fullness and, in particular, experienced the full range of human emotions. So it seems appropriate for me to discuss one of the most emotionally charged passages of the entire NT, where Jesus becomes irate with a poor leper who begs to be healed and, after cleansing him of his disease, rebukes him and drives him away.

This is not the Jesus one would expect to find in the Gospels. It is no wonder that early Christian scribes modified the passage to remove its offense and that modern commentators who accept the original reading have tried to explain it away. Most readers, though, are unaware of the problem, since the scribes who decided to alter the text were by and large successful, so that most Greek MSS — and the English translations that are based on them — indicate not that Jesus became angry but that he felt compassion. Originally, though, it was not that way at all. What follows is a discussion of the text and interpretation of Mark 1:39-45, in which we find a leper in the hands of an angry Jesus.

Overview

I begin with a rather literal translation of the passage:

> 39And he [Jesus] came preaching in their synagogues in all of Galilee and casting out the demons. 40And a leper came to him beseeching him and saying to him, "If you will, you are able to cleanse me." 41And [feeling compassion (σπλαγχνισθείς)/becoming angry (ὀργισθείς)] reaching out his hand, he touched him and said to him, "I do will, be cleansed." 42And immediately the leprosy went out from him, and he was cleansed. 43And rebuking him severely, immediately he cast him out 44and said to him, "See that you say nothing to anyone, but go, show yourself to the priest and offer for your cleansing that which Moses commanded, as a witness to them." 45But when he went out he began to preach many things and to spread the word, so that he [Jesus] was no longer able to enter publicly into a city.[1]

This passage involves numerous complications that have exercised scholars over the years. What was the leper's actual medical condition — are we to think of leprosy in the modern sense (Hansen's disease) or some other skin disorder? Why was he publicly associating with Jesus, in evident violation of the Jewish law (Lev 13)? Why does Jesus first instruct the leper not to tell *anyone* what has happened but then instruct him to tell someone (the priest)? Is it possible that two different oral traditions have been combined in this account? Could one of the accounts have originally been an exorcism narrative? This at least would explain some of the story's features — including the odd statement that Jesus "cast him out" (ἐκβάλλω), a term normally reserved for demons in Mark's narrative. How does this story portray Jesus' relationship to the law? Why, that is, does he explicitly

---

1. All translations are mine, unless otherwise indicated.

break the law by touching the leper (see Lev 13) but then seem to affirm the law by telling him to do what Moses commanded? Is Jesus in favor of the law? Against the law? Above the law? And what does it mean that the leper's healing will be a witness to *them?* To whom? To the priests (only one is mentioned)? To the people (as in some translations)? But what people? The entire population of Israel? Is it to be a positive witness (*for* the priests/people), to show that salvation now has arrived? Or a negative witness (*against* the priests/people), to show that the one they reject brings salvation?[2]

The questions go on and on, but most of them, at least, are rooted in words that are secure in the text. Not so with the question on which I want to focus in this article, while bracketing all the rest: What was Jesus' emotional reaction to this poor leper — did he feel compassion, as in most of the MSS, or anger, as in several others? And if — as I have already intimated — it was anger, what exactly was he angry about?

Before dealing with the interpretive question, we must establish the text. The grounds for thinking that Mark originally spoke of an angry, rather than a compassionate, Jesus are compelling, as most recent commentators have realized.

The Text

External Evidence

It is true that the reading ὀργισθείς is not found in an abundance of MSS of Mark, only in the fifth-century Codex Bezae and several Old Latin MSS (a ff² r¹). But textual scholars have long recognized that readings attested in such "Western" witnesses almost certainly go back at least to the second century.[3] Even Hort, the greatest champion of the "Alexandrian" text as "original," had to concede that such Western readings were an obstacle to

---

2. For discussion of these issues, see the critical commentaries. In my opinion, far and away the best discussion is Joel Marcus, *Mark 1–8: A New Translation with Introduction and Commentary* (AB 27A; New York: Doubleday, 2000), 205-11.

3. See D. C. Parker, *Codex Bezae: An Early Christian Manuscript and Its Text* (Cambridge: Cambridge Univ. Press, 1992), 261-78; and, more briefly, B. D. Ehrman, "The Text of the Gospels at the End of the Second Century," in *Codex Bezae: Studies from the Lunel Colloquium, June 1994* (ed. D. C. Parker and C.-B. Amphoux; NTTS 22; Leiden: Brill, 1996), 95-122.

his argument; they could often claim the greatest antiquity in terms of external support, despite the paucity of their attestation, as they are frequently cited by church fathers of the earliest periods when MSS of any kind are virtually nonexistent.[4] This view has been supported by additional research since Hort's day.[5] Some hard evidence exists in the present case. From the fourth century, Ephrem's commentary on Tatian's Diatessaron (produced in the 2d century) discusses that when Jesus met the leper he "became angry." If the Diatessaron did have this reading, then it is the earliest witness that we have — no papyri survive for this portion of Mark, and our earliest surviving MS for the verse is Vaticanus, from the mid-fourth century, nearly three hundred years after Mark actually wrote the account.

So, even though the vast majority of MSS indicate that Jesus felt compassion for the leper, their number is not in itself persuasive. It is easy to imagine, as we will see more fully below, why scribes may have been offended by the notion of Jesus' anger in such a situation and so changed the text to make him appear compassionate instead (whereas it is difficult to see why any scribe would have changed the text the other way around). Once the change was made, it could easily have spread like wildfire, as scribes adopted this more comfortable reading instead of the more difficult one, until the original text came to be virtually lost except in a few surviving sources.

But fortunately we do not need to wait for the fourth or fifth century to find witnesses to the original text of Mark, for the scribes who produced our surviving MSS were not the first to reproduce Mark's text. Strictly speaking, the earliest surviving copyists of Mark were Matthew and Luke (assuming for the time being — safely I think — Markan priority), who, of course, modified the text they reproduced far more than any subsequent scribe would dare to do. Still, Matthew and Luke reproduced entire stories of Mark wholesale, changing them here and there when it suited their purposes. Luckily for us, both took over the story in question, and so we can get some sense of what *their* version(s) of Mark looked like. Did their copies indicate that Jesus felt compassion or anger?

4. See the introduction to *The New Testament in the Original Greek* (ed. F. J. A. Hort and B. F. Westcott; New York: Harper & Brothers, 1882). See also B. D. Ehrman, *The Orthodox Corruption of Scripture: The Effect of Early Christological Controversies on the Text of the New Testament* (New York: Oxford Univ. Press, 1993), 223-27.

5. See, e.g., B. D. Ehrman, "Heracleon and the 'Western' Textual Tradition," *NTS* 40 (1994): 161-79.

In fact, the parallel accounts from Matthew and Luke ascribe neither emotion to Jesus, as can be seen in the following synopsis.[6]

Matt 8:2-3	Mark 1:40-42	Luke 5:12-13
		¹²Καὶ ἐγένετο
		ἐν τῷ εἶναι αὐτὸν ἐν μιᾷ τῶν πόλεων καὶ
²καὶ		ἰδοὺ ἀνὴρ ⌜πλήρης λέπρας⌝. ⌜ἰδὼν δὲ⌝ τὸν
ἰδοὺ λεπρὸς ⌜προσελθὼν	⁴⁰Καὶ ἔρχεται πρὸς αὐτὸν λεπρὸς	⌜Ἰησοῦν, ⌜πεσὼν ἐπὶ πρόσωπον □ἐδεήθη
προσεκύνει αὐτῷ	παρακαλῶν αὐτὸν ⌜[καὶ γονυπετῶν]⌝	αὐτοῦ⌝ λέγων· κύριε, ἐὰν θέλῃς δύνασαί
λέγων· κύριε, ἐὰν θέλῃς δύνασαί	□καὶ λέγων⁰¹ αὐτῷ ⌜ὅτι ἐὰν θέλῃς δύνασαί	με καθαρίσαι. ¹³ καὶ
με καθαρίσαι. ³ καὶ	με καθαρίσαι. ⁴¹ ⌜καὶ ⸆ σπλαγχνισθεὶς	
ἐκτείνας τὴν χεῖρα ⸆ ἥψατο αὐτοῦ	ἐκτείνας τὴν χεῖρα ⌜αὐτοῦ ἥψατο	ἐκτείνας τὴν χεῖρα ἥψατο αὐτοῦ
⸆ λέγων· θέλω, καθαρίσθητι· καὶ	καὶ λέγει ⁰αὐτῷ· θέλω, καθαρίσθητι· ⁴²καὶ	⌜λέγων· θέλω, καθαρίσθητι·
εὐθέως ἐκαθαρίσθη αὐτοῦ ἡ λέπρα.	⌜⌐εὐθὺς □ἀπῆλθεν ἀπ' αὐτοῦ ἡ λέπρα,	εὐθέως ⌜ἡ λέπρα ἀπῆλθεν ἀπ' αὐτοῦ⌝.
	καὶ⌝ ἐκαθαρίσθη.	

6. K. Aland, ed., *Synposis Quattuor Evangeliorum* (11th ed.; Stuttgart: Deutsche Bibelstiftung, 1976), 59.

Several points can be made about these Synoptic accounts. First, they are verbally identical up to and past the point at which the participle describing Jesus' emotion is given in Mark. Second, Matthew and Luke both omit the participle — whichever one it was — altogether.

This is commonly taken, quite rightly I think, as evidence both that Matthew and Luke had copies of Mark indicating that Jesus became angry (ὀργισθείς) and that they omitted the term because they both found it offensive. Before giving additional support for this view, I should point out that this is one of the "minor agreements" between Matthew and Luke (there are several others in the passage) that scholars have used to show the problems in the traditional understanding of Markan priority. But in most instances such agreements (which are often omissions, as in this case) can easily be explained as accidental agreements — that is, of the thousands of places where both Matthew and Luke changed Mark, some dozens of them happen to coincide. The accidental agreement in the present case is understandable if — and only if — the participle in question may have caused offense or dissatisfaction to both authors.

There are solid reasons for thinking that Jesus' anger would have offended Matthew and Luke but that his compassion would not. The data are these: on only two other occasions in Mark's Gospel is Jesus explicitly described as compassionate, 6:34 (the feeding of the five thousand) and 8:2 (the feeding of the four thousand).[7] Luke completely recasts the first story and does not include the second. Matthew, however, has both stories and retains Mark's description of Jesus being compassionate on both occasions (14:14; 15:32). On two additional occasions in Matthew (9:36; 20:34), and yet one other occasion in Luke (7:13), Jesus is explicitly described as compassionate, using this term (σπλαγχνίζομαι). In other words, Matthew and Luke have no difficulty describing Jesus as compassionate. Why would they both, independently, have eliminated that description of Jesus here, in a story that they otherwise adopted verbatim?

On the other hand, we have good reason for thinking that Matthew and Luke would have each omitted ὀργισθείς if it were in their texts of Mark, for they did so in both of the other instances in Mark in which Jesus is explicitly said to become angry. In Mark 3:5 Jesus looks around "with anger" (μετ' ὀργῆς) at those in the synagogue who were watching to see if he

---

7. On one other occasion he is *asked* to be compassionate (9:22). Strikingly, he replies by giving a rebuke (9:23). See the discussion of this passage below.

would heal the man with the withered hand. Luke has the verse almost the same as Mark, but removes the reference to Jesus' anger (Luke 6:10). Matthew completely rewrites this section of the story and says nothing of Jesus' wrath (Matt 12:12-13). Similarly, in Mark 10:14 Jesus is aggravated (ἀγανακτέω) at his disciples for not allowing people to bring their children to be blessed. Both Matthew and Luke have the story, often verbally the same, but both delete the reference to Jesus' anger (Matt 19:14; Luke 18:16).

In sum, Matthew and Luke have no qualms about describing Jesus as compassionate. But they never describe him as angry. In fact, whenever one of their sources, Mark, did so, they both independently rewrite the term out of their stories. Thus it is hard to understand why they would have removed σπλαγχνισθείς from the account of Jesus healing the leper but easy to see why they might have removed ὀργισθείς.

My conclusion at this point is that even though most Greek MSS describe Jesus as feeling compassion for this leper, the earliest datable textual tradition (the Western witnesses, in this case) and the work of the oldest surviving "copyists" of Mark's Gospel (Matthew and Luke) indicate that the older form of the text depicted him as becoming angry.

Transcriptional Probabilities

Corroborating evidence for this conclusion comes in the form of "transcriptional probabilities" — the technical term used by textual scholars to indicate which form of the text was the more likely to be changed by a scribe. The logic of the criterion is that scribes were more likely to make a text more grammatically correct than less, more internally consistent than less, more in harmony with other accounts than less, more theologically acceptable than less. Any text, therefore, that is less grammatical, consistent, harmonious, or orthodox, on these grounds, is correspondingly *more* likely to be original. Or, to give the traditional formulation, "the more difficult reading is to be preferred."

In the present case there can be little question about which reading scribes would have been likely to prefer. It may be difficult to understand why Jesus would get angry under any circumstance; but that he might become angry when approached by a poor soul like this leper is completely mystifying — especially to those (like ancient scribes and modern commentators) who assume that Jesus must have been compassionate at all times and reserved his anger only for his hardhearted and willful enemies. Confronted with a text such as this, it is no wonder that scribes would have wanted to change it.

Some modern critics, though, have argued otherwise. In his influential *Textual Commentary on the Greek New Testament,* for example, Bruce Metzger maintains that since scribes did not modify the two other passages in which Jesus is explicitly said to become angry in Mark (3:5; 10:14), it is unlikely that they would have modified this one either.[8]

The argument sounds convincing at first, but not when the passages themselves are actually examined. In the other two instances it makes perfect sense for Jesus to get angry: in one he is angry at his enemies who have hardened hearts and misinterpret God's law in a way that allows them to perpetuate suffering (3:5); in the other he becomes irritated with his disciples for not allowing children to come to him so that he can lay hands on them (10:14). But why would Jesus get angry in the story of the leper? The answer is far less obvious, and therefore far more open to misconstrual. Scribes would thus be likely to change this text, but not the others.

Moreover, Metzger's discussion of transcriptional probabilities (in which he is reporting the sentiment of the entire United Bible Societies' Greek New Testament Committee) leaves open the much larger question: if scribes were unlikely to change Jesus' anger to compassion, how is it that they were *likely* to change his compassion to anger? That is to say, one still has to account for the change. The committee proposes two solutions. First they suggest that a scribe may have been influenced by the harsh verb of v. 43, ἐμβριμάομαι ("severely rebuked him," literally something like "snorted at him"), and, to explain this subsequent emotionally charged language, modified the earlier description of Jesus' emotional state. This might work as a solution; but one wonders why, if the problem involved ἐμβριμάομαι from v. 43, the scribe would not have simply changed *that* text — especially since it (a) involves a rare word, (b) ascribes a confusing emotion to Jesus, and (c) is the text that was copied *second* (i.e., would not a scribe be more likely to change what he was currently writing in light of what he had already written, rather than in light of what he was about to write?).

The second proposal is that a scribe changed σπλαγχνισθείς to

8. B. M. Metzger, *A Textual Commentary on the Greek New Testament* (2d ed.; Stuttgart: Deutsche Bibelgesellschaft, 1994), 65.

ὀργισθείς because in *Aramaic* (Jesus' native tongue) the words for compassion and anger are spelled almost exactly alike.[9] I have to say that arguments like this have always struck me as completely mystifying; I have never heard anyone explain how exactly they are supposed to work. Why, that is, would a Greek scribe proficient in Greek and copying a Greek text be confused by two words that look alike in *Aramaic?* We should not assume that Greek scribes spoke Aramaic (virtually none of them did), or that they copied Aramaic texts, or that they translated the Gospel from Aramaic to Greek. This Gospel was composed in Greek, transmitted in Greek, and copied in Greek by Greek-speaking scribes. So how does the accidental similarity of two Aramaic words relate to the issue? Moreover, even if this *were* the reason for the confusion between the two words, why would the change go in this direction (from compassion to anger) rather than the other?

We are left with no good explanation for why scribes might have wanted to change the text if it originally indicated that Jesus felt compassion. But we have plenty of reasons for thinking they may have changed the text to eliminate Jesus' anger. In fact, as we will see below, there are also less obvious reasons for early scribes wanting to make this change (less obvious to us, that is, but more obvious to them).

Before explaining these reasons, I should point out that there is evidence in the MSS themselves that scribes felt some consternation over the emotional response that Jesus has toward the leper. Several other textual witnesses (W b c [e]) — all of which read "felt compassion" in v. 41 — have modified his evident lack of compassion in the subsequent verses by omitting vv. 42b-43, where he rebukes the man and then casts him out as if he were a demon. True, these scribes may have done so because the verses are absent from Matthew and Luke (who may have omitted them for the same reason: the portrayal of Jesus as something less than compassionate). Nonetheless, the net affect is striking: now Jesus is not only said to be compassionate instead of angry, he also does nothing that might appear to compromise the emotion later!

---

9. "Compare Syriac *ethraḥam,* 'he had pity,' with *ethra'em,* 'he was enraged'" (Metzger, *Textual Commentary,* 65).

Intrinsic Probabilities

We are now in a position to move beyond the question of what the MSS and the proclivities of scribes might suggest about the original text and ask which of the two readings — Jesus as angry or as compassionate — fits better with the portrayal of Jesus in Mark's Gospel. This will lead us, then, at a later stage, to take on the task of interpreting the passage more closely, once we are still more confident of its original wording.

Which reading, then, makes better sense in the context of Mark's broader narrative? This is a question that rarely gets asked, oddly enough; or perhaps it is not so odd, since even the commentators who realize that the text originally indicated that Jesus became angry are embarrassed by the idea and try to explain it away, so that the text no longer means what it says.[10]

We might begin our exploration of intrinsic suitability by giving the benefit of the doubt to the other reading (σπλαγχνισθείς) and ask if indeed it does not make the better sense in context. Is it not more plausible that Jesus would respond to the pleas of this poor leper with compassion rather than anger?

That certainly does resonate with common sense — especially with a common sense that sees Jesus as the all-gentle Good Shepherd concerned above all for the well-being of all his children (and intent never to hurt their feelings). We need constantly to remember, though, that the question is not about which portrayal of Jesus we ourselves find most comfortable, but about which portrayal of Jesus was originally presented by the author of the Gospel of Mark. Even critical commentators sometimes fail to make this distinction. Evidently, few readers of Mark (including some of its commentators) have realized that Jesus is never described in this Gospel as exercising compassion when he heals. Instead, the emotion commonly associated with him — odd as this might seem — is anger.

As I have already indicated, on two occasions Jesus is explicitly said to feel compassion in Mark. Interestingly enough, both are in the same context: Jesus is in a wilderness area and feels compassion for the crowds with him, because they are hungry. He then miraculously provides food for them by multiplying the loaves and fishes (6:41; 8:6-7). On only one occasion does the term "compassion" (σπλαγχνισθείς) occur in a story in which Jesus heals anyone with a disease or a demon; and in that instance the term is not

---

10. See the discussion of the commentators' various interpretations below.

used to describe him. Mark 9 presents the account of a man pleading with Jesus to cast an evil demon from his son, since the disciples have proved unable to do so: "Often," he tells Jesus, "it casts him into the fire and into water to destroy him; but if you are able, show us compassion (σπλαγχνισθείς) and help us" (9:22). The man, in other words, asks for compassion. Strikingly enough, Jesus replies not with compassion but a rebuke: "*If* you are able?! All things are possible to the one who believes" (9:23). The man then continues to plead: "I do believe; help my unbelief!" (9:24).

One might be tempted to conclude that Jesus does after all show compassion by healing the boy. It should be noted, though, that Mark says no such thing. Instead, he indicates that Jesus healed the boy only because he saw that a crowd was starting to form (9:25a). It may be that interpreters have read compassion into the account rather than out of it (and that they do so with all the other healing stories in Mark, since Mark himself never ascribes the emotion to Jesus when he heals). In any event, Mark does not describe Jesus as compassionate in chapter 9 but shows him rebuking a man for doubting his ability to heal.

This leads us now to the other side of the coin. If Mark never indicates that Jesus heals out of compassion, what does he say about his anger? As we have seen, Jesus gets angry on several occasions in Mark's Gospel; what is most interesting to note is that each account involves Jesus' ability to perform miraculous deeds of healing.

One possible instance is much debated among scholars. In Mark 8:11-12 the Pharisees begin to argue with Jesus and demand that he show them a sign from heaven (evidently to prove who he is). Jesus "sighed deeply" (ἀναστενάζω) in his spirit and replied that he would give no sign to "this generation." Commentators have commonly taken the term ἀναστενάζω to imply anger at his opponents for doubting his abilities, but the most recent and thorough lexical study of the term (it is fairly rare, even outside the NT) has maintained that it connotes dismay rather than indignation.[11] Thus we should probably leave it to one side. But if the majority of commentators is correct, that it suggests anger, the anger has come in the context of a request for a miracle.[12]

---

11. J. B. Gibson, "Another Look at Why Jesus 'Sighs Deeply': ἀναστενάζω in Mark 8:12a," *JTS* 47 (1996): 131-40.

12. One might note that in the Synoptic parallels the request comes as a response to a *healing* (of a demoniac): Matt 12:22-42; Luke 11:14-32.

Among the explicit references already mentioned is the interesting passage of Mark 10, in which the disciples prevent unidentified people ("they," 10:13) from bringing children to Jesus so that he might touch them. Jesus responds by becoming indignant (ἀγανακτέω), and tells his disciples: "allow the children to come to me, do not hinder them; for the kingdom of God belongs to such as these." He then takes the children in his arms, blesses them, and lays his hands on them (10:13-16).

Jesus' actions here, of course, allow him to make some comments about children and the kingdom; but the actions themselves should not be so quickly overlooked. In our culture laying on hands may be simply a symbolic gesture of blessing; but in Mark's Gospel it is usually a sign of healing, or at least the transmission of divine power (cf. 1:31, 41-42; 5:41-42; 6:5; 8:23-25; 9:27). When Jesus "blesses" these children and "lays his hands" on them, is he actually *doing* something that "heals" them or transmits his divine power to them ("such as these enter the kingdom of God")?

If so, then not only in chapter 9 but also in chapter 10 Jesus' anger has to do with his response to someone in a healing setting: in the first he rebukes a man for not having sufficient faith in his ability to heal ("*If* you are able?!"), in the second he rebuffs his disciples for not seeing that he wants to welcome the children and place his hands of healing on them.

The most explicit account of Jesus' anger occurs earlier in Mark, in chapter 3. Here, at the climax of a cycle of five controversy stories,[13] Jesus finds himself in a synagogue with a group of Pharisees and a man with a withered hand. The Pharisees are watching Jesus closely to see if he will heal the man on the Sabbath, in violation of (their interpretation of) the law of Moses. Jesus tells the man to come forward and asks his opponents the rhetorical question: "Is it permitted to do good on the Sabbath, or to do evil? To save a life or destroy it?" (3:4). When they respond with silence he looks around at them "with anger" (μετ' ὀργῆς), grieving at the hardness of their hearts. He then tells the man to stretch out his hand, which is restored (3:5). This — coming after a series of other confrontations in rapid succession that take up all of Mark 2 — proves to be too much for the Pharisees; they leave to make common cause against Jesus with the Herodians and plot from then on to have him killed (3:6).

Another healing narrative, another instance of Jesus' anger. In this instance, at least, the object and reason for his wrath are evident. The

---

13. Mark 2:1-12, 13-17, 18-22, 23-28; 3:1-6.

Pharisees are the object, and the reason is that they have hardened hearts, not realizing that it is right to do what is good on the Sabbath but wrong to do what is bad. As Jesus indicates earlier, in the first of the controversy accounts in chapter 2, the Sabbath was made for the sake of humans, not humans for the Sabbath (2:27). Thus his healing power is particularly appropriate on the Sabbath, the day given by God for the benefit of his people; how much better to provide real assistance on this day for someone in need? The Pharisees, though, are overly concerned with their scrupulous regulations of what is and is not permitted for the people of God (according to Mark at least [see 7:1-8]; the question of the *historical* Pharisees is another matter). Above all, they oppose Jesus' authority to do miracles on the Sabbath, seeking to kill him precisely because he stands over against their interpretations of the law and of God's will for his people. Mark, of course, takes the opposite stand and portrays Jesus as angered by his opponents' refusal to see that his ability to heal in fact comes from God.

To summarize: we have seen several instances of Jesus' anger in Mark. In one instance it is at least possible as an interpretation of his sighing over the request of his enemies for a miraculous sign from heaven (8:12); in another it is implicit in his rebuke of the man who seeks healing for his demon-possessed son (9:23); in another it comes in reaction to his disciples who refuse to allow children to enjoy his blessing, and possibly healing, through the laying on of hands (10:14); and in yet another it is in direct response to the Pharisees who refuse to acknowledge that his authority to heal comes from God and is a right understanding of the will of God (3:5).

We now can move to chapter 1 and the healing of the leper. Here too is another healing narrative. What is Jesus' emotion on this occasion? Never in the Gospel of Mark is the term "compassion" associated with Jesus healing; on several occasions anger is. Which is more likely to be associated with him here? Apart from the question of consistency with the rest of Mark's narrative as a whole, we may pursue the question by digging somewhat deeper into several aspects of the story itself and its literary context.

First, the story itself. As briefly noted above, it is hard to explain the subsequent actions of Jesus if a gentle sense of "compassion" was wafting over him, for after he heals the man he "sternly rebukes" (or "warns") him and then "throws him out." The first term, ἐμβριμάομαι, is rare and difficult to translate. It is sometimes used of "snorting" horses. In its other occurrence in Mark it almost certainly means "rebuke" or "reproach" (14:5, when the disciples react to the woman who anointed Jesus); that should probably determine its meaning here. The only other occurrence in the Synoptics is at Matt 9:30, which appears to be dependent on this passage in Mark. Otherwise in the NT it is used only in the Gospel of John (11:33, 38), and there somewhat idiosyncratically.[14] John's usage, of course, would not have been available to Mark, some thirty years earlier; the LXX, though, would have been, and interestingly enough, the term occurs there in contexts that also speak about "anger" (ὀργή; Lam 2:6; Dan 11:30). On balance it seems easier to understand that Jesus would severely rebuke the man if he were angry with him than if he felt sorry for him.

The other term in question points in the same direction. After Jesus rebuked the man, he "threw him out" (ἐκβάλλω), a term typically used in Mark when Jesus casts out demons (eleven of sixteen occurrences), but also of his driving out the money changers and merchants from the temple (11:15) and of the wicked tenants who cast out the "son" in the parable of the vineyard (12:8).[15] In every instance in the Gospel, it is used of some kind of aggressive action.

We still have not explored fully why Jesus might have acted so aggressively and angrily toward a leper who wanted, after all, simply to be healed. But first we should deal directly with the more common objection to the reading, that it just does not seem consistent with how one would expect Jesus to react in the Gospels.

Here again I need to emphasize that our personal sense of how Jesus should react or our unreflective notions of how he does react in the Gospels have very little bearing on exegesis. One of the most striking and interesting aspects of Mark's Gospel is precisely how contrary to expectations the portrayal of Jesus is. Any Jew who began to read that this was the story of "Jesus the Messiah" (1:1) would be completely shocked or confused

---

14. In John ἐμβριμάομαι is used reflexively to refer to Jesus' inner state. Some have solved the problem of Mark 1:43 by proposing that there too ἐμβριμάομαι should be understood similarly. But there is no reflexive here in Mark (the verb is used transitively; the ex-leper is the object) — a problem sometimes solved by appealing to a reputed discrepancy in translation from the Aramaic. So M. Wojciechowski, "The Touching of the Leper (Mark 1,40-45) as a Historical and Symbolic Act of Jesus," *BZ* 33 (1989): 116. Again, one wonders how Aramaic confusions can have any bearing on *Greek* terms. See above.

15. Mark 1:34, 39, 43; 3:15, 22, 23; 6:13; 7:26; 9:18, 28, and 38 use ἐκβάλλω with reference to exorcism; additional uses for the verb occur in 1:12; 5:40; 9:47; 11:15; 12:8.

by the story line. This is a messiah who gets crucified by the Romans as a political insurgent. On the macrolevel, that is a portrayal that simply makes no sense (unless you are a Christian and understand that the term "messiah" no longer means what it used to mean). But even on the microlevel of the immediate context, consider how Jesus is portrayed in the first part of this Gospel. John the Baptist announces that the one who comes after him will provide a baptism in the Holy Spirit. The reader might well then expect Jesus to do so. Instead, we are told the Spirit "drives him out" (ἐκβάλλω — the same aggressive word as above) into the wilderness for a bizarre encounter with the devil and the wild beasts. Jesus and the Spirit do not appear to be on friendly terms; in any event there is nothing here to suggest that Jesus has the power over the Spirit to bestow it.

Throughout these early chapters — and contrary to what one might expect or hope — Jesus is not portrayed as a proponent of what we might call "family values." He rips his would-be followers away from their homes and families, sometimes leaving their parents in the lurch (1:16-20). He rejects his own family, who think, as it turns out, that he has gone out of his mind (3:21); and when they come to see him, he publicly spurns them (3:31-35).

When people seek after Jesus for help, he refuses to see them (1:37-38). He fails to behave in recognizably religious ways (2:18-22); he condones lawless behavior (2:23-28); he defies religious authority (3:1-6). He associates with lowlifes (2:16-17); he drags his followers away from their livelihood (1:16-20; 2:13-14); he keeps to himself in the wilderness and refuses to be acknowledged for who he is, even by his enemies (1:25, 34; 3:7-12).

This, of course, is not the whole picture — but it is the predominant one. Jesus is not at all what we would expect him to be, and in none of these instances is "compassion" (or any related term) ascribed to Jesus.[16] In any event it simply will not do to say that Jesus must not have gotten angry with the leper seeking healing since that would have been out of character. It may be out of character with popular portrayals and understandings of Jesus, but it would not be out of character with the Jesus we meet in the early chapters of Mark.

This brings us, then, to the key interpretive question. When a leper

---

16. Of course, he does acquire a huge following by doing his miracles (1:45). And his early miracles have suggested to some a good dose of compassion. In chap. 1, after all, he does raise Simon Peter's mother, bedridden with a fever. More than one wry observer has noted, though, that after he does so she gets up to feed them supper (1:30-31).

approached Jesus and said "If you will, you are able to make me clean," why did he become angry?

Explaining Jesus' Anger

Most commentators who accept ὀργισθείς as the original text have difficulties explaining it and either pass over it quickly or make it say something other than it does. Over the years numerous interpretations have been proposed; it seems odd that no one has thought to consider the other occasions on which Jesus gets angry in this Gospel. Still, one must admit that some of the explanations are highly creative.

Some interpreters have argued that the participle refers not to Jesus but to the leper, who in anger touched Jesus and so was healed (cf. the woman with a hemorrhage in 5:25-34).[17] Unfortunately, this explanation cannot account for the next words, since the subject of λέγει is surely the same as that of ἥψατο. Others have thought that Jesus became angry because he knew that the man would disobey orders, spreading the news of his healing and making it difficult for Jesus to enter into the towns of Galilee because of the crowds.[18] But it seems unlikely that Jesus would be angry about what the man would do later — before he actually did it! Others have suggested that he was angry because the man was intruding on his preaching ministry, keeping him from his primary task.[19] Unfortunately, nothing in the text indicates this as a problem, and it seems odd as an interpretation in Mark's Gospel in particular, where healings and exorcisms play a much greater role than preaching.

Another suggestion is that Jesus was angry with the leper for breaking the law by coming up to him to be healed, instead of avoiding human contact and calling out "unclean, unclean," as the law commands (Lev 13:45).[20]

17. So K. Lake, "'ΕΜΒΡΙΜΗΣΑΜΕΝΟΣ and 'ΟΡΓΙΣΘΕΙΣ, Mark 1,40-43," HTR 16 (1923): 197-98.

18. So W. L. Lane, The Gospel according to Mark (NICNT; Grand Rapids: Eerdmans, 1974), 87.

19. Suggested but not taken by V. Taylor, The Gospel according to St. Mark (London: Macmillan, 1963), 189. See also G. Telford, "Mark 1:40-45," Int 36 (1982): 55.

20. So A. E. J. Rawlinson, The Gospel according to St. Mark (Westminster Commentaries; London: Methuen, 1949), 22; Rawlinson accepts σπλαγχνισθείς as the reading in the text at hand but sees Jesus' anger in his reaction to the leper after healing him.

But this fails to explain why Jesus himself would then have broken the law by initiating physical contact with the person. Other interpreters have thought that the anger is not to be taken personally. For example, some scholars have maintained that anger was simply part of an exorcist's repertoire, used as part of the emotional energy needed to cast out demons.[21] Even if that were true, it would not explain the situation here, in the final form of Mark's Gospel, since this is a healing story with no mention of any demons (the prehistory of the story notwithstanding).

Probably the most common argument, in one form or another, is that Jesus is not angry with the leper at all but with the state of the world that has caused him to suffer. What is most intriguing about this interpretation is its rhetorical effect — it turns out that the story is really about Jesus being compassionate, even though the text says he became angry! Thus Vincent Taylor can maintain that Jesus is angry that there is such suffering in the world; Eduard Schweizer can argue that Jesus is angry at the misery caused by such a disease; and John Painter, who prefers σπλαγχνισθείς, indicates that if ὀργισθείς were original, it would mean that Jesus is angry at the situation of the leper who has to be isolated from normal human contact because of the law of Moses.[22] This final interpretation, I should point out, would appear to suggest that the problem is the Jewish law — a dubious notion, since at the end of the story Jesus seems to affirm the law, by telling the healed leper to do what the law commands. In any event all of these interpretations have two things in common: they avoid making Jesus appear angry with the man, and they avoid dealing directly with the words of the text in order to do so.

Somewhat better is the understanding of Morna Hooker, who situates Jesus' angry reaction in relation to his reaction to the world elsewhere in Mark's Gospel, where he is in constant conflict with the forces of evil in order to bring about the good kingdom of God here on earth. For Hooker, then, Jesus is angry not at the leper or at his disease or at the world in general, but at Satan, the one whose evil works have put people in bondage, as particularly evident in the case of the demon possessed.[23] This interpreta-

---

21. The classic study is C. Bonner, "Traces of Thaumaturgic Technique in the Miracles," *HTR* 20 (1927): 171-81.

22. Taylor, *Mark*, 189; E. Schweizer, *The Good News according to Mark* (trans. D. H. Madvig; Richmond: John Knox, 1970), 58; J. Painter, *Mark's Gospel: Worlds in Conflict* (London and New York: Routledge, 1997), 49.

23. M. D. Hooker, *The Message of Mark* (London: Epworth, 1983), 42; followed by Marcus, *Mark*, 209.

tion is moving in the right direction because, unlike the others, it has Mark's overarching message in mind. Unfortunately, there is not a word about Satan in this passage; moreover, the interpretation does not consider the more obvious question of where and why Jesus is said to become angry elsewhere in Mark.

The two key passages are the ones we have already considered at length (3:1-6; 9:20-25) — both of which have important parallels with the story of the leper. The first reference to anger comes in the account of 3:1-6, the man with the withered hand. It is striking, and probably worth noting, that 1:39-45 and 3:1-6 bracket the cycle of conflict stories in chapter 2. In some sense the conflicts begin with Jesus' heightened popularity at the end of chapter 1 (the result of the healing of the leper); they climax in 3:6 with the Pharisees' decision to seek Jesus' life (the result of the healing of the man with the withered hand). Both of these accounts describe a healing of a debilitating bodily ailment; both narrate a conflict involving Jesus' anger (with the leper, with the Pharisees); both appear to relate a violation of the law (Jesus touches the leper in one; he appears — to the Pharisees at least — to violate the Sabbath in the other). In other words, these two stories are placed around 2:1–3:6 for a reason — they serve as interpretive brackets for Jesus' conflicts with the Jewish authorities. Strikingly, in both he gets angry, and in both places the anger has to do with how people perceive his healing powers. This is especially clear, of course, in the second story, where the Pharisees do not believe that Jesus is authorized by God to heal on the Sabbath. But what about the first? Why would Jesus become angry when the leper says to him, "If you will, you can make me clean"? Is it because the leper is not sure that Jesus (or God, whom Jesus represents) *wants* to heal him ("if you *will* . . .")?

Consider the second story where Jesus appears to be angry. In 9:22-23 the man with the demon-possessed son entreats Jesus: "If you are able, have pity and help us." Jesus replies angrily, "If you are able?!" Here again is a question about Jesus' miracle-working power; but in this case it is not a question of authorization (as in 3:1-6) but of ability. When Jesus sees a crowd forming — and only then — he performs the miracle.

Jesus is angered when anyone questions his authority or ability to heal — or his desire to heal. Consider the other passage that explicitly mentions his anger, when the disciples prevent people from bringing their children to have Jesus "lay his hands" on them (10:13-16). Jesus not only *can* provide the healing touch that brings blessing, he *wants* to; and anyone who hinders him from doing so becomes the object of his wrath.

So too in our account, 1:39-45. Jesus is approached by a leper who says, "If you are willing, you are able to cleanse me." But why would Jesus *not* be willing to heal him? Of course he is willing, just as he is authorized and able. Jesus is angered — not at the illness, or the world, or the law, or Satan — but at the very idea that anyone would question, even implicitly, his willingness to help one in need. He heals the man before rebuking him and throwing him out.

The Modification of the Text

Mark described Jesus as angry, and, at least in this instance, scribes took offense. This comes as no surprise: apart from a fuller understanding of Mark's portrayal, Jesus' anger is difficult to understand. Moreover, scribes never did think of Mark's fuller portrayal of Jesus per se, in the way modern exegetes do. They thought instead about the Gospel narratives (all four of them) as one harmonious whole. Jesus' anger in this instance did not seem to fit, and so the text was altered. It had been changed previously by the prescribal copyists, Matthew and Luke, who omitted his anger; and it was changed by the scribes themselves, who transformed his anger into compassion. But there may have been something more at stake in this scribal alteration than a simple offense at Jesus' unexpected outburst.

Only in relatively recent years have textual scholars begun to explore fully the social world of Christian scribes to understand reasons they may have had for modifying the text. Even so, there have been only two major studies to date, one dealing with the effect of anti-Judaism on an important part of the textual tradition, the other with the effect of early christological controversies.[24] But other areas of interest could be pursued — for exam-

---

24. For the former see E. J. Epp, *The Theological Tendency of Codex Bezae Cantabrigiensis in Acts* (SNTSMS 3; Cambridge: Cambridge Univ. Press, 1966). The problem with Epp's otherwise excellent and groundbreaking study is that although he showed that Codex Bezae incorporates "anti-Jewish" tendencies, he did not situate these in a plausible *Sitz im Leben* — i.e., in the social setting of the scribes responsible for the alterations. This was a shortcoming I tried to overcome in my study of christologically motivated variations, *The Orthodox Corruption of Scripture.* See the bibliography there. For shorter discussion of such issues, see my "Text of the Gospels," and "The Text as Window: New Testament Manuscripts

ple, the ways scribes were affected by the attempts to silence women in early Christianity, the rise of asceticism, and the apologetic movement. The final matter, the effects of early Christian apologia on our anonymous scribes, has been comprehensively explored by Wayne Kannaday.[25] Here I might say just a few words about this as it relates to the text at hand.[26]

By the late second century, virtually the only resource for learning about the actions and words of Jesus were the Christian Gospels (and later oral traditions that ultimately derived from them). We know that by 180 C.E. or so, some of the better-informed pagan opponents of Christianity, such as the Middle-Platonist Celsus, had read the Gospels and used their portrayals of Jesus as weapons against the Christians. A heated debate commenced — in literary circles, at least — over whether the things Jesus said and did were appropriate to one who was revered as the Son of God. The background to these debates lay in the widespread notion throughout the Mediterranean that divine beings occasionally roamed the earth. There were, of course, numerous stories about other superhuman individuals, who like Jesus were also said to have been supernaturally born, done miracles, healed the sick, cast out demons, raised the dead, and been exalted to heaven to live with the gods. These other individuals were also sometimes called "sons" of God.[27]

Based on the fragmentary evidence at our disposal, it appears that there were general expectations of what such a person would be like within the broader culture of the Greco-Roman world. Part of the confrontation between pagans and Christians, at least in the rarified atmosphere of the apologetic literature, involved determining whether Jesus carried himself with the dignity and deportment of a son of God. Pagan critics like Celsus argued on the contrary that Jesus was a fraud who did not benefit the hu-

and the Social History of Early Christianity," in *The Text of the New Testament in Contemporary Research: Essays on the Status Quaestionis* (ed. B. D. Ehrman and M. W. Holmes; SD 46; Grand Rapids: Eerdmans, 1995), 361-79.

25. "Apologetic Discourse and the Scribal Tradition: Evidence of the Influence of Apologetic Interests on the Textual Tradition of the Canonical Gospels" (Ph.D. diss., Univ. of North Carolina, Chapel Hill, 2002).

26. The following paragraphs are based on my "Text of the Gospels."

27. A solid study of these issues from the perspective of the early Christian apologist Origen is E. V. Gallagher, *Divine Man or Magician? Celsus and Origen on Jesus* (SBLDS 64; Chico, Calif.: Scholars Press, 1982). My comments here on these individuals are not dependent on the thorny question of the terminology (e.g., θεοὶ ἄνδρες) used to describe them.

man race, and that as a consequence he was not a true son of God but a deceiver, a worker of dark craft, a magician.[28]

It appears that the debates over Jesus' identity and the appropriateness of his designation as the Son of God made an impact on the texts of the NT. One of the best candidates for "apologetic" variation of the text is in a passage that occurs somewhat later in the Gospel of Mark. This is the account in 6:3, where in most of our Greek and versional witnesses, the townspeople of Nazareth identify Jesus as the "carpenter, the son of Mary." We know that Celsus himself found this identification of Jesus as a τέκτων significant, possibly (though not certainly) because it situated Jesus among the lower classes and thereby showed him not to be worthy of divine stature. The response of Celsus's principal Christian opponent, Origen of Alexandria (whose quotations of Celsus are our main sources of information about him), may have been disingenuous, although there is no way to know for certain: he claims that there is no MS of the Gospels that provides this identification. Possibly all of Origen's texts agreed with P[45], f^{13}, and 33 in changing Mark 6:3 to identify Jesus as "the son of the carpenter," rather than "the carpenter"; or possibly he had forgotten the passage in Mark. In any event, given the second-century modification of the text — that is, its change precisely in the period when Jesus' own socioeconomic status and employment history had become an issue for apologists — we might be inclined to think that it was precisely the apologetic impulse that led to the corruption.[29]

Or take a different, even simpler, example, drawn this time from the Gospel of Luke: a change of word order in 23:32, where the original statement that Jesus was crucified with "two other evildoers" is modified in Codex Bezae to read "two others, who were evildoers." For the scribes who effected the change, there was evidently no reason to allow the text to be misread as saying that Jesus was to be numbered among the ranks of the miscreants. The change was yet more effective in some of Bezae's versional allies (c e sy[s]), where the offensive term is omitted altogether, so that Jesus is crucified along with "two evildoers."

My point is that Christian scribes who wanted to defend Jesus' character against the assaults of hostile pagan critics may have had real-life

---

28. Cf. Origen, *Contra Celsum*. See the full discussion by Gallagher, *Divine Man or Magician?*

29. As can be inferred from Origen's discussion; see *Contra Celsum* 6.36.

motivations for changing the texts of the Gospels in places where Jesus did not appear, at first glance at least, to be portrayed as one who merited the appellation "Son of God." Is it possible that this is what lies behind the alteration of Mark 1:41? In this text Jesus becomes angry with a poor leper who begs to be healed. In the broader context of Mark's account, the anger makes sense. Here is a man who questions Jesus' willingness to heal those in need. Jesus similarly became angry when the Pharisees questioned his authorization to heal, when the father of a demon-possessed boy questioned his ability to heal, and when his own disciples questioned his desire to heal. But anyone not intimately familiar with Mark's Gospel on its own terms — with concordance in hand — may not have understood why Jesus became angry. Matthew certainly did not; neither did Luke. Nor did later scribes, who may have been perplexed by this account of a leper in the hands of an angry Jesus and changed the text to make Jesus both more compassionate and more acceptable to the Christian claim, made in the face of pagan opposition, that "truly this man was the Son of God."

Liar Liar and "This Woman" in John 7:1–8:59: From Rhetorical Analysis to Intertextual Rereading

Jeffrey L. Staley

This essay has a prepublication history almost as long as my friendship with Jerry Hawthorne, my college Greek professor, to whom this volume is dedicated. I began writing this paper in 1985, just after completing my dissertation,[1] and I presented it in an unpolished form at the 1986 meeting of the Pacific Northwest regional SBL in Portland, Oregon. That paper had the rather mundane title, "The Rhetorical Structure of John 7:14–8:59," and in it I argued that a close reading of the Johannine dialogue revealed an intricate rhetorical unity. At the time I knew that "reading" was a problematical category for many literary critics, but for me the words "reading" and "reader" were unambiguous terms that referred to a textual entity and process evoked by those little black marks on white paper. For me, "reading" and "reader" had no existence apart from texts. They were, in fact, rhetorical constructs within texts, constituent elements of an "implied reader" that could be carefully reconstructed by eagle-eyed critics like myself.[2]

As this essay will make clear, today I believe in many other kinds of readers besides just an implied, textually encoded reader. I now give credence to supplied and replied readers; to the single-plied and the double-

---

1. J. L. Staley, *The Print's First Kiss: A Rhetorical Investigation of the Implied Reader in the Fourth Gospel* (SBLDS 82; Atlanta: Scholars Press, 1988).

2. So carefully defined as "an intratextual entity evoked by the temporal quality of narrative" (ibid., 34).

plied; to the real and the unreal; to historical and hysterical readers; and to multiplied combinations of all of these. Even more importantly, I believe that all these readers and their attendant reading processes are fictional constructs in some way, whether I am talking about an intratextual "implied reader," a first-century reading audience, or myself as a "real, intertextual reader." Every reader is an intentional, fictional construct with its own distinct rhetorical purpose and ideology.[3] This essay is an attempt to explore some of those intergalactic intercalations of contemporary readers and ancient texts.

A Brief History of Reading

It is an early fall morning at Holden Village in Washington's North Cascade Mountains. Shadows from a recent snow shroud the east side of 8,500-foot-high Dumbell Mountain. A coppery crush of leaves spin lazily in an eddy of Railroad Creek. The sky is sapphire blue. The air is crisp and clean. I do not want to be sitting here at a table, writing. I want to be outside, hiking up to Copper Basin, someplace I have never been before.

When I first started writing about John 7–8, I wanted to show how a literary and rhetorical analysis of the text could reveal the unity of one of the most fragmented Johannine scenes.[4] I had not spent much time thinking about lengthy direct speech segments like John 7–8 when I wrote my dissertation. But I knew that in the history of the text (both real and imagined), this direct speech section of John seemed to have undergone more corruption than any other Johannine monologue or dialogue. So, if I could show that there was a rhetorical unity to John 7–8 in its present canonical state, then my literary reading of the entire Gospel would gain credibility, and my construction of its "implied reader" would be vindicated in the academic world.

---

3. See J. L. Staley, *Reading with a Passion: Rhetoric, Autobiography, and the American West in the Gospel of John* (New York: Continuum, 1995), esp. 113-46, 198-99.

4. "Die Kapitel 7–10 sind ihm 'ein sinnloses Durcheinander,'" wrote E. Schwartz in 1908 (quoted by L. Schenke, "Joh 7–10: Eine dramatische Szene," *ZNW* 80 [1989]: 172). Similarly Gérard Rochais quotes Wellhausen as saying about John 7:14–8:59, "'On ne peut pas découvrir un fil conducteur, un progrès. C'est toujours la même chose qui est répétée, dans quantité de variantes, et l'on n'avance pas d'un pouce'" ("Jean 7: Une construction littéraire dramatique, à la manière d'un scénario," *NTS* 39 [1993]: 355).

The most obvious corruption of this Johannine text is, of course, that lady come lately — "the woman caught in adultery" (7:53–8:11). "This woman" somehow forced her way into the canonical Gospels, and from there was thrust into the midst of Jesus' Johannine conversation. Eventually she strutted out into the open, into the heated exegetical conversations of contemporary scholarship.[5] But she was no concern of mine. She did not play any role in my interpretation of John 7–8, since there was excellent MS evidence for excluding her from the text. In the imaginations of many Johannine scholars who studied John 7–8, however, not far beneath this woman's abrupt textual eruption were the text displacement theories of Bultmann, Schnackenburg, and others before them. These scholars proposed transposing chapters 5 and 6, and then parts of chapters 7 and 8, in order to make sense out of the peculiar narrative sequencing of John 4–8.[6] Thus the multiple narrative disjunctions and aporiae of John 7–8 (whether real or imagined) were the perfect grounds on which to test my unitary theories of the Johannine implied reader.

While working on my dissertation, I thought I had detected a certain argumentative pattern in Johannine dialogical style, one that consistently moved from what I termed a "less personal" to a "more personal" tone and content.[7] This movement could be seen in the specific metaphors that the

---

5. See esp. B. D. Ehrman, "Jesus and the Adulteress [Jn 7:53–8:11]," *NTS* 34 (1988): 24-44; J. P. Heil, "The Story of Jesus and the Adulteress (John 7,53-8,11) Reconsidered," *Bib* 72 (1991): 182-91; G. R. O'Day, "John 7:53–8:11: A Study in Misreading," *JBL* 111 (1992): 631-40; D. B. Wallace, "Reconsidering 'The Story of Jesus and the Adulteress Reconsidered,'" *NTS* 39 (1993): 290-96; J. P. Heil, "A Rejoinder to 'Reconsidering "The Story of Jesus and the Adulteress Reconsidered,"'" *EgT* 25 (1994): 361-66; J. I. H. McDonald, "The So-Called *Pericope de Adultera*," *NTS* 41 (1995): 415-27; T. van Lopik, "Once Again: Floating Words, Their Significance for Textual Criticism," *NTS* 41 (1995): 286-91; B. H. Young, "'Save the Adulteress!' Ancient Jewish *Responsa* in the Gospels?" *NTS* 41 (1995): 59-70; A. Watson, "Jesus and the Adulteress," *Bib* 80 (1999): 100-108; L. J. Kreitzer and D. W. Rooke, eds., *Ciphers in the Sand: Interpretations of the Woman Taken in Adultery (John 7.53–8.11)* (Biblical Seminar 74; Sheffield: Sheffield Academic Press, 2000); L. A. Guardiola-Sáenz, "Border-crossing and Its Redemptive Power in John 7.53–8.11: A Cultural Reading of Jesus and the Accused," in *Rewriting the Ground: John's Gospel and the Postcolonial Era* (ed. M. W. Dube and J. L. Staley; Sheffield: Sheffield Academic Press, forthcoming); J. Kim, "Adultery or Hybridity? Reading John 7:53–8:11 from a Postcolonial Context," in *Rewriting the Ground.*

6. R. Bultmann, *The Gospel of John: A Commentary* (trans. G. R. Beasley-Murray; Philadelphia: Westminster, 1971), 209-325; R. Schnackenburg, *The Gospel According to St. John*, vol. 1 (trans. K. Smyth; New York: Crossroad, 1990), 55-56.

7. Staley, *Print's First Kiss*, 55-56, 69. No doubt some would call my choice of the word

narrator used to describe Jesus, in terms of Jesus' own argumentative strategies, and in the broad, overall outline of the book's plot. For example, with regard to the narrator's language, many scholars have noted how the Johannine prologue moved the Logos from God to the world and back to God again.[8] But what had not been observed were the changes in metaphors that went along with this progression. Curiously, in the chiastic structure of the prologue, the abstract language of Logos, light, and God (1:1-4) moves to the more personal language of kinship (only child, bosom, father) in 1:17-18.[9] Moreover, in the narrative's second monologue (5:19-47) the same progression can be found. There Jesus begins in 5:19-29 by speaking vaguely about "the father" (ὁ πατήρ), "the son" (ὁ υἱός), and "everyone" (πάντες). But then, in the second half (5:30-47), his language becomes more direct and personal with "I" (ἐγώ), "my" (ἐμοῦ), "you" (ὑμεῖς), and "my Father" (ὁ πατήρ μου) becoming more prevalent. Finally, this same movement can be traced in the general plot of the book as a whole. For example, in the second half of the Gospel (John 11–21) Jesus speaks for the first time of his love for friends and followers, the narrator describes Jesus' love for individuals, and Jesus gives a lengthy farewell speech to his disciples. These elements all point to a more personal turn in the narrative.[10] Thus, in my early reading of the Fourth Gospel, a remarkable argumentative unity permeated the book's narrative design.

I turn my wooden chair to face a window in the cramped Holden Village Library, hoping to catch a glimpse of the late afternoon sun as it filters through dusky green cedars. A sharp blast from an air horn stirs me out of my imaginary hike to Copper Basin, and I stare outside as a group of staff members chase a stubborn yearling brown bear down the village main street.

"personal" ethnocentric (B. J. Malina and R. L. Rohrbaugh, *Social-Science Commentary on the Gospel of John* [Minneapolis: Fortress, 1998], 163-64). Nevertheless, the language of the monologues does change, with many more personal pronouns being used in the second halves of each.

8. For example, R. A. Culpepper, "The Pivot of John's Prologue," *NTS* 27 (1981): 1-31.

9. Staley, *Print's First Kiss*, 55-56.

10. Staley, *Reading with a Passion*, 63-66.

A Rhetorical Analysis of the Text

I began my 1986 SBL paper by arguing that despite the seemingly confused, disjunctive dialogue of John 7–8, there was a clear chiastic structure
to the narrative unit and an overarching progression in its argument.
Thus, despite any proposed source-critical or displacement theories, the
final form of John 7–8 was coherent and unified on at least two rhetorical
levels: symmetry (stylistics) and argumentation. An underlying subtext in
the paper made the additional point that if one really wanted to enjoy
Johannine rhetoric, one needed to move beyond the mere analysis of narrative symmetry. The critic should also explore the narrative's argumentative structure — which might or might not follow its symmetric, chiastic divisions.[11]

What I did not say in the title of that 1986 paper (or explain anywhere in the body) was why I excluded John 7:53–8:11 from my rhetorical
analysis of 7:1–8:59. The answer to that implicit question was all too obvious. John 7:53–8:11 just did not belong in John. It was a late addition to the
text, as proven by textual research and linguistic analysis. But still, why
leave 7:53–8:11 out of my analysis, especially since I was struck at the time
(though I did not voice the opinion out loud) with the fact that "this
woman's"[12] story was actually positioned near the center of my chiastic
structure and fit into it rather nicely?

But with or without "this woman," my 1986 analysis of Johannine
narrative structure argued that John 7–10 stood together as a narrative unit
whose primary focus was on two central Jewish institutions: synagogue
and temple. Surrounded by the two dialogical temple scenes with its "po-

---

11. This could be one of the real values of Malina and Rohrbaugh's work on John
(Social-Science Commentary), which has an appendix arguing for a chiastic structuring of
the entire Gospel (295-319). For other models of the symmetrical structuring of John 7–8,
see J. Breck, *The Shape of Biblical Language: Chiasmus in the Scriptures and Beyond*
(Crestwood, N.Y.: St. Vladimir's Seminary Press, 1994), 191-232; W. Howard-Brook, *Becoming Children of God: John's Gospel and Radical Discipleship* (Maryknoll, N.Y.: Orbis, 1994),
171-210; S. Motyer, *Your Father the Devil? A New Approach to John and 'the Jews'* (Carlisle,
UK: Paternoster, 1997), 141-59. Although there are quite a few differences between other
scholars' structural analyses of John 7–8 and my own, I will not attempt to delineate all those
differences here. For the most part, other analyses do not see any overarching chiastic structure in John 7–8, nor do they see an argumentative progression between John 7 and 8 (but cf.
Howard-Brook, *Becoming Children of God,* 172).

12. Cf. 2 Sam 13:17; 2 Kgs 6:28.

lice" (7:14–8:59; 10:22-39) was the story of the man born blind and Jesus' monologue about the good shepherd, both of which seemed to focus on the synagogue and the Pharisees.[13]

Here, then, is my 1986 analysis of 7:14–8:59, now filtered through the bifocals I was finally forced to purchase not too long ago. My first look at the text focused on stylistic analysis, that is, on the text's chiastic structure and the repetition of ideas or vocabulary within that structure. I hoped that by highlighting the repetition of certain words and ideas I would convince the uninitiated reader of a symmetrical structure that might otherwise appear highly imaginative or grossly idiosyncratic. My second look at the Johannine text focused on its argumentative structure, borrowing heavily from Chaim Perelman's analysis of rhetoric in *The New Rhetoric*.[14]

Now, as anyone working with chiasms knows, their beginnings and endings are often the easiest parts to delineate, because those segments usually deal with important plot developments.[15] In John 7–8, for example, the rhetorical unit 7:14–8:59 is clearly marked off by Jesus' entrance into and exit from the temple. But, as I mentioned earlier, I did not include the textually suspect 7:53–8:11 in my analysis, even though it lay near the center of the exposed chiasm and made reference to another exit and reentrance to the temple (7:53–8:2).

The second movement of the chiasm was not as easy for me to delineate. But, after many hours of slow, tortuous reading, I was able to isolate the next inward chiastic step. This segment focused on the crowds' (ὄχλοι) arguments with Jesus over the authority of his teaching (7:15-24). I believed its seven argumentative points were paralleled in chapter 8, but with important new elaborations and developments in plot. There "the Judeans" ('Ιουδαῖοι)[16] argue with Jesus over the implications of his teach-

13. Staley, *Print's First Kiss*, 64-66. There I called this section "The Third Ministry Tour." Fernando Segovia is much clearer on the issue of the Johannine plot than I originally was; see "The Journey(s) of the Word of God: A Reading of the Plot of the Fourth Gospel," *Semeia* 53 (1991): 22-35, 42-43. See also Schenke, "Joh 7–10," 172-92; Rochais, "Jean 7," 355-78; C. Cory, "Wisdom's Rescue: A New Reading of the Tabernacles Discourse (John 7:1–8:59)," *JBL* 116 (1997): 95-116.

14. C. Perelman and L. Olbrechts-Tyteca, *The New Rhetoric: A Treatise on Argumentation* (trans. J. Wilkinson and P. Weaver; Notre Dame, Ind.: Univ. of Notre Dame Press, 1969).

15. G. A. Kennedy, *New Testament Interpretation through Rhetorical Criticism* (Chapel Hill: Univ. of North Carolina Press, 1984), 34.

16. In my original 1986 regional SBL presentation I called the Judeans "the Jews." I am still not entirely convinced of the value of the word "Judean" over "Jew" for the Fourth Gos-

ing (8:31-58).[17] I tried not to worry about the fact that the segment in John 8 was nearly twenty verses longer than its parallel segment in John 7.[18] Furthermore, the only way that I could come up with a convincing delineation of these two parallel segments was by not requiring that their seven argumentative points be repeated slavishly in consecutive order.

Up to this point, the argumentative points I highlighted in 7:10–8:59 were these:

A Jesus goes up secretly to Jerusalem, enters the temple, and begins to teach (7:10-14)

A′ Jesus hides himself and leaves the temple (8:59)

B The crowds argue with Jesus over the authority of his teaching (7:15-24)

  i. "if any one wants to do his will he shall know about the teaching . . ." (7:17)

  ii. "the one who speaks from himself seeks his own glory . . ." (7:18)

  iii. "Moses gave you law, but none keep (ποιεῖ) the law" (7:19)

  iv. "Why are you seeking to kill me?" (7:19)

  v. "You have a demon!" (7:20)

  vi. "I performed one work" (7:21)

  vii. an analogy: circumcision on the Sabbath (7:22-23) (an allusion to Abraham ["the fathers," Gen 17:9-14])

B′ The Judeans argue with Jesus regarding the implications of his teaching (8:31-58)

---

pel, but like Agrippa in Acts 26:28, I am "very nearly persuaded" by recent anthropological arguments (Malina and Rohrbaugh, *Social-Science Commentary*, 44-46).

17. Raymond E. Brown's commentary on the Gospel of John had made this same text division (*The Gospel According to John I–XII* [AB 29a; Garden City, N.Y.: Doubleday, 1966], 315, 361). However, Brown was not particularly interested in dividing Johannine narrative into large chiastic segments (Breck, *Shape*, 192; cf. Brown, *John*, 343). But if Brown had been so inclined, he might well have divided John 7–8 exactly the way I have.

18. I can now take solace in Breck's argument that one should not be overly concerned about the "unequal length of parallel subsections" (*Shape*, 196-97), even though I am not completely convinced by this argument.

    i. "if you remain in my word you are truly my disciples, and you will know the truth . . ." (8:31-32)

       ("if anyone keeps my word he will never taste death," 8:51)

   ii. "I do not seek my own glory" (8:50)

  iii. "if you were sons of Abraham, you would do (ἐποιεῖτε) the works of Abraham" (8:39)

  iv. "you are seeking to kill me" (8:40)

   v. "Aren't we right in saying . . . you have a demon?" (8:48)

  vi. "You do the works of your father" (8:41)

 vii. an analogy: a slave in a household (8:34-38) (an allusion to the Abraham story [Gen 21:8-18; cf. Gal 4:21-31])[19]

The third symmetrical movement of the chiasm was the most difficult for me to frame. For, although John 7:25-36 is easily delineated by the arguments Jesus has regarding his identity,[20] 8:13-30 does not fall as easily into a discernible segment.[21] However, a certain parallel framework became evident when I compared the latter with 7:25-36.

C Arguments with Jesus regarding his possible identity (7:25-36) (the first subdivision emphasizes *who* Jesus might be [the Messiah], the one who sent him, the *Jerusalemites*, and Jesus as one *doing* signs; 7:25-31)

    i. "you know me and you know where I am from" (7:28)

   ii. they were seeking to arrest him, but no one laid a hand on him (7:30)

  iii. his hour had not yet come (7:30)

  iv. many in the crowd believed in him (7:31)

     (the second subdivision emphasizes *where* Jesus might be going and the *Pharisees;* 7:32-36)

   v. "you will search for me and you will not find me" (7:34)

19. Jerome Neyrey makes a strong case for connecting this seemingly innocuous metaphor of slavery with the ancient Abraham story ("Jesus the Judge: Forensic Process in John 8,21-59," *Bib* 68 [1987]: 522).

20. Again, I seem to be tracing over Raymond Brown's fingerprints (*John*, 317).

21. Brown, *John*, 342.

vi. "will he go to the Dispersion . . . ?" (indirect question) (7:35)

vii. "where I am you cannot come" (7:36)

C′ Arguments with Jesus regarding his true identity (8:13-30)
(the first subdivision asks *where* Jesus' Father is, emphasizes the *Pharisees,* and Jesus as *witness;* 8:13-20)

  i. "you do not know where I have come from" (8:14)

 ii. no one arrested him (8:20)

iii. his hour had not yet come (8:20)

  (the second subdivision asks *who* Jesus is, emphasizes *the
  Judeans,* and Jesus as one *doing* what is pleasing to his Father; 8:21-30)

 iv. many [Judeans] believe in him (8:30)

  v. "you will search for me but you will die in your sin" (8:21)

 vi. "is he going to kill himself . . . ?" (indirect question) (8:22)

vii. "where I am going you are not able to come" (8:21-22)

So far this chiastic arrangement looks rather cleverly constructed.
However, I may have cheated a bit to make it look as clear-cut as it does. To
be honest, in 1986 I thought that both 7:25-36 and 8:13-30 could be broken
down into two additional segments (7:25-31, 32-36 and 8:13-20, 21-30). But
when I did that, the following imperfection was revealed:

C The Jerusalemites wonder whether Jesus might be the Messiah, and
Jesus responds by talking about the one who sent him (7:25-31)

  i. "you know me and you know where I am from" (7:28)

 ii. they were seeking to arrest him, but no one laid a hand upon
 him (7:30)

iii. his hour had not yet come (7:30)

 iv. many in the crowd believed in him (7:31)

D The Pharisees and Judeans wonder whether Jesus might be going
to the Dispersion when he talks about where he is going and
about the one who sent him (7:32-36)

  v. "you will search for me and you will not find me" (7:34)

vi. "will he go to the Dispersion . . . ?" (indirect question) (7:35)

vii. "where I am you cannot come" (7:36)

C′ The Pharisees challenge Jesus' testimony and ask where his father is (8:13-20)

   i. "you do not know where I have come from" (8:14)

   ii. no one arrested him (8:20)

   iii. his hour had not yet come (8:20)

D′ The Judeans wonder whether Jesus is going to kill himself when he talks about where he is going and about the one who sent him (8:21-30)

   iv. many [Judeans] believe in him (8:30)

   v. "you will search for me but you will die in your sin" (8:21)

   vi. "is he going to kill himself . . . ?" (indirect question) (8:22)

   vii. "where I am going you cannot come" (8:21-22)

Clearly, if one wants a "perfect" chiasm, 8:13-20 should come *after* 8:21-30 (i.e., C-D, D′-C′). Thus the only way that I could keep my chiasm "perfect" was by combining C and D under one general heading (C). A generation ago I could easily have reconstructed an "Urtext" with these two segments reversed, and invented a redactional argument for the present (corrupt) state of the text. No doubt a reputable journal would have published the "research." But my training has been in literary and rhetorical criticism, and a reconstruction like that was not a viable option for me. Back in 1986 I still wanted perfection in my John, but it would have to come from the argumentative and stylistic structure of the text as it now stood (excluding 7:53–8:11), rather than from some hypothetical, reconstructed pre-text.

Thankfully, the final two segments of the chiastic structure of 7:10–8:59 were much easier to identify than B and C.

D Jesus' metaphorical proclamation regarding his true identity (7:37-39)[22]

22. Malina and Rohrbaugh dislike the word "identity" when talking about ancient Mediterranean constructions of personhood (*Social-Science Commentary*, 143-45, 163-64), but that is the term I used in my 1986 presentation.

(the one who believes in me . . . shall flow rivers of living water)

D′ Jesus' metaphorical proclamation regarding his true identity (8:12)

(the one who follows me . . . shall have the light of life)

E   Arguments among the crowd regarding Jesus' identity (7:40-43)

    i. the Christ is not to come from Galilee

    ii. Jesus is not on the scene

E′ Arguments among the authorities regarding Jesus' identity (7:45-52)

    i. no prophet is to arise from Galilee

    ii. Jesus is not on the scene

F   The second attempt to arrest Jesus ends in failure (7:44)

Thus the simplified chiastic structure that appeared in 7:10–8:59 was:

A   Jesus goes up secretly to Jerusalem, enters the temple, and begins to teach (7:10-14)

  B   The crowds argue with Jesus over the authority of his teaching (7:15-24)

    C   Arguments with Jesus regarding his possible identity (7:25-36)

      D   Jesus' metaphorical proclamation regarding his true identity (7:37-39)

        E   Arguments among the crowd regarding Jesus' identity (7:40-43)

          F   A second attempt to arrest Jesus ends in failure (7:44)

        E′ Arguments among the authorities regarding Jesus' identity (7:45-52)

      D′ Jesus' metaphorical proclamation regarding his true identity (8:12)

    C′ Arguments with Jesus regarding his true identity (8:13-30)

  B′ The Judeans argue with Jesus regarding the implications of his teaching (8:31-58)

A′ Jesus hides himself and leaves the temple (8:59)

It gradually became apparent to me as I struggled to make John 7–8 chiastically coherent that I was operating on two different rhetorical levels. While my large chiastic segments focused on the development of Jesus' arguments with his opponents, the miscellany of words and themes simply isolated common material — regardless of plot or direct discourse arguments. So, I wrote in my 1986 paper,

> We have clearly established that the narrative unit delineated by Jesus' entrance and exit from the temple has a chiastic structure, determined by the clustering of certain themes and motifs (a kind of "surface structure"). However, we want to show that there is also a rhetorical cohesiveness from an argumentative perspective. Here we will be looking not so much at the repetition of similar motifs, as at the differences and development of thought in John 7–8.

Jerome Neyrey has published extensively on the argumentative structure of John 7–8 since I first wrote these lines.[23] In his analysis of the text he argues that John 7 and 8 are best understood as a "trial" in which Jesus undergoes a "formal forensic process."[24] "Forensic" rhetoric is simply another term for what Perelman and Kennedy call judicial rhetoric: a species of argumentation in which the speaker "is seeking to persuade an audience to make a judgment about events occurring in the past."[25] More appropriate to John 7–8, however, is Malina and Rohrbaugh's term "challenge and riposte," an expression Neyrey also uses.[26]

---

23. J. H. Neyrey, *An Ideology of Revolt: John's Christology in Social-Science Perspective* (Philadelphia: Fortress, 1988), 37-58; idem, "The Trials (Forensic) and Tribulations (Honor Challenges) of Jesus: John 7 in Social Science Perspective," *BTB* 26 (1996): 107-24.

24. Neyrey, "Trials," 110; cf. 109, 116. See also Mark W. G. Stibbe, *John* (Readings: A New Biblical Commentary; Sheffield: Sheffield Academic Press, 1993), 99; and Motyer, *Your Father the Devil?* 141-59.

25. Kennedy, *New Testament Interpretation*, 19. Following Aristotle, Kennedy identifies three species of rhetoric: judicial, deliberative, and epideictic (19-20, 23-24; cf. Perelman and Olbrechts-Tyteca, *New Rhetoric*, 47). "Deliberative . . . aims at effecting a decision about future action, often in the very immediate future; and epideictic . . . celebrates or condemns someone or something, not seeking an immediate judgment or action, but increasing or undermining assent to some value" (Kennedy, *New Testament Interpretation*, 36).

26. Malina and Rohrbaugh, *Social-Science Commentary*, 146-67; Neyrey, "Trials," 116-23. Interestingly, Malina and Rorhbaugh do not use the terms "forensic" and "trial" in their social-scientific analysis of John 7–8, even though they list Neyrey's essay in their bibliography.

When I first analyzed the argumentative structure of John 7–8, the two chapters seemed to reflect the deliberative genre of rhetoric rather than the judicial or forensic genre as Neyrey has argued.[27] The deliberative genre is directed toward persuading an audience of a future decision. This made the most sense to me at the time, since Jesus' opponents raise questions about the authority of his teaching (7:15), after which he reacts with a statement that is oriented toward the future ("Anyone who resolves to do the will of God will know whether the teaching is from God or whether I am speaking on my own," 7:17).[28] A judicial argument would have focused more on the past; for example, "Rabbi Joseph was my teacher, and you all respect him, so go ask him what he taught me" (cf. 18:21). Obviously, Jesus cannot put forward a judicial argument in his own defense, since the origin of his teaching is not open to the same kind of external verification (God is his teacher, not a human).[29] Thus challenge and riposte, insinuation, innuendo, and gossip — all informal means of argumentation and exhortation — will play a more prominent role in John 7–8 than any formal "forensic trial."[30]

27. Neyrey, "Jesus the Judge," 510-11.

28. Kennedy shows how important exhortation and the future tense are in deliberative rhetoric (*New Testament Interpretation*, 145-47); cf. John 7:24, 28, 34, 37; 8:12, 21, 24, 28, 31-32, 36, 46, 51.

29. By way of contrast, Jesus' hearing before the high priest (John 18:19-24) is clearly couched in judicial rhetoric. There, when asked about his teaching, Jesus responds with references to the past: "*I have spoken* openly to the world; *I have always taught* in synagogues and in the temple. . . . Ask those *who heard* what *I said* to them . . ." (my emphasis).

30. The classification of rhetorical species is not always easy to make, as Kennedy has made abundantly clear through his rhetorical interpretation of the NT. In his argument with Hans-Dieter Betz over the classification of Paul's rhetoric in Galatians, Kennedy states, "the basic argument of deliberative oratory is that an action is in the self-interest of the audience, or as Quintilian prefers to put it, that it is right (8.3.1-3)" (*New Testament Interpretation*, 146). Kennedy therefore categorizes Galatians as deliberative rhetoric rather than as judicial rhetoric, which Betz had earlier argued for.

Like the rhetorical species of Galatians, that of John 7–8 is not easy to define. But following Kennedy's lead in Galatians, I believe that the language of judgment and the strategy of attack and defense evident in John 7–8 are not in themselves proof of judicial ("forensic") rhetoric. The key question is, to what end are these argumentative devices being used? In John 7–8 I believe that Jesus' use of the future tense and his focus on future benefits clearly show that these argumentative devices are being used in a deliberative framework. Jesus is acting as a prophet. His audience recognizes this, but is unconvinced by his prophetic message.

In 8:12-59 Jesus manages to put the issue of his authoritative teaching back into the maelstrom of ultimate authority — "the Father who sent me" (8:18; ". . . though you do not know him," 8:55) — which is an issue he has been trying to raise since John 7:15. But the changes in vocabulary between John 7 and 8 are significant here. Now the personal pronouns ἐγώ and ὑμεῖς are more prevalent, as is kinship language (πατήρ, υἱός, and Ἀβραάμ). The pronoun ἐγώ occurs in the nominative four times in 7:14-52, but twenty-one times in 8:12-59. Similarly, ὑμεῖς is only found four times (in the nominative) in 7:14-52, but fourteen times in 8:12-59. Moreover, the kinship nouns πατήρ, υἱός, and Ἀβραάμ are found respectively in the two chapters: one and nineteen times; zero and three times; and zero and eleven times. The noun θεός is found only one time in 7:14-53, but eight times in 8:12-59. Finally, the climactic inclusio ἐγώ εἰμι (8:12, 24, 28, 58) exemplifies the heightened drama of the challenges and ripostes between Jesus and his opponents.[31] Now theology mutates into Christology as Jesus' deliberative claims begin to center more and more on himself: "if anyone wants to do *his* will" (7:17), "if you remain in *my* word" (8:31), and "if anyone keeps *my* word" (8:51); and "you will seek me and will not find me" (7:34) and "you will seek me and die in your sins" (8:21). Just as in the prologue, the monologue of 5:19-47, and the Gospel as a whole, the movement from John 7 to 8 is always toward a more personal, revelatory, and confrontational climax.

I concluded my 1986 paper with the following paragraph:

John 7–8 is framed by the inclusio of Jesus' entrance and exit from the temple, and within this inclusio the plot to arrest Jesus and put him to death is highlighted. These repetitions, along with others, help to separate the text into a chiastic superstructure. But this seemingly static superstructure undergirds a deliberative argument that is only revealed by subtle changes in the language between John 7 and 8. These changes are similar to other argumentative developments in the Fourth Gospel, and thus they are not isolated argumentative devices. What once were thought to be aporiae and editorial glosses in John 7–8 are, in reality, evidence of a remarkable narrative unity.

But my interaction with John 7–8 is much messier than this antiseptic textual analysis would lead one to surmise. I spill my coffee on the white

---

31. This increasingly agonistic language is well noted by Malina and Rohrbaugh (*Social-Science Commentary*, 162).

pages of my Greek text, smudging the black letters. My children interrupt my early morning study with their cries of "What's for breakfast, Dad?" and I hurry off to meet their needs. I am much more easily distracted now than when I wrote the first draft of this essay back in 1986. I work in fitful starts. My body cannot take long periods of sitting without aches and pains intruding on my consciousness, and I cannot stay up as late at night as I once could. Then there is my preoccupation with my son, my only son. He is nearly grown now, and already I miss him. He is only fourteen, but I know I will not have him forever. Yet I will have him forever. I am not ready for him to go away, and so I let him talk me into doing strange things. He pulls me away from my writing, from the Johannine text with its blotches and stains, and I am quickly in another place. It is not my study, and it is not Copper Basin above Holden Village.

An Intertextual Rereading

My son. He is the one who made this intertextual rereading possible.[32] He is in junior high and out of control. He is standing beside me, begging me to take him to the most recent Jim Carrey movie. Carrey is his favorite actor, and my son has seen every major movie that Carrey has been in. Carrey is responsible for making my son the way he is.

"Is it supposed to be better than *Dumb and Dumber*?" I start at a point below which I will not go.

"Oh yeah, way better." He replies much too quickly, and there is a tenor of conviction in his pubescent voice that I find somewhat unsettling.

"Better than *Ace Ventura, Pet Detective*?" I am holding out for something more intellectually challenging — maybe a film like *The Cable Guy* or *Mask*.

"No contest, Dad. My friends say this is his best movie yet."

"What friends?"

"Jeez, Dad, come on! Just look at his initials! J.C. Don't you get it, Dad? J.C.? Carrey's got the same initials as Jesus does, and you're always talking about Jesus. So maybe you need to see this movie too! Come on! Please? Maybe this is one you'll be able to use in one of your classes."

---

32. For an excellent introduction to the theoretical issues of postmodern intertextuality, see G. Allen, *Intertextuality* (New Critical Idiom; New York: Routledge, 2000).

"Oh, I'm sure. Well, do your chores first and then we'll see."

My son finishes his Saturday tasks in record time, and against my better judgment I take him to the movie. It is called *Liar Liar*,[33] and I manage to sit through the entire show without taking even one twenty-minute break. In fact, I watched the film and came away a believer. *Liar Liar* is, indeed, a Bible film. Jim Carrey, a.k.a. Fletcher Reede,[34] actually quotes the NT in the movie — John 8:32, to be exact. With arms raised in triumph, after having just won a settlement for Mrs. Samantha Cole, he shouts out the much abused phrase to a packed courtroom: "And the truUuuth shall seEeet you freEEEE!"

The film begins with nothing, with a blank, black screen. Then a voice speaks out in the darkness, just as in Gen 1:1. It is the feminine voice of a schoolteacher — wisdom personified — spelling out the word "work" for her students. Work is an important theme of Genesis 1 and one that the film develops in some detail. Furthermore, the implications of Jesus' teaching and his "work" (ἔργον) just happen to be the starting point of Jesus' volatile argument with the Judeans in John 7–8 (7:14-17, 21; cf. 5:17-20; 6:27-29).

"W-O-R-K. Today we are going to share what our parents do for work."

Suddenly we are in the light, in an elementary school classroom.

A little girl pipes up, "My mommy is a doctor."

A boy chimes in, "My dad is a truck driver."

Then a third child adds, "My mom is a teacher."

"And your dad?" the teacher asks the same child.

"Mmm, my dad? He's a liar."

"A liar? Oh, I'm sure you don't mean a liar!"

"Well, he wears a suit and goes to court and talks to the judge."

"Oooh, I see, you mean he's a *lawyer!*" the teacher says with a relieved smile.

But the boy just shrugs bewilderedly.

Thus we are introduced to Max (Maximilian), only child of Fletcher

---

33. Directed by Tom Shadyac and written by Paul Guay and Stephen Mazur, the movie was released in March 1997. Interestingly, Shadyac's next film, *Patch Adams,* also combined christological themes with a Gospel-like plot.

34. Note that Carrey's character (Fletcher *Reede*) perhaps carries within himself a homonym for the reading experience.

Reede, and two important themes from John 7–8: lying (8:44) and the law (7:19-24).

The premise of the film is a simple one: Can a white, upper-middle-class, male lawyer make it through one business day without lying? Fletcher has recently divorced and is trying to make senior member in a southern California law firm. His son Max is almost five years old, and Fletcher seems to care about him — but can rarely fit the boy into his busy schedule. So he never keeps his promises to his son. After Fletcher fails to show up to his son's fifth birthday party, Max makes a wish: "Please, make it so my daddy won't be able to tell a lie for one whole day."

And unbeknownst to Fletcher, the little boy's wish comes true. But Fletcher has a twofold problem. First, to remain true to his own materialistic values, he must lie in order to win a large monetary settlement for his client Samantha, who is divorcing her husband and wants half of his wealth. According to her signed prenuptial agreement, however, she is not entitled to any of her husband's wealth if she has committed adultery. And she has — with several different men. Fletcher, therefore, cannot represent her without lying, and his future status in the law firm depends on his winning this case. His second problem is that his former wife is planning to re-marry and move across the country to Boston to be with her new husband. If she does that, father and son will seldom see each other.

With his son's birthday wish fulfilled, Fletcher is forced to find a way to win both the court case and his son — without ever lying. So the plot goes careening off in the wacky style typical of Jim Carrey films. Faithful to the genre, Fletcher finds a way to win in the end.

I must confess, the quote of John 8:32 in this film has gotten to me. Over the next year or so I rented the movie a number of times and watched it again and again, looking for other hints of Johannine themes. I did not really expect to find any, but then I did not expect to hear Carrey quote John 8:32 either. Suddenly I am struck by another Johannine thunderbolt.

Liar Liar seems to evoke explicit christological metaphors from the Gospel of John. John is well known for its seven "I am" metaphors, and the film quotes what is perhaps the best-known secular "I am" saying in contemporary American culture — the one from Dr. Seuss's *Green Eggs and Ham*.[35]

---

35. T. Seuss Geisel, *Green Eggs and Ham* (New York: Random House, 1960). Interestingly, Carrey's next feature film role was "the Grinch" in Dr. Seuss's *How the Grinch Stole Christmas*.

When Fletcher finally discovers the wish his son made on the night of his fifth birthday, he shrieks "Oh my God!"[36] and drives off to Max's school to try to get him to reverse the wish.[37] Fletcher bursts into his son's classroom in the middle of storytime, just as the teacher is reading the famous lines, "I do not like them Sam *I am,* I do not like green eggs and ham."

But I hesitate to put this "finding" in my essay. Surely I have watched the film too many times by now. I am giving the producer far too much intellectual credit. This connection is too bizarre to be "real." But then I remember that someone once published a book arguing that the Gospel of John was a midrash on the book of Esther.[38] Can my intertextual reading be any stranger than that? At least there was an actual quotation from John in *Liar Liar* that got me started on this adventure. So far as I know, no one has ever found an explicit quotation from Esther in the Gospel of John.

Now I am on a roll. I notice other Johannine motifs in the film. For example, "the hour" is a significant plot device in both the film and the Fourth Gospel. Unlike Jesus or his Father, however, Fletcher is never able to keep his promises about the "appointed hour." The father/son relationship (Fletcher/Max) is also central to the film, as is the son's leaving (on a jet plane to Boston). All three are interconnected, foundational metaphors in the film and the Gospel of John.

Water also plays a significant symbolic role in John and the film. In the movie, a revelatory moment occurs when Fletcher sees a pitcher of water sitting in front of him in the courtroom, during Samantha's divorce hearing. He pours himself one glassful after another until he drinks the en-

---

36. This is the first reference to God in the film, and the very next sentence is the "I am" saying from *Green Eggs and Ham.* The close temporal connection between Fletcher's informal use of the word "God" and the "I am" saying may be more than coincidental. It is the narrative marker of Fletcher's first revelatory experience, and a subtle interpretive key to the film's central miracle. Interestingly, Shadyac uses the same strategy in *Patch Adams* to help the viewer make the association between Patch's metaphoric death and resurrection and Jesus' passion. The technique also occurs in the science fiction thriller *The Matrix,* where it functions as a marker to connect the main character, Neo, with Christ.

37. As in the first two Johannine signs (2:1-11; 4:46-54), we as viewers know a miracle has happened long before the characters in the film know it. As I have argued elsewhere, John is unique among the Gospels in employing this rhetorical device (*Print's First Kiss,* 84-86). Furthermore, the proof that the "miracle" has occurred comes to us through the experience of someone (Fletcher) who has no idea a miracle has happened.

38. J. Bowman, *The Fourth Gospel and the Jews: A Study in R. Akiba, Esther, and the Gospel of John* (PTMS 8; Pittsburgh: Pickwick, 1975).

tire pitcher empty. He then takes a break and goes to the bathroom. His ensuing prolonged absence from the courtroom represents his desperate attempt to postpone the trial for a few hours. The ruse works, and he is granted a reprieve. As a result, he is able to "save" Samantha and himself the next day. Thus in both the film and the Gospel, water is linked to salvation.

The film is beginning to look like a piece of art to me, a grand theological expression, the work of a mastermind. I begin to worry about myself. Do I see John everywhere, anywhere I look? I know the answer to that is no. I am not insane. But I am beginning to think I need to go for a walk to clear my head. I need an interruption — my son, to sneak up behind me and wrestle me to the ground. But my son is across the street babysitting, and my mind continues to work, long after I have asked it to shut down.

Then suddenly I realize I have missed the film's most obvious connection to John 7–8: Samantha Cole, the woman Fletcher is asked to represent in court. Because I had excluded John 7:53–8:11 from my original rhetorical analysis of John 7–8, I had overlooked what was the clearest narrative connection between the Gospel of John and the film.

As with Fletcher, Samantha Cole's entire life is held together by lies. She lied about her age in order to get married at the age of seventeen, without parental consent; she lied about her weight and hair color on her driver's license; and she now is lying in court about her voice caught on a tape recorder, as she was in the very act of committing adultery. She is the adulterous woman of John 7:53–8:11 and is so carefully set into the plot of the film that her story is easily overlooked — until J.C. shouts out: "The truth shall set you free!"

No one in the film picks up stones to throw at Samantha because of her sin — or at Fletcher either, for that matter (John 8:5, 7, 59; cf. 10:31). However, throwing is an important motif in the film. Fletcher gives his son Max a baseball and glove for his birthday, and although father and son never actually play catch, they make plans to. The only person who throws anything in the film is Fletcher himself, who throws his shoes at a jet plane as it taxis down the runway, with his ex-wife and son on board. After the shoes bounce off the plane's windshield, the pilot stops taxiing, and Fletcher saves his son and ex-wife from leaving him. In the film, then, the act of throwing is a motif that reflects familial love and brings about ultimate redemption. The motif is not connected with violence and hatred as it is in John 8 and 10.

117

Postmodern Intertextuality and Canonical Authority

A postmodern sense of text and intertextuality does not require that the writers or director of *Liar Liar* have John 7–8 in mind when making the film. Rather, it argues that all texts, simply by being texts, are intertwined with other texts.[39] They feed on each other and nourish each other. So, by explicitly quoting John 8:32, *Liar Liar* invites biblically attuned viewers to look for other Johannine allusions in it. Surprisingly, there are fragmentary connections. For some people, how they assess the significance of the allusions will be a matter of political and/or religious importance. Minimally, one can argue that viewing the film against the backdrop of John 7–8 gives the viewer an appreciation for a Jim Carrey movie that otherwise might appear to have no redeeming qualities. But a postmodern sense of intertextuality moves in more than one direction.

Unlike the adulterous woman of John 7:53–8:11, Samantha Cole is not an arbitrary addition to the plot of *Liar Liar*. However, she is a flat character with no positive character traits. She is a "bad" woman who only cares about herself, and Fletcher feeds upon her selfishness. Yet without her, Fletcher himself would not be redeemed. Samantha's one true insight — that her husband, who has just divorced her, is a good father — is the catalyst that causes Fletcher to see himself in a new light and sends him running after his former wife and son. By way of contrast, the adulterous woman in John 8 has been viewed as an unnecessary intrusion into Jesus' controversy with the Judeans, with no particular plot function. But can the film *Liar Liar* lead one to reassess "this woman's" connection to John 7–8? Can she somehow redeem the biting challenges and ripostes of Jesus and the Judeans?

For a Johannine scholar and first-time viewer of *Liar Liar*, Fletcher's grand exclamation, "The truth shall set you free," was my entrance to another intertextual level of the film. Until that moment, nothing in the film would have made me think about the Gospel of John. It was pure entertainment. Funny, but not worth watching more than once. The divorce proceedings with Samantha Cole were easily forgotten, since they seemed like an unnecessary subplot to the "lying" conceit that drove the film. That is, any type of legal proceeding, any cast of characters could have been used to make fun of Fletcher, the stereotypical lying lawyer. However, once the

---

39. Allen, *Intertextuality*, 174-99.

choice was made for an *adulterous woman* to be the catalyst for Fletcher's turnabout, she became a necessary character in the movie's plot.

When the Johannine intertext is evoked (8:32), "this woman's" voice, Samantha's voice — caught on tape in the very act of adultery — becomes another important Johannine connection. But in John 7–8 "this woman" intrudes, interrupts, and arrests the fierce diatribe in the temple. In contrast to Samantha Cole, she has no name. She also has no voice, except when she says, "No one, sir" (8:11). In the Johannine text she is a narrative interlude, a glaring, in-your-face, disconnected question mark that turns the virulent voices of John 7–8 into an intensely personal confrontation. She literally brings the rhetorical situation of John 7–8 down to stony earth. She is the canonical counterpoint to Fletcher's intrusive, jarring quote of John 8:32, that intertextual connection that raised the movie to another level.

I have come a long way from the reading of John 7–8 I did in 1986, where the boundaries of "text," "rhetoric," and "reader" were clear and distinct, where I was careful to keep my personal experience out of my scholarly discourse on the biblical text. Today I am more apt to find John anywhere, and apt to consider all sightings seriously. Some people may challenge what seems to be an idiosyncratic reading, wondering at the end whether I am even reading John at all. What is at stake in a postmodern sense of rhetoric and intertextuality? If *Liar Liar* gains some credulity from its intertextual repertoire, is it not conceivable that John 7–8 could also gain something from its connection to *Liar Liar*? Need it lose in the exchange? If Jesus can stoop so low as to write in the gritty dirt of ordinary human experience, then perhaps we should feel empowered to lift up popular culture's allusions to the Christian canon into serious dialogue with postmodern rhetoric and textuality.[40] So I shall go back and read John 7:53–8:11 once again. Perhaps this time, in the midst of a complex Johannine chiasm, I will find Jim Carrey poised, contorted in silence, ready to cast the first shoe. And perhaps I will find this woman, now named, shouting with a voice that moves her beyond the confines of patriarchal stereotypes, with a voice strong enough to redress the judicial subtleties that have thrust her and her rescuer so dangerously into the spotlight of imperial power.

---

40. I have written to this issue recently, arguing that Leslie Marmon Silko's novel *Ceremony* opens up a new way of envisioning biblical border women ("Changing Woman: Postcolonial Reflections on Acts 16.16-40," *JSNT* 73 [1999]: 134-35).

The Spirit and Jesus "on Mission" in the Postresurrection and Postascension Stages of Salvation History: The Impact of the Pneumatology of Acts on Its Christology

William J. Larkin Jr.

Introduction

In *The Presence and the Power,* Professor Hawthorne makes a strong case for the significant role the Holy Spirit played in Jesus' earthly life and ministry.[1] At many points he uses Acts, especially Acts 10:37-40, to support his case.[2] In the course of his discussion, he refers to Acts and the Epistles as the "developed Christological reflection of the earliest church."[3] In a *Festschrift* that honors his life and work, it is most fitting that we enter into his labors by extending his work to the next stages of salvation history: Jesus' postresurrection period and his postascension reign. This should prove most beneficial since Acts recounts the formative period for the church's developed theological reflection. Indeed, to understand the role of the Holy Spirit in the life and ministry of the exalted Lord with and through his church will be to comprehend a key factor in the direction and final shape of that maturing reflection.

The resulting profile of the impact of Acts' pneumatology on its Christology will reveal the dynamic interplay between the Holy Spirit and

---

1. G. F. Hawthorne, *The Presence and the Power: The Significance of the Holy Spirit in the Life and Ministry of Jesus* (Dallas: Word, 1991).

2. Ibid., 101, 128-29, 147, 153, 155, 166-67, 237-38, 240.

3. Ibid., 128.

the exalted Lord Jesus that will prove to be a fruitful seedbed for trinitarian thought. Indeed, Luke portrays the Spirit as the expression of the immanence of the transcendent Lord Jesus, who continues to be actively engaged in ministry to the ends of the earth until the end of human history.

The Holy Spirit in Jesus' Postresurrection Ministry

Jesus, the Spirit-Empowered,
"Not Yet Ascended" Prophetic Revealer

Critical to Luke's pneumatology in Acts are references to the Holy Spirit during Jesus' postresurrection ministry (Acts 1:1-11/Luke 24:13-53). Luke begins with a note that the Spirit of God empowers Jesus in this postresurrection period as he "gives command through the Holy Spirit to the apostles whom he had chosen" (ἐντειλάμενος τοῖς ἀποστόλοις διὰ πνεύματος ἁγίου οὓς ἐξελέξατο, Acts 1:2). Some see this as a reference to Jesus' Spirit-inspired choice of the apostles during his earthly ministry. They say Luke moved the prepositional phrase διὰ πνεύματος ἁγίου forward to emphasize the legitimacy of the apostles' authority. But it is better to let the word order syntactically guide the sense so that the prepositional phrase, though awkwardly placed, links its object to the nearest verb: ἐντειλάμενος.[4] Jesus, by the power of the Spirit, gives a command to the apostles during the postresurrection period to await the coming of the Spirit (Luke 24:49; Acts 1:4, 8).[5] In fact, διὰ πνεύματος ἁγίου heightens the authority of the command. Since the command is to wait for God to act, this phrase also heightens the certainty that God will fulfill his promise. Indeed, Jesus speaks with the same authority, the same inspiration, as the prophets of old when they prophesied the events of salvation history (cf. Acts 1:16; 4:25).

---

4. C. K. Barrett, *A Critical and Exegetical Commentary on the Acts of the Apostles* (ICC; 2 vols.; Edinburgh: T&T Clark, 1994-98), 1:69; contra E. Haenchen, *The Acts of the Apostles: A Commentary* (trans. R. McL. Wilson et al.; Philadelphia: Westminster, 1971), 139; and I. H. Marshall, *The Acts of the Apostles: An Introduction and Commentary* (TNTC; Grand Rapids: Eerdmans, 1980), 57. Note also the Western text's apparent attempts to overcome this more difficult reading of the risen Lord acting through the Spirit (B. M. Metzger, *A Textual Commentary on the Greek New Testament* [2d ed.; Stuttgart: Deutsche Bibelgesellschaft, 1994], 237-38).

5. So G. F. Hawthorne, "Holy Spirit," *DLNT* 492.

Pneumatology, then, contributes to Christology by underscoring that even in his time of triumph, Jesus is still the prophetic revealer of subsequent events of salvation history. With the phrase διὰ πνεύματος ἁγίου, Luke's pneumatology further contributes to his Christology by identifying stages of exaltation — resurrection, ascension, and session at the right hand.[6] The risen, but not yet ascended, Jesus acts "through the Spirit," because he is not yet glorified.[7]

Jesus' Teaching on the Promised Spirit's Arrival from Above

When we consider what Jesus taught about the Spirit during his post-resurrection appearances, we need to keep in mind Luke's use of functional redundancy for recapitulation as he begins his second volume.[8] In this way he highlights for us those aspects of the promise of the Spirit's coming that are most significant to him, saving mention of them until a later point, as well as avoiding extensive repetition on matters he has already covered.[9] Functional redundancy is exhibited in the parallels of Luke 24:36-49 and Acts 1:4-5, which describe an incident during the forty days when Jesus teaches his disciples about the coming of the Spirit. Likewise, Luke 24:50-53 and Acts 1:6-11 are parallel accounts of events surrounding Jesus' ascension.[10]

In the first set of parallel accounts, Luke, explicitly in the Gospel, then less explicitly in Acts, portrays the ascended Jesus as the source of the baptism with the Holy Spirit (Luke 24:49/Acts 1:4-5). It is described as the

---

6. W. J. Larkin Jr., "Ascension," *DLNT* 96-98.

7. Hawthorne uses Acts 1:2 to emphasize the continuity between the relation of the Holy Spirit and Jesus during his earthly ministry and in his postresurrection period (*Presence and the Power*, 153).

8. R. D. Witherup, "Functional Redundancy in the Acts of the Apostles: A Case Study," *JSNT* 48 (1992): 67-86; L. C. A. Alexander, *The Preface to Luke's Gospel: Literary Convention and Social Context in Luke 1.1-4 and Acts 1.1* (SNTSMS 78; Cambridge: Cambridge Univ. Press, 1993), 143.

9. Cf. R. P. Menzies's discussion of Jesus' "Pre-Ascension Promise (Luke 24.49; Acts 1.4-5, 8)," in *Empowered for Witness: The Spirit in Luke-Acts* (JPTSup 6; Sheffield: Sheffield Academic Press, 1994), 168-72. (Rev. ed. of *The Development of Early Christian Pneumatology with Special Reference to Luke-Acts* [JSNTSup 54; Sheffield: Sheffield Academic Press, 1991].)

10. See M. C. Parsons, *The Departure of Jesus in Luke-Acts: The Ascension Narratives in Context* (JSNTSup 21; Sheffield: JSOT Press, 1987).

"promise of the Father" in both instances. In the Gospel, Luke relates Jesus' assertion: "And behold, I am sending the promise of my Father on you."[11] In Acts all we meet is a "divine passive" — "you shall be baptized with the Holy Spirit" (ἐν πνεύματι βαπτισθήσεσθε ἁγίῳ, probably an instrumental, not locative, use of ἐν + the dative, echoing the Hebrew preposition בְּ).[12]

In both instances there are further hints from the immediate context that it is the ascended Lord who will send the baptism. In Luke 24:49 Jesus' sending of the Spirit is a matter of "being endued with power from on high." It is an event the disciples are to wait for. Since the ascension intervenes, the outpouring of the Spirit will evidently occur subsequent to Jesus' exaltation (24:49, 51). In Acts 1:4, 8, the phrases used are "the promise of [or "from"] the Father" (τὴν ἐπαγγελίαν τοῦ πατρός) and "the Holy Spirit coming upon you" (ἐπελθόντος τοῦ ἁγίου πνεύματος ἐφ' ὑμᾶς; cf. Isa 32:15 LXX). Again, the ascension intervenes between the command to await the Spirit and the actual arrival of the Spirit. This too points to the baptism coming from heaven, although the phrasing points less clearly to the ascended Lord as its source.

If we strictly identify the coming of the Spirit as "empowerment for witness," then this "coming upon" is an inspiration.[13] But if we understand the baptism of the Spirit to include more than that — namely, all the activities of the Spirit in the church that make for salvation,[14] and, indeed, the salvation blessings themselves (cf. Acts 2:38) — then we may take the imagery more generally as "arrival from above."

Luke recounts Jesus' vagueness about the fact that he will be the immediate source of baptism with the Spirit. This displays a historical sensitivity to the wise way the risen Lord, during his postresurrection period, would have prepared his Jewish followers to embrace a truth that would have explosive implications for understanding his true nature as God incarnate. The OT consistently speaks of the Spirit's bestowal as directly from

---

11. All Scripture translations are my own unless otherwise noted.

12. Barrett, *Acts*, 1:74.

13. Ibid., 1:79.

14. Max Turner, "The 'Spirit of Prophecy' as the Power of Israel's Restoration and Witness," in *Witness to the Gospel: The Theology of Acts* (ed. I. H. Marshall and D. Peterson; Grand Rapids: Eerdmans, 1998), 347. See also idem, *Power from on High: The Spirit in Israel's Restoration and Witness in Luke-Acts* (JPTSup 9; Sheffield: Sheffield Academic Press, 1996), esp. his section on "The Promise of the Spirit to the Disciples (Luke 24.47-49; Acts 1.4-5, 8)," 341-46.

God, not mediated by any other person (e.g., Isa 32:15; 44:3; 59:21; Ezek 36:25-27; 39:29; Joel 2:28; Zech 12:10). It is true that the Messiah was to be anointed with the Spirit (Isa 11:1-2; 42:1; 61:1), but only in intertestamental literature do we find a messianic figure pouring out the Spirit, and then only during his earthly mission (*T. Jud.* 24:1-6; cf. *T. Levi* 18:1-2, 5-12; *T. Benj.* 9:2-3).[15] Jesus, still from a "promise" perspective, to some extent downplays his own role in sending the Spirit. In continuity with the ot perspective, he consistently says that the Spirit is the promise of the Father — it comes from God (Luke 24:49/Acts 1:4). However, the one statement that Jesus would send the Spirit (Luke 24:49), when combined with other features in the text — the phrases "promise from the Father" (Luke 24:49; Acts 1:4); the divine passive (Acts 1:5); the Spirit's coming "from on high" (Luke 24:49) and "coming on" the disciples (Acts 1:8); the command to wait for it as a postascension event (Luke 24:49; Acts 1:4-5, 7-8) — set the trajectory of the disciples' thought in a direction that, when the Spirit does come, they can readily draw a trinitarian conclusion. The Father who sends the Spirit, and Jesus, the ascended Lord, who baptizes them with it, though distinct persons, must participate in the same divine nature. Thus Luke's pneumatology contributes to his Christology from a promise perspective and in seminal form.

Jesus also reveals the eschatological and missionary contexts of the Spirit's coming during his postresurrection appearance teaching. He clearly demarcates a time when the Spirit will be present as an end-time blessing, but a time that is not itself the end. So he can promise the baptism with the Spirit in circumstances that are not the final restoration of the kingdom to Israel (Acts 1:4-8). In this way Jesus continues the tension between the "now" and the "not yet." The Spirit's outpouring, that promised end-time deluge, would come "not many days from now" (Acts 1:5; cf. 2:1-13; Isa 66:15; Ezek 36:25-27; 39:29; Joel 2:28). Yet it would not be that final, decisive "baptism with the Spirit and fire" (Luke 3:16) that would bring judgment on all the enemies of God's people and establish the Messiah's kingdom in complete triumph. Rather, the outpouring would be missionary in nature. Jesus, king of peace, the servant-king, through the Spirit-empowered witness of his followers, would take away the burden of sin,

---

15. E. R. Stuckenbruck, "The Spirit at Pentecost," in *Essays on New Testament Christianity: A Festschrift in Honor of Dean E. Walker* (ed. C. R. Wetzel; Cincinnati: Standard, 1978), 92-96.

the law, and corruption and lead many to know forgiveness and the gift of the Spirit (Acts 1:8; cf. Luke 24:46-47; Acts 13:36-39).[16]

Initially, Luke places the commission to witness side by side with the promise of the Spirit's coming (Luke 24:47-48, 49). Yet he clearly implies that they are inseparable. The disciples are commissioned to be witnesses beginning in Jerusalem. The call to wait tells them to stay in that city until they are "endued with power from on high." In the recapitulation in Acts, Luke brings out the connection much more clearly as he relates new information: a commission given at the ascension — "You shall receive power, after the Holy Spirit has come upon you, and you shall be my witnesses" (Acts 1:8). Though the Spirit's coming at Pentecost meant more than empowerment for witness, it certainly entails that empowerment. Indeed, Jesus' last words let us know that the Spirit's presence must always be understood in the context of mission.[17] The Spirit is an enabler for witness about Jesus to the ends of the earth. The miraculous effect of the Spirit's coming at Pentecost — that persons from the ends of the earth each hears in his or her own language the great deeds, the saving acts, of God (Acts 2:4-11) — confirms that it is the Spirit that empowers those on mission to the ends of the earth.

Luke's pneumatology contributes to his Christology at this point in such a way that it rewrites the Jewish understanding of biblical eschatology. We now know that this missionary Spirit is empowering a mission that not only characterizes the "between the times" (cf. Luke 21:13; Acts 1:6-8), but also, in so doing, brings "times of refreshing" (Acts 3:20) — foretastes of the final salvation now. All this, again, comes from the risen and exalted Jesus Messiah, who begins his reign in this interim period (Acts 2:33; 5:31; 26:23). The presence of the Spirit as both mediating and being the salvation blessing (cf. 2:38; 5:31-32) is evidence that this is truly Jesus' position and role during this stage of salvation history.

Luke's pneumatology further contributes to Christology at this point by promoting an understanding of the christocentric nature of the gospel message and its warrant. The Spirit will empower persons who are μου μάρτυρες (Acts 1:8 — note the use of *hyperbaton* for emphasis, "my wit-

16. L. Legrand, "The Angel Gabriel and Politics: Messianism and Christology," *ITS* 26 (1989): 19.

17. See G. W. H. Lampe, "The Holy Spirit in the Writings of St. Luke," in *Studies in the Gospels: Essays in Memory of R. H. Lightfoot* (ed. D. E. Nineham; Oxford: Blackwell, 1955), 159-200.

nesses"). They will proclaim "repentance unto the forgiveness of sins" ἐπὶ τῷ ὀνόματι αὐτοῦ — "in his name" (Luke 24:47), that is, in the authority of the risen and soon to be ascended Lord. This message is no dead letter of loyalty to a past religious leader and his teachings, but living truth of a divinely empowered witness. This Spirit will energize the witness to the ends of the earth.

The Holy Spirit and Jesus' Postascension Ministry

As for Jesus' postascension reign and ministry, Acts 1:1, with its reference to the Third Gospel as "the things Jesus began to do and to teach," strongly implies that in some sense what Luke is about to write in Acts will encompass what Jesus "continued to do and teach." Yet within ten verses Jesus departs via the ascension (Acts 1:9-10). How will Jesus continue his mission? Luke indicates a variety of ways. Jesus, as exalted Lord, is described as being the source of the present application of salvation blessings (2:33; 5:31; 26:23). Jesus is presented as intervening directly in history to heal, bear witness by signs and wonders, or spiritually save (9:34; 14:3; 16:14). Jesus directly intervenes to commission, guide, and comfort his witnesses (9:3-19; 18:9-11; 22:6-21; 23:11; 26:13-18). Significantly, in a number of these contexts and at other places in Acts, the Holy Spirit, as one would expect from Jesus' postresurrection teaching, plays a key role in Jesus' postascension ministry in human history (2:33-36; 5:31-32; 7:55-56; 8:39; 13:2, 4 [cf. 9:15-16; 20:24; 22:14-16; 26:16-18]; 16:7; 19:21; 20:22-24; 21:4, 11-14). In the process, again Luke's pneumatology contributes to his Christology.

The NT letters speak every so often of Christ's position and activity in and from heaven (e.g., Rom 8:34; 1 Cor 15:25; Eph 1:20-23; Heb 4:14-16), and the book of Revelation, of course, expresses this in the form of visions (cf. Rev 4–5). Only Acts, by means of narrative, relates the ascended Lord's continued ministry and the contribution that the Spirit makes to it. Here there are four basic themes: Jesus is the sender of salvation blessings (Acts 2:33-36; 5:31-32); Jesus is the reigning Lord (7:55-56); Jesus is he who deploys for mission (8:39; cf. 9:15; 13:2, 4); and Jesus is the guide in mission (16:7; 19:21; 20:22-24; 21:4, 11-14; 23:11).[18]

---

18. For further discussion of the Holy Spirit "on mission" in Acts see J. B. Sheldon, *Mighty in Word and Deed: The Role of the Holy Spirit in Luke-Acts* (Peabody, Mass.:

Jesus, the Sender of Salvation Blessings

Peter's preaching on the day of Pentecost, which interprets to the crowd both the cause and the significance of the outpouring of the Holy Spirit, climaxes with a chiastic construction that persuasively argues for the immediate cause of this phenomenon (Acts 2:25-36). First, for Jesus' resurrection, Peter provides scriptural proof (2:25-28; cf. Ps 16:8-11); a christocentric interpretation (Acts 2:29-31); and finally a kerygmatic proclamation (2:32) of Jesus' resurrection. Then in reverse parallelism he proclaims Jesus' ascension/session at the right hand of God and pouring out of the Spirit (2:33); a brief christocentric interpretation of Ps 110:1 (Acts 2:34a); and a quotation of this scriptural proof (2:34b-35). Peter exclaims in his conclusion, "Let all the house of Israel know certainly that God has made him Lord and Christ, this Jesus, whom you crucified" (2:36).

As Peter describes the process that has made Pentecost possible, he begins with the ascension: "being exalted to the right hand of God" (2:33). Barrett views the precise function of the dative in the phrase τῇ δεξιᾷ τοῦ θεοῦ as ambiguous both here and at Acts 5:31.[19] Is it instrumental — "by the right hand of God" — or locative — "to the right hand of God"? The parallel phrasing in the proof text, which clearly points to position ("Sit at my right hand"), brings clarity. The dative phrase in v. 33 is, therefore, locative. Peter's next statement, "Receiving the promise of the Holy Spirit from the Father," adjusts the phrasing from "promise of the Father" (Luke 24:49) to "promise of the Holy Spirit" (τὴν ἐπαγγελίαν τοῦ πνεύματος τοῦ ἁγίου, Acts 2:33). Luke is probably now moving from a "genitive of source" understanding to an epexegetical genitive.[20] What Jesus receives is "the promise, that is, the Holy Spirit."

This statement also gives us new information about the role relationships between Father and Son in the "heaven to earth" transaction. Previously, Luke has given us only glimpses of it as he set side by side the christocentric origin and the divine origin of the Spirit's coming (Luke 3:16, "He [the Messiah] will baptize you with the Holy Spirit"; 24:49, "I [Jesus] am

Hendrickson, 1991); W. H. Shepherd Jr., *The Narrative Function of the Holy Spirit as a Character in Luke-Acts* (SBLDS 147; Atlanta: Scholars Press, 1994); J. H. E. Hull, *The Holy Spirit in the Acts of the Apostles* (London: Lutterworth, 1967).

19. Barrett, *Acts*, 1:149, 290.

20. L. T. Johnson, *The Acts of the Apostles* (SP; Collegeville, Minn.: Liturgical Press, 1992), 52.

sending the promise of the Father"; vs. the divine passives of Luke 24:49 and Acts 1:5 — "you have been endued with power from on high . . . you will be baptized with the Holy Spirit"; and, of course, the phrase "promise of the Father," Luke 24:49; Acts 1:4). Now that the Spirit has been given, Peter with Spirit-aided insight can clearly proclaim the cooperation of Father and Son in the Spirit's coming. In doing so, Peter draws out a very important facet of the reality of Jesus. He is the Father's Son.[21] The main clause, "he [Jesus] has poured out this [the Spirit]," completes the "heaven to earth" transaction. It provides a counterpoint to Jesus' "subordination" to the Father and reveals his essential role as the immediate imparter of salvation blessings.

John J. Kilgallen notes the observation of the Venerable Bede, the medieval commentator, that both natures of Christ are manifested in this outpouring. He received the Spirit as a man and poured it forth as God.[22] Indeed, when this action is understood against the backdrop of the univocal ΟΤ teaching that God pours out the Spirit,[23] its significance for Jesus as divine becomes clear. Indeed, the final exclamatory conclusion, "God has made him Lord and Christ, this Jesus, whom you crucified" (2:36), should not be understood as "adoptionist Christology,"[24] but should be viewed as an "instating" of Jesus in a unique, lofty position from which he functions as the exclusive medium of salvation, Lord over all, and Messiah, something that he had always been (Luke 2:11).[25]

While the apostles serve as eyewitnesses to Jesus' resurrection (Acts 2:32), the crowd is called on to consider itself a witness to Jesus' ascended, exalted state. For it is "that which you are seeing and hearing" (ὃ ὑμεῖς [καὶ] βλέπετε καὶ ἀκούετε, present tense continuous action) that is evidence that Jesus has poured out the Spirit (2:33).

Before I sum up the contribution of pneumatology to Christology in this thematic area, we need to look at one other passage that brings Christ's continuing ministry and the work of the Spirit into close contact: Acts 5:31-32. In his reply to the Sanhedrin's accusation of an apostolic vendetta (5:28), Peter declares that Christ's death, resurrection, and ascension/exaltation were not supposed to bring judgment but salvation blessing. God has exalted

---

21. J. J. Kilgallen, "A Rhetorical and Source-traditions Study of Acts 2,33," *Bib* 77 (1996): 196. Barrett (*Acts*, 1:150) calls the phrasing "mildly subordinationist."

22. Kilgallen, "Rhetorical Study," 196.

23. See above, n. 14 and text.

24. Contra Barrett, *Acts*, 1:152.

25. L. W. Hurtado, "Christology," *DLNT* 171.

Jesus "to his right hand" (again locative, not instrumental)[26] as ruler and savior so that he "might give repentance and forgiveness of sins to Israel" (5:31). This infinitive phrase of purpose ([τοῦ] δοῦναι μετάνοιαν τῷ Ἰσραὴλ καὶ ἄφεσιν ἁμαρτιῶν) does not have an explicitly stated subject. Grammatically, it is normal to assume that it would be the same as the subject of the main clause that the phrase modifies, namely God. If v. 32 refers to the same salvation blessings in the person of the Holy Spirit, then it would confirm that God is the giver. As we shall see, however, the Holy Spirit does not refer to salvation blessings in that verse. Further, when we note the role of Jesus as savior, the sense of the sentence seems to be that God gives repentance and forgiveness through Jesus (cf. 3:19-20; 26:23). In fact, reading Acts 5:31 in light of the clear description in Acts 2:33 helps us understand that Peter is pointing to Jesus' decisive role in the dispensing of salvation blessings here as well.[27] The OT is marked by the parallel themes that God will bring the final salvation and that the Messiah will bring it (Ps 106:47; 118:25-26; Isa 63:8; Jer 17:14; Joel 2:32). The ambiguity at Acts 5:31 may be revealing again that God and the Messiah are one and the same person, namely the Savior Jesus (cf. Acts 2:21, 36, 38-39). The title "Savior," as the title "Lord," aids the Jewish believer in making the transition from unitary monotheism to trinitarian monotheism.

Peter goes on immediately to say, "We are witnesses of these things, and the Holy Spirit whom God gave to those who obey him" (5:32). Some see the Holy Spirit as a witness to the presence of salvation blessings now in the sense of being the salvation blessing itself (cf. 2:38).[28] Others see the witness as outward miraculous manifestations that salvation has come (8:15-17; 10:44-47; 15:8).[29] Rather, the Spirit bears witness by empowerment in witness. Spirit-empowered, bold witness produces in the hearers a recognition that the gospel message about an unseen Lord ready to apply salvation — "repentance and forgiveness of sins" — is true and for them (4:8-13; 6:5, 8-10; John 16:8-11).[30]

---

26. B. Witherington III, *The Acts of the Apostles: A Socio-Rhetorical Commentary* (Grand Rapids: Eerdmans, 1998), 232; contra F. F. Bruce, *The Book of the Acts* (rev. ed.; NICNT; Grand Rapids: Eerdmans, 1988), 113.

27. G. Schneider, *Die Apostelgeschichte*, 2 vols. (HTKNT; Freiburg: Herder, 1980-82), 1:397.

28. Marshall, *Acts*, 120.

29. J. B. Polhill, *Acts* (NAC; Nashville: Broadman, 1992), 170.

30. J. D. G. Dunn, *The Acts of the Apostles* (Narrative Commentaries; Valley Forge, Pa.: Trinity Press International, 1996), 70.

The contribution of the pneumatology of Acts to its Christology in this thematic area is to bear witness to Jesus' ascended, exalted position and also to his divine nature, for Christ assumes the divine prerogative of giving both the Spirit and salvation blessings. As the crowd sees and hears the speaking in tongues, the outpouring of the Spirit, they, by inference, become witnesses to its source: the exalted Lord Jesus at God's right hand (Acts 2:33). The apostles' Spirit-filled preaching — the Holy Spirit bearing witness — is, at one and the same time, the exalted Lord Jesus giving repentance and forgiveness of sins (5:31-32). Just as the OT presents the Spirit of God as the way in which God is immanent, so in Acts the Spirit's presence becomes a way of speaking of Jesus' immanence.[31] More than just representing Jesus, the Holy Spirit mediates, indeed, extends the personal presence of the exalted Lord as he "continues to do and teach" (Acts 1:1) on mission in the world.

Jesus, the Reigning Lord

A second theme, Jesus the reigning Lord (termed in context, "Son of Man standing at God's right hand"), reveals that the Holy Spirit also bears witness from "earth to heaven" — granting a Spirit-filled vision of Jesus and the Father in glory (7:55-56). At the climax of Stephen's speech, he, full of the Holy Spirit and "gazing into heaven, saw the glory of God and Jesus, standing at the right hand of God." Though this may be a momentary prophetic vision, it does come to one who through all his life has so yielded to the Holy Spirit that he can now be described not simply as being "filled with the Spirit" but as "full of the Spirit" (cf. 6:5, 8, 15). As here, Luke consistently uses "gazing" (ἀτενίζω) for viewing a supernatural sight (1:10; 3:4, 12; 6:15). As Stephen describes the scene, he says he sees "the Son of Man *standing* at the right hand of God" (7:56). Commentators have often sought the significance of that posture in this description of the Son of Man ("standing" vs. "sitting"; cf. Ps 110:1).[32] It probably has to do with position, however. Stephen is emphatically confessing Jesus' transcendent place in heaven, and by that his deity.[33] The crowd's reaction points in this

---

31. H. D. Buckwalter, "The Divine Saviour," in *Witness to the Gospel*, ed. Marshall and Peterson, 116.

32. See Barrett (*Acts*, 1:384-85) for a comprehensive list of options.

33. E. Richard, *Acts 6:1–8:4: The Author's Method of Composition* (SBLDS 41; Missoula, Mont.: Scholars Press, 1978), 295.

direction. They shout in order to drown out what they see as blasphemy. They cover their ears with their hands so as to prevent such words from entering their ears (so the rabbinic practice, *b. Ketub.* 5a).

The significance of this vision for the identity of Jesus is not lost on Stephen. By witnessing to him as "Son of Man standing at the right hand of God," Stephen declares to be true what, according to Luke, Jesus said at the Sanhedrin trial (Luke 22:69/Ps 110:1; Dan 7:13): "From now on the Son of Man will be seated at the right hand of the power of God." The universal, heavenly reign of that heavenly being from Daniel 7, "one like the Son of Man," and the literal, messianic understanding of Ps 110:1 (cf. Acts 2:34b-35) so worked in Stephen's thinking that his subsequent words show the fullness of his confession of Jesus' divine nature. For he addresses Jesus both in a prayer of "spirit committal" at death and with a request that he grant forgiveness to others (Acts 7:59-60).

Some commentators say it is a mistake to lay too much stress on the christological significance of the vision, since in it Stephen only confirms what he has already said in his sermon.[34] This is not entirely accurate. In his sermon we have learned two seemingly unrelated facts: God does not dwell in temples made with hands (7:48) and Jesus was the Righteous One, the Messiah (7:52). Now we learn that he is not dead, but standing as the Son of Man in God's very presence at his right hand in heaven.

Not to think about the christological implications of the vision is to disregard what, for Luke, is a key piece of evidence concerning Jesus in his postascension ministry. Luke does tell us of other visions and appearances from heaven, but they are reported either in the third person or by the recipient after the fact (e.g., 9:3-4, 17; 10:11; 22:6-7, 14; 26:13-16). But only this vision involves a witness to others of what is seen in heaven itself, during the very experience of the vision. From the way Stephen relates to Jesus, it is indeed a "trinitarian vision."[35] What pneumatology contributes to Christology with this theme is to take us a step beyond the Spirit-filled witness of Acts 2. God grants one on earth, full of the Spirit, to see Jesus standing at God's right hand in heaven and to bear witness of it to others during the very experience of the sight. In this way a clearer view of who Jesus is — that divine Son of Man — and where he is — standing in transcendent authority — is gained.

---

34. Barrett, *Acts*, 1:383.

35. H. C. Kee, *To Every Nation under Heaven: The Acts of the Apostles* (New Testament in Context; Harrisburg, Pa.: Trinity Press International, 1997), 103.

Jesus, the Deployer in Mission

Another activity of Jesus during his postascension ministry from heaven is to commission and deploy his witnesses in missionary activity. The most extensively treated example in Acts, of course, is Paul. In the multiple accounts of his conversion experience, we become increasingly aware that on the Damascus road Jesus not only converted Paul but commissioned him to missionary service (9:15-16; 22:14-15; 26:16-18; cf. a subsequent commissioning in the temple, 22:21). Even though Luke does not directly report Jesus' commissioning of Paul on the Damascus road until the third account of his conversion, we should not conclude it is unimportant to him. Quite the contrary. Luke is using the rhetorical device of "functional redundancy," by which he reserves the clearest statement of this important theme until the last account.[36] Note also Paul's description of his life's work to the Ephesian elders: "to complete . . . the ministry I have received from the Lord Jesus, to bear witness to the gospel of the grace of God" (20:24).

It is curious, then, that at the deployment of Paul and Barnabas we meet a command from the Spirit, "Set apart to *me* Barnabas and Saul unto the work to which I have called them" (13:2; cf. 13:4). The use of the perfect tense (προσκέκλημαι, "I have called"), referring as it does to a completed act in past time with continuing results, probably points to, in Paul's case, Jesus' commissioning of him on the Damascus road. From the standpoint of Acts 13:1-3, it was a completed act with continuing results in terms of continuing validity. If both Acts 13 and Acts 9, 22, and 26 point to the same event, the questions arise: How are the calling of Jesus and of the Holy Spirit related? What implications do these accounts have for our understanding of the Godhead? The answer to the first question is that Luke provides no answer. Though we might try to harmonize the two accounts by saying that, in Acts 13:2, the Holy Spirit is serving as a mouthpiece for God or Jesus,[37] Luke does not indicate such a relationship in the immediate context. He simply lets the two assertions stand side by side in his work, though separated by chapters. Jesus calls Paul; the Holy Spirit has called Paul. Some commentators say that such evidence leads to interesting trinitarian speculation that was neither in Luke's mind nor in that of the first-century church.[38] Though we

36. See Witherup, "Functional Redundancy," 68-70, 83-85.
37. Dunn, *Acts*, 173.
38. Barrett, *Acts*, 1:604; Dunn, *Acts*, 173.

may agree that Luke betrays no conscious trinitarian expression, we should not overlook the fact that he has presented evidence for the unity of the members of the Trinity in the Godhead by simply attributing the same actions to more than one member. From such evidence develops naturally, even necessarily, the trinitarian understanding of Christian monotheism. This, then, becomes the contribution of pneumatology to Christology in the area of commissioning and deploying on mission.

Another potential piece of evidence in this same area with similar christological significance is Acts 8:39-40. "The Spirit of the Lord snatched away Philip . . . now he was found at Azotus."[39] If κυρίου ("of the Lord") refers to Jesus,[40] then in one phrase we have Jesus' active engagement by his Spirit in deploying his witnesses in mission, even miraculously. Some say the text does not require that Philip's removal be a supersonic ride of miraculous velocity.[41] Yet the fact that all of a sudden the eunuch does not see Philip anymore, though the evangelist had arrived on foot, and the fact that the verb ἁρπάζω is used (cf. 2 Cor 12:2; 1 Thess 4:17; cf. also 1 Kgs 18:12; 2 Kgs 2:16; Ezek 3:14; 8:3) indicate that we are dealing with a miraculous translation.

Jesus, the Guide in Mission

A final theme of Jesus' postascension ministry is guidance in mission. When Paul and his missionary band tried to enter Bithynia at the beginning of their second missionary journey, "The Spirit of Jesus would not allow them" (Acts 16:7).[42] Barrett sees only literary significance in the turn of

39. Since it makes explicit the reception of the Spirit at the eunuch's baptism and regularizes the inclusio — Philip is guided at the beginning and the end by an angel of the Lord (8:26) — and since it is less attested than the shorter reading, the predominantly Western longer reading (A^c 36^a 94 103 307 322 323 385 467 1739 1765 2298 it^p vg^mss syr^h with* arm Ephraem Jerome Augustine [D is defective here], πνεῦμα ἅγιον ἐπέπεσεν ἐπὶ τὸν εὐνοῦχον, ἄγγελος δέ, "the Holy Spirit fell on the eunuch, and an angel of the Lord caught up Philip") is probably secondary and not original (Metzger, Textual Commentary, 316).

40. S. J. Kistemaker, Exposition of the Acts of the Apostles (New Testament Commentary; Grand Rapids: Baker, 1990), 321.

41. J. Stott, The Message of Acts: The Spirit, the Church, and the World (repr. Downers Grove, Ill.: InterVarsity Press, 1990), 162.

42. According to Metzger (Textual Commentary, 390-91), the expression τὸ πνεῦμα Ἰησοῦ is so unusual (found only here in the NT) that the textual tradition contains a number of substitutes for or omissions of Ἰησοῦ.

phrase.[43] It is introduced for the sake of variety, given the similar statement in v. 6 (κωλυθέντες ὑπὸ τοῦ ἁγίου πνεύματος, "hindered by the Holy Spirit"). Yet when understood within the context of the contribution of pneumatology to Christology in Acts, especially as it concerns Jesus' postascension ministry from heaven, this verse creates an important stage in the thematic development of the ascended Lord Jesus on mission.

As I have noted, in the early chapters of Acts (1–7), the focus was on the ascended Lord's provision of salvation blessings from heaven through Spirit-empowered witness (Acts 2:33-36; 5:31-32). Such an emphasis is present even in the very last evangelistic speech of Paul (cf. 26:23). In Acts 8–14 we encountered the ascended Jesus' ministry as active engagement in mission through calling/commissioning his witnesses. Here his involvement is more direct, since Jesus and the Spirit act in parallel — Jesus calls and the Spirit calls (Acts 9, 22, 26, and Acts 13). Now as we head into the last half of Acts and study the contribution of pneumatology to Christology in the theme of Jesus' guidance of his mission, the activity of the Spirit and Jesus become one. For it is "the Spirit of Jesus" who does not allow the band to enter Bithynia (16:7). As was true with the deployment by the Spirit at the beginning of the first missionary journey (13:2, 4), we are not told what means the Spirit used to communicate this prohibition. In the former case, that the guidance comes during corporate worship, particularly to leaders labeled "prophets and teachers" (13:1), leads many to conclude that the Spirit spoke to these leaders through some of their own number.[44] At 16:7 there are no such clues. The psychologizing of David French, who says this is a periphrasis for Paul's trepidation and discretion as he sought to avoid further official trouble from Rome by not using the major public roads in Asia, is supported neither by Luke's presentation nor by our knowledge of the Roman road system in that part of Asia Minor.[45] Though some suggest that the Spirit possibly spoke through prophets,[46] and others say it was

---

43. Barrett, *Acts,* 2:770.

44. Polhill, *Acts,* 290.

45. D. French, "Acts and the Roman Roads of Asia Minor," in *The Book of Acts in Its Graeco-Roman Setting* (ed. D. W. J. Gill and C. Gempf; Book of Acts in Its First Century Setting 2; Grand Rapids: Eerdmans, 1994), 57; R. Jewett, "Mapping the Route of Paul's Second Missionary Journey from Dorylaeum to Troas," *TynBul* 48 (1997): 1-22.

46. G. Stählin, "Τὸ πνεῦμα 'Ιησοῦ (Apostelgeschichte 16:7)," in *Christ and Spirit in the New Testament: Studies in Honour of C. F. D. Moule* (ed. B. Lindars and S. S. Smalley; Cambridge: Cambridge Univ. Press, 1973), 250.

neither prophet nor vision but inner conviction (at least on Paul's part), it is best to recognize that Luke simply does not tell us.[47] What he does tell us is that the Spirit of the one who gave the great commission (1:8) and called Paul to participate in that mission (9:6, 15) now provides guidance, in terms of location, for prosecuting that mission.

The dynamic interplay of the Holy Spirit and Jesus in guiding his witnesses in mission is brought out more fully at the conclusion of Paul's third missionary journey (Acts 19:21; 20:22-24; 21:4, 11-14; 23:11). The phrases ἔθετο . . . ἐν τῷ πνεύματι ("purposed in the s/Spirit" — 19:21) and δεδεμένος . . . τῷ πνεύματι ("bound in the s/Spirit" — 20:22) are ambiguous. Do they refer to Paul's inner self or to God the Holy Spirit? Barrett appeals to lexical matters: τίθημι will only mean "purpose" when taken with πνεῦμα meaning "human spirit" (cf. Homer, *Od.* 4.729).[48] Most commentators, however, follow indicators from the immediate and larger context, which they conclude point to a reference to the Holy Spirit in both Acts 19:21 and 20:22.[49] In expressing what he has "purposed in the Spirit," Luke uses his favorite term for divine necessity (δεῖ, 19:21; cf. 1:21-22; 3:21; 5:29; 9:16; 23:11; 27:24). In further expounding the direction he is receiving (20:22-23), Paul speaks of the Holy Spirit's warnings.

Again, we are not told how Paul received the Spirit's communication. As the ambiguity of expression indicates (it is stated in such personal terms: "Paul purposed in the Spirit"; "I go bound in the Spirit"), it seems to be less an experience that would involve a third party and more the Spirit's direct dealing with Paul.

There is, however, a more objective, complementary work of the Spirit guiding these series of events (20:23; 21:4, 11-14). Paul speaks of the Spirit "warning him in every city" of the suffering that awaits him in Jerusalem (20:23). Again, Luke does not tell us the means of these warnings, and commentators continue to be cautious. I. Howard Marshall says it might be by means of prophets or a personal revelation.[50] Acts 21:4 has the very compressed expression "they were saying through the Spirit" (ἔλεγον διὰ τοῦ πνεύματος), which introduces not just a warning but a prohibition. The range of meaning for διά + the genitive, which extends from efficient

---

47. Barrett, *Acts,* 2:769; Dunn, *Acts,* 217.

48. Barrett, *Acts,* 2:919.

49. For example, Kee, *To Every Nation,* 233; Witherington, *Acts,* 588; Dunn, *Acts,* 262, 272; J. A. Fitzmyer, *The Acts of the Apostles* (AB 31; New York: Doubleday, 1998), 677.

50. Marshall, *Acts,* 331.

cause through modal, accompanying circumstance, and occasion, to ultimate cause, permits us to see Luke's description, not (at worst) as contradictory to 20:23 and 21:11, or (at best) as an inadequate expression of the process.[51] Rather, this phrase combines the church's conclusion — an urging not to go up to Jerusalem — with its prophetic occasion or basis — the Spirit's warning (cf. 20:22-23). If we take the Agabus incident — the final and most extensive account of the Spirit speaking a warning in the assembly (21:11-14) — as an indicator, then the means in each instance could well have been through a prophet. The function of this complementary guidance seems to have been "exhortation," in the sense of testing Paul's resolve to follow through on his commitment both to his lifelong mission and to the immediate, Spirit-impressed direction of it to bear witness in Jerusalem and Rome. There was also a comforting aspect to the warning, for it let Paul know that the negative circumstances — suffering and imprisonment — were not outside God's will.

In this series of events, Paul and Luke see the ascended and reigning Lord Jesus' role in guidance as threefold. First, he has given Paul his lifelong mission: "the service which I have received from the Lord Jesus, to bear witness to the gospel of the grace of God" (20:24). To this Paul must remain true, even if it means denying a desire for self-preservation and embracing martyrdom for the sake of the name of the Lord Jesus (20:24; 21:13). Second, Jesus has a will, "the will of the Lord" (21:14), by which he is prosecuting his mission in and through Paul. The church recognizes it, indeed embraces it, as that which should happen: "Let the will of the Lord be done!" (cf. Luke 22:42). Though some would see this as a submission to the will of God the Father,[52] the consistent reference to Jesus as "the Lord Jesus" and "the Lord" in the immediate and larger context (Acts 20:19, 21, 24, 35; 21:13) leads to the conclusion that the reference here is to Jesus' will.[53] Paul participates in "the will of the Lord" as he, with resolve, although amid warnings about impending suffering, follows his "Spirit-impressed" purpose, which will allow him to fulfill his service for Christ. Third, Jesus, through a night appearance, further guides and directs Paul (23:11): "Be encouraged! For as you were bearing witness to the things concerning me at Jerusalem, so you must (δεῖ) also witness at Rome." Here Jesus not only

---

51. Contra Barrett, *Acts*, 2:990; see A. J. Hess, "διά," *EDNT* 1:296-97.
52. Fitzmyer, *Acts*, 690.
53. Dunn, *Acts*, 283.

shows his approval of Paul's witness at Jerusalem, he also confirms to Paul that purpose conceived "in the Spirit" to bear witness at Rome. By telling Paul that this is, indeed, a divine necessity (δεῖ), Jesus directs him toward a divinely ordained and certain end goal. This direction and assurance will guide Paul's responses to circumstances, often life-threatening, which would keep him from that goal (cf. 23:17-22; 25:10-11; 27:31-35).

The contribution of pneumatology to Christology in this final thematic area is to reveal again the unity of action among members of the Trinity in prosecuting the church's mission. The "Spirit of Jesus" guides the witnesses' steps (16:7). What we learn, too, is that Jesus not only gives the great commission, dispenses salvation blessings, and calls his witnesses to embark on mission, but he also actively engages in directing the mission and determining the timing and the location of mission. The Spirit is the agent for such direction and works personally. But the Spirit also promotes growth in character, mercifully informing the witnesses in advance of the suffering that lies ahead and giving them opportunity to display their resolve. The Spirit, as the way the ascended and exalted Lord expresses his immanence, works so personally and powerfully that Jesus' transcendent, universal sovereignty over the course of history is immediately recognized. Recognizing that a given course of events is a "Spirit-impressed" path, the church can exclaim, "Let the will of the Lord [i.e., Jesus] be done!" (21:14).

Conclusion

In sum, the contribution of the pneumatology of Acts to its Christology is to glorify Jesus in a number of different ways. During his postresurrection ministry, the Spirit so empowers Jesus that, in his resurrected but preascension state, he becomes an authoritative prophetic revealer of subsequent events in salvation history — particularly the Spirit-graced interim period before the end and its Spirit-empowered christocentric kerygmatic mission (Acts 1:1-11). In its description of both the promise and the fulfillment of the Spirit's coming, Acts' pneumatology plants the seeds for understanding Jesus as the exalted, divine Second Person of the Trinity (Luke 24:46-49; Acts 1:4-5, 8; 2:33-36). At the same time, it shows how that deity is immanent, pouring out salvation blessings to all who call on the name of the Lord in response to Spirit-empowered witness (2:33-38; 5:31-32). Not only does the Spirit enable us to understand the "heaven to earth" transaction, which is Jesus "continuing to do and teach" (1:1) on mission to the ends of the earth, but through the eyewitness testimony of one full of the Spirit; but we are also able to glimpse "earth to heaven" and see Jesus for who he is, reigning Son of Man, coequal with the Father (7:55-60). Finally, in terms of both commission and guiding on mission, the Spirit in its parallel or unified action with Jesus creates a further basis for a trinitarian understanding of Christology (9:15; 13:2; 16:7). Again, Acts' pneumatology helps us see the ascended Lord's immanence as he, by the Spirit, is indeed active in prosecuting his mission in a character-forming and unstoppable way, particularly in the midst of suffering, to the ends of the earth (13:4; 19:21; 20:22-23; 21:4, 11-14; 23:11).

Moral Character and Divine Generosity: Acts 13:13-52 and the Narrative Dynamics of Luke-Acts

Bruce W. Longenecker

Since the work of H. J. Cadbury in the 1920s, it has become standard within scholarly circles to view the Gospel of Luke and the Acts of the Apostles as two volumes of a single work.[1] Nonetheless, the relationship between the two texts continues to require definition. The requirement is all the more pressing in light of the content of the two texts. The Gospel of Luke focuses on the figure of Jesus, whose public profile includes that of a Jewish peasant teacher, and whose message as one anointed "to preach good news to the poor" (4:18) incorporates a significant emphasis on the "material" implica-

---

1. H. J. Cadbury, *The Making of Luke-Acts* (New York: Macmillan, 1927). The 47th Colloquium Biblicum Lovaniense (1998) considered the topic "The Unity of Luke-Acts." For a summary of the colloquium's offerings, see J. Verheyden, "The Unity of Luke-Acts," *HvTSt* 55 (1999): 964-79. He summarizes the colloquium's findings in this way: "these two impressive documents . . . should be read and studied as the one great work by the same great author and theologian they were meant to be" (979).

This article is offered with great respect to the honoree of this volume, Jerry Hawthorne. As an undergraduate student in the early 1980s, I was unaware of the extent to which Jerry's scholarship was respected. What impressed me most in those days was his own character — not least his personable disposition, his educational prowess, and his embodied devotion to God. Twenty years later I am in a better position to recognize that Jerry's scholarly and personal profiles have fed each other, for the benefit of many, of which I am one.

tions of the Christian message (e.g., 1:52-53; 6:20-26; 10:25-37; 11:41; 12:13-21, 33-34; 14:16-24; 16:14-31; 18:22; 19:8). The Acts of the Apostles, on the other hand, focuses on the universal spread of the news that God has made this Jesus to be Lord and Christ of all (Acts 2:36); the financial and materialistic aspects of Jesus' message, so carefully articulated in the Gospel of Luke, fail to have the same prominent profile or to carry the same weight in Acts (e.g., 2:42-47; 4:32-37; 9:36-38; 11:29-30). Perhaps, then, this relative neglect of material concerns in Acts might be additional fodder for those who demure from the Cadbury consensus and find the two Lukan texts not to be two tightly woven volumes of the same work but simply two distinct texts from the same author, whose concerns are somewhat different.[2]

This essay seeks to address the issue of the relation of material and universal interests in Luke and Acts, if only by means of a circuitous route. I intend to demonstrate that a common theological interest underlies both the material interests of Luke's Gospel and the universal interests of the Acts of the Apostles. This will be done by (1) noting significant exegetical features of Acts, particularly in 13:13-52, and (2) placing them within the larger flow of Luke's narrative. While it will not be possible to demonstrate that the Gospel of Luke and the Acts of the Apostles are, in fact, two volumes of one larger narrative, the findings of this essay demonstrate that such a scenario is not problematic with regard to the relatively distinct interests of the two Lukan texts.

Acts 13:13-52: Paul's Maiden Speech

In Acts 13:13-52 Luke recounts Paul's sermon before the Jews and God-fearers of the synagogue in Pisidian Antioch and records the intriguing re-action of the Antiochene Jews to his message. The first thing to note about this passage is its paradigmatic character. This is the first time that the reader hears Paul speak in extended fashion in a context of Christian public proclamation.[3] The preceding passage (13:9-12) raises the readers' inter-

2. See esp. M. C. Parsons and R. I. Pervo, *Rethinking the Unity of Luke and Acts* (Minneapolis: Fortress, 1993); G. Bouwman, *Das dritte Evangelium: Einübung in die formgeschichtliche Methode* (Düsseldorf: Patmos, 1968), 62-67; G. Schneider, *Die Apostelgeschichte* (2 vols.; HTKNT; Freiburg: Herder, 1980-82), 1:76-82.

3. Prior to this, the reader has only heard Paul confess that Jesus "is the Son of God" (9:20) and denounce the Jewish magician and false prophet Bar-Jesus (13:9-12).

est in Paul, since it is there that Paul rather than Barnabas takes the lead, and henceforth becomes the principal character in the narrative of Acts.

Here, then, is the maiden speech of an emerging Christian leader. As such, it largely defines Paul's identity as a public ambassador for Christ, just as the maiden sermon of Jesus in Luke 4 serves as a defining moment that is unpacked throughout the rest of his ministry.[4] The significance of this event is evident also in that it is the only time that Luke records an extended sermon by Paul in a synagogue context. Moreover, the episode establishes Paul's normal pattern of ministry that is practiced throughout most of the Acts narrative: he first preaches in the synagogue and then preaches to Gentiles beyond its scope.

In various ways, then, this episode in Acts 13 stands as the Lukan template of Paul's normal pattern of ministry.[5] Moreover, the Antiochene episode also serves a paradigmatic role in displaying important facets of Luke's view on the origins and nature of Jewish opposition to Paul's Gentile mission. To demonstrate this, we need to take careful note of the two dissimilar responses of the Antiochene Jews to Paul's message in two different situations, an issue to which we now turn.

Paul's Encounters with the Jews of Pisidian Antioch

The Antiochene episode of Acts 13 comprises two encounters between Paul and those in the synagogue. In the first encounter Paul and Barnabas are asked to address the synagogue congregation, which receives them positively (13:13-43). The second encounter is vastly different, resulting in Jewish animosity against Paul and Barnabas (13:44-51).

The difference in these two synagogue receptions is crucial to discerning Luke's theological and narrative program and requires explanation. In the first encounter, Paul's sermon contains a plethora of claims that were standard in early Christian preaching: the messianic identity of Jesus, his salvific death and resurrection, the fulfillment of Scripture, the forgiveness of sins, the insufficiency of the law, the benefits for Israel of

---

4. For parallels between Paul and Jesus on this score, see L. T. Johnson, *The Acts of the Apostles*, 7th ed. (Collegeville, Minn.: Liturgical Press, 1992), 237.

5. So E. Haenchen, *Die Apostelgeschichte* (KEK; Göttingen: Vandenhoeck & Ruprecht, 1977), 402; W. H. Shepherd Jr., *The Narrative Function of the Holy Spirit as a Character in Luke-Acts* (SBLDS 147; Atlanta: Scholars Press, 1994), 213.

what God has done, and a warning about not believing the Christian message. Judging from the immediate reaction of those whom Paul was addressing, however, none of these tenets was thought to be necessarily incompatible with, or offensive to, synagogal Judaism. Luke gives no hint that these particulars have transgressed the boundaries of acceptability within synagogal Judaism. Indeed, Luke records that, after Paul's speech, many Jews and converts to Judaism followed him and Barnabas, asking to hear more on the next Sabbath (13:42-43).[6] The reader should not be surprised by this. Earlier, in 13:5, Luke speaks of Paul preaching "the word of God in the synagogues of the Jews" and makes no mention of Jewish offense or persecution. As Luke shifts his overarching focus from Peter and Palestinian Christianity (Acts 1–12) to Paul and the spread of Christianity worldwide (Acts 13–28), he demonstrates from the start that the message of Paul and Barnabas was not in essence antagonistic to synagogal Judaism in the Diaspora.[7]

If, then, the synagogal opposition does not originate in these tenets of the early Christian movement, where does it lie? The answer to this cannot be found in the first Antiochene encounter, but emerges from the second, where it becomes obvious that the controversy has to do with the attraction of Christianity for Gentiles (and vice versa). The same Jews who one week earlier had approved of Paul and Barnabas are now shown to be antagonistic toward them, maligning Paul and (thereby) blaspheming (βλασφημεῖν in its agonistic and theological semantic fields).[8] Whereas one week earlier the synagogal Jews were enamored with what Paul had spoken, the next week these same Jews contradict his speech (cf. λαλεῖν in both 13:43 and 13:45). In 13:44-45 Luke makes clear why their attitude has

6. In the phrase οἱ σεβόμενοι προσήλυτοι (13:43), the noun should carry the greater weight. Luke does not have God-fearing Gentiles in mind here (cf. 13:50; 16:14; 17:4, 17; 18:7) but former Gentiles who have converted to Judaism. On this matter, see the discussions by M. Wilcox, "The 'God-fearers' in Acts — A Reconsideration," *JSNT* 13 (1981): 102-22, esp. 108-9; and I. A. Levinskaya, *The Book of Acts in Its Diaspora Setting* (Book of Acts in Its First Century Setting 5; Grand Rapids: Eerdmans, 1996), 35-49.

7. Cf. J. Jervell, *The Theology of the Acts of the Apostles* (Cambridge: Cambridge Univ. Press, 1996), 89.

8. M. L. Soards (*The Speeches in Acts: Their Content, Context, and Concerns* [Louisville: Westminster/John Knox, 1994], 79-88) overemphasizes the negative tone of Paul's speech in 13:16-43. He unhelpfully allows the dynamics of the second encounter of 13:44-51 to spill over into the first (so 84-85) and imagines that Paul's criticism of Jewish leaders in Jerusalem takes on life of its own in the intervening week (87).

changed so drastically: "the whole city" (πᾶσα ἡ πόλις), a veritable "multitude" of Gentiles (τοὺς ὄχλους), had gathered to hear Paul.

Gentiles had already frequented this Antiochene synagogue, of course, as Paul's initial speech itself makes clear, being addressed not only to "Israelites" (ἄνδρες Ἰσραηλῖται, 13:16) but also "those who fear God" (οἱ φοβούμενοι τὸν θεόν, 13:16; cf. 13:26). Gentile attendance at Jewish synagogues was nothing exceptional. On this occasion, however, the Jewish constituency reacted with hostility to what was transpiring in the synagogue. The reason for this reaction seems to be that the implications of Paul's message became clear: the scope of God's salvation was now being extended to universal proportions in ways that eclipse the institutions and practices of synagogal Judaism. Although the Gentiles are said to have been gladdened by this message (13:48), these particular Pisidian Jews were having none of it and resorted to assembling a posse of those whom they could influence to persecute Paul and Barnabas and eventually drive them out of the region (13:50).[9]

We might think that the Pisidian Jews should have been alert to the universalistic implications of Paul's earlier sermon, but this is not necessarily the case. There is little in that sermon (13:16-41) that requires a universalistic interpretation of Paul's message. The statement most in accord with the universalistic gospel that Paul expresses elsewhere is the assurance that "everyone who believes is freed from everything from which you could not be freed by the law of Moses" (ἀπὸ πάντων ὧν οὐκ ἠδυνήθητε ἐν νόμῳ Μωϋσέως δικαιωθῆναι, ἐν τούτῳ πᾶς ὁ πιστεύων δικαιοῦται, 13:38-39 in Greek, 13:39 in most translations). Granted, the law of Moses is shown here not to have a fully salvific function. Nonetheless, especially in view of the Israel-centeredness of Paul's speech in general, this saying alone does

---

9. Doing justice to the full dynamics of the situation would involve a fuller depiction of synagogal universalism than can be afforded here. The reader is observing the clash of two forms of universalism, a typical synagogal form (which Luke leaves undefined) and a distinctively Christian form (as defined by Luke in the narrative he constructs). Luke, of course, is partial to the latter. The advocates of each would have viewed themselves as heirs of Israel's heritage. Moreover, Luke seems to envisage Gentile converts to Christianity as sojourners in the midst of Israel (see esp. R. Bauckham, "James and the Gentiles (Acts 15.13-21)," in *History, Literature, and Society in the Book of Acts* [ed. B. Witherington III; Cambridge: Cambridge Univ. Press, 1996], 154-84), similar perhaps to the way synagogal Jews viewed God-fearing Gentiles. Where the two forms of universalism and inclusivism primarily part company is not so much in theological conviction but in the way convictions are given concrete expression in terms of practice and socialization.

not necessitate a full-blown Christian universalism without regard for ethnicity.[10] It could be taken simply as implying that traditional forms of Jewish piety and practice are to be intertwined with faith in the Jewish messiah if they are to have their full effect.[11]

Nine points help to demonstrate that Paul's speech is styled in a manner that leaves any implications of Christian universalism indeterminate at best:

1. It is given in the synagogue, after an invitation to speak offered by the officials, who asked for a "word of exhortation for the people" (λόγος παρακλήσεως πρὸς τὸν λαόν, 13:15).
2. It is directed to the "Israelites" (ἄνδρες Ἰσραηλῖται, 13:16)[12] and descendants of Abraham's family (13:26), along with those God-fearers who attached themselves to the Jewish synagogue (οἱ φοβούμενοι τὸν θεόν, 13:16, 26).
3. It concerns "the God of this people Israel" (ὁ θεὸς τοῦ λαοῦ τούτου Ἰσραήλ, 13:17).
4. It incorporates the phrase "our ancestors" on two occasions (τοὺς πατέρας [ἡμῶν], 13:17, 32; cf. 13:26).
5. It affirms that the promised savior has been brought to Israel (13:23).
6. It depicts John as a prophet who sought the repentance of the people of Israel and pointed to Israel's Messiah (13:24-25).
7. It claims that recent events have involved the fulfillment of Israel's Scriptures (13:27-37).

10. Criticism of the law is not without precedent in non-Christian forms of Judaism; cf., e.g., 1 Enoch 42.

11. P. Vielhauer ("On the 'Paulinism' of Acts," in Studies in Luke-Acts: Essays Presented in Honor of Paul Schubert [ed. L. E. Keck and J. L. Martyn; Nashville: Abingdon, 1966], 33-50, here 41) argues that the Paul of Acts 13 simply preaches that faith is to accompany observance of the law. It is closer to the truth, however, to see this as one case in which the reader is in a privileged position, knowing more than the narrative figures. The reader knows that the Paul of Acts 13 thinks of salvation as being through faith alone, although the narrative characters of the Antiochene synagogue might be forgiven for concluding along Vielhauer's lines.

The same situation of irony operates with regard to the phrase "the grace of God" in 13:43. There is no reason why synagogal Jews should have understood this phrase to make traditionally essential practices nonessential. The reader, however, is privileged to know from 11:20-26 (esp. 11:23) that this phrase is to have precisely that implication.

12. Notice, moreover, that this same form of address can be uttered by nationalistic Jews from Asia in 21:28. Paul's terminology and theirs overlap.

8. It suggests that all this has been for the benefit of those descended from Israel (13:33; cf. 13:38).[13]

9. It highlights that the Christian message is being proclaimed to the people of Israel (πρὸς τὸν λαόν, 13:31).

Points eight and nine are especially significant. No doubt the first seven points could easily have been incorporated into a speech that explicitly articulated a Christian universalism. Even the eighth and ninth points could be incorporated within a message that broadened out to include Gentiles within its scope. But there is nothing in Paul's sermon that harnesses such features in the service of Christian universalism. Indeed, the beneficiaries of recent salvific events are simply said to be the people of Israel.

Accordingly, it is possible to suggest that, if the synagogue audience is unaware of the universalistic implications of Paul's speech, that is precisely because Paul has not articulated anything along those lines on this occasion. Universalistic implications become clear to the synagogue participants only in the events of the following Sabbath (13:44). Paul left the way open for a distinctively Christian universalistic application of his message, but a lucid articulation of the matter fails to appear in this first Antiochene episode. Paul's maiden speech in the narrative of Acts is Christian throughout, but it does not showcase the full Christian portfolio.[14]

The point, then, is clear. Only when the synagogal Jews of Pisidian Antioch realize the universalistic implications of Paul's message does their opposition to Paul arise. Prior to that realization, points of theological import were not in and of themselves problematic.

The same is evident in Acts 22. Paul, allowed to speak to the people and addressing them in Hebrew as "brothers and fathers" (ἀδελφοὶ καὶ πατέρες, 22:1), recounts his personal history, including his days as a persecutor of the church, his conversion experience, his time in Damascus, his vision of the exalted Jesus, and his commission to witness to the Gentiles. At the mention of "Gentiles," Luke writes: "Up to this point they listened

---

13. I take αὐτῶν to be the original possessive pronoun modifying τοῖς τέκνοις in 13:33; the alternative reading (τοῖς τέκνοις ἡμῶν) "gives a most improbable sense" (B. M. Metzger, *A Textual Commentary on the Greek New Testament* [2d ed.; Stuttgart: Deutsche Bibelgesellschaft, 1994], 362).

14. See the discussion in B. Witherington III, *The Acts of the Apostles: A Socio-Rhetorical Commentary* (Grand Rapids: Eerdmans, 1998), 413-14.

to him, but then they shouted, 'Away with such a fellow from the earth! For he should not be allowed to live,'" after which they cried out, threw off their cloaks, and tossed dust into the air (22:22-23).

Here, then, is a second occasion in which Luke clearly highlights the decisive factor in Jewish opposition to Christianity: the nonconformity to the Torah proffered by Paul's Gentile mission. Apart from that factor, syna-gogal Jews are shown to tolerate the christological and soteriological distinctives of Paul's speech. They may not have agreed with Paul's claims that one who was known to have been crucified is now known as the Righ-teous One and the Lord, that sins are forgiven as one calls on his name, and that the temple has been the locale for a vision of this exalted one. But lack of agreement was not the cause of their alarm about Paul's gospel; that re-action is explained solely by Paul's contention that he has been divinely commissioned to offer the message of salvation "to the Gentiles" without the requirements expected by the synagogue community.

These significant episodes should warn us against seeing the Jewish antagonism toward Paul in Acts as if it were simply the product of a theo-logical debate about Christology (e.g., 18:5-6) or the resurrection (e.g., 23:6; 24:21; 26:6-8).[15] Luke is concerned with pinpointing as the root cause of opposition a more fundamental phenomenon than theological niceties of this sort, focusing ultimately on the matter of moral character. The key word here appears in 13:45, where the synagogal Jews are depicted as being filled with "jealousy" (ζῆλος). This word, descriptive of an inner attitude, clearly falls within the arena of social character. What is less clear, however, is its precise meaning, since ζῆλος was used by ancient writers to denote various things depending on the particular situation in view. Accordingly, Luke's use of this moral term to describe the Jewish response to Christian universalism requires closer examination.

The Significations of Jealousy

In a nontechnical sense, ζῆλος carries simple meanings such as "eagerness," "intense interest," and "impassioned commitment." In the ancient world,

---

15. Paul's speech in Acts 26 is intriguing since it cites two reasons for Jewish opposi-tion to his message: resurrection (26:6-8) and universalism (26:20-23). Indeed, as is made clear in 26:20-23, the two are integrally related.

however, ζῆλος frequently carried a more technical meaning, having one of three primary significations.[16]

First, and perhaps most frequently, ζῆλος signifies "emulation," denoting the desire to match or replicate the stature, reputation, character, attributes, or fortunes evident in another person or group. When ζῆλος is used to describe a person in this situation, it refers to the desire to possess what another person owns and to acquire it not by depriving the other but by equaling the other in pertinent respects. The zealous one is spurred on toward personal betterment, in order thereby to obtain the desired object. The process involves acquisition by means of imitation.[17]

Second, the term occasionally overlaps with "envy" (φθόνος). In this case, the desire to possess something belonging to another (person or group) is accompanied by a covetous desire to deprive the other of that possession. Rather than being emulated, the possessor is attacked in any way possible, the jealous one seeking to acquire the desired object from its rightful owner without having to earn it through proper channels. The goal is acquisition by means of plunder.[18]

Third, instead of overlapping with "envy," the term can frequently denote the protective response of those who possess something that is in danger of being taken away by those who are envious. When one possesses what others are desirous of, one's zeal involves the defense of that possession in the face of antagonistic attempts to acquire it. Here denunciation of others is a strategy for retaining the honor or possession that others are seeking to confiscate from the rightful owner.[19]

---

16. Cf. A. C. Hagedorn and J. H. Neyrey, "'It Was Out of Envy that They Handed Jesus Over' (Mark 15.10): The Anatomy of Envy and the Gospel of Mark," *JSNT* 69 (1998): 15-56, esp. 18-19.

17. A small sampling would include Aristotle, *Rhetorica* 2.11.1-7; Isocrates, *Ad Demonicum* 36; and (with παραζηλοῦν) Rom 10:19; 11:11, 14.

18. Examples of this use in ancient literature are far less frequent than other uses, since "envy" (φθόνος) is the term regularly used to denote this attribute (cf., e.g., Aristotle, *Rhetorica* 1387b-1388a). But occasionally this overlap of meaning is evident (cf. Hesiod, *Opera et dies* 195). Interestingly, the best examples from the 1st century c.e. of this use of ζῆλος are found in the NT itself: Acts 5:17; 7:9; Rom 13:13; 2 Cor 12:20; Gal 5:20; Jas 3:14, 16; 4:2; cf. 1 Cor 3:3; 13:4.

19. Cf. Paul's use of ζῆλος in 1 Cor 10:22 and 2 Cor 11:2.

The Jealousy of "the Jews"

Having outlined three of the connotations of the word, we can now assess Luke's claim that the Jews were filled with ζῆλος. Of these three meanings, only the first ("emulation") is inappropriate to the Antiochene context of 13:45; either of the last two would fit the context.[20]

To a certain extent, however, the interpretation given to the term "the Jews" (οἱ 'Ιουδαῖοι) in 13:45 influences the way ζῆλος is understood in the same verse. For instance, some argue that the Jews envisaged here are solely the synagogue leaders, rather than the Jews in general.[21] In this interpretation ζῆλος connotes "envy." As Paul's honor increases, that of the synagogue officials decreases.[22] In an effort to undermine the one who had damaged their honor, these leaders speak out against Paul's reputation (the agonistic aspect of βλασφημεῖν) and contradict him with the hopes of discrediting his public speech. What had begun as an irenic relationship between synagogue leaders and invited guests the week before has become, for the Jewish leaders anyway, a public contest for honor. Their jealousy involves them in an envious attempt to regain the honor that they had previously enjoyed. Seeking to inflate their status and honor, the synagogue leaders denounce the Christian apostles in agonistic strains. The reader is witnessing a tension between those who had benefited from "ascribed

---

20. L&N (1:760, §88.162) find ζῆλος in Acts 13:45 to involve "a particularly strong feeling of resentment and jealousy against someone." This offers little assistance in determining the precise nuances of the term, since "resentment" could accompany either the desire to acquire or the desire to protect against the acquisitive advances of another.

21. Cf. H. C. Kee, *Good News to the Ends of the Earth: The Theology of Acts* (Philadelphia: Trinity Press International, 1990), 56; F. S. Spencer, *Acts* (Readings, a New Biblical Commentary; Sheffield: Sheffield Academic Press, 1997), 147. Some see the differentiation of the two groups already in 13:42-43. So F. F. Bruce (*The Book of the Acts* [NICNT; rev. ed. Grand Rapids: Eerdmans, 1988], 264) maintains that the synagogue authorities "had listened to the [Paul's] discourse [in 13:16-41] with misgivings" and prudently dismissed the congregation prematurely rather than letting Paul continue. This is unlikely. Those who gave the invitation to return are likely to be the same ones who gave the first invitation earlier in the day: the synagogue officials. Luke gives us no reason to think that it was the common people alone, and not the leadership, who wanted to hear more.

22. So B. Rapske speaks of "a diminution of power for the ruling élites in the Jewish community" ("Opposition to the Plan of God and Persecution," in *Witness to the Gospel: The Theology of Acts* [ed. I. H. Marshall and D. Peterson; Grand Rapids: Eerdmans, 1998], 235-56, here 247n.32).

honor" (i.e., the synagogue officials) and those "Johnny-come-latelies" who have manipulated a situation to gain "acquired honor" (i.e., Paul and Barnabas).

There is some merit in finding "the [jealous] Jews" in 13:45 to refer solely to the Jewish leadership. Luke has already used the word ζῆλος in connection with a contest between Christian apostles and Jewish leaders earlier in his narrative. In 5:17, for instance, "the high priest and all who were with him, that is, the party of the Sadducees," are said to have been "filled with jealousy" (ἐπλήσθησαν ζήλου, as in 13:45). In this they are responding to the fact that "many signs and wonders were done among the people through the apostles" so that "the people held them in high esteem" (5:12-13). These people are said to have been great in number, coming from the towns around Jerusalem (5:14, 16). This rechanneling of the people's esteem would have involved a reduction in esteem toward the Jerusalem leaders. Consequently, it is natural to expect "jealousy" on this occasion to indicate the envy of these leaders.

It is unlikely, however, that Luke intended his readers to interpret "the Jews" in 13:45 simply as Jewish synagogue leaders. He has used the word "Jews" just two verses earlier (13:43) to refer to the collective people rather than the leadership in particular, and he gives no indication that a different referent is envisaged here. Moreover, in the earlier Antiochene episode he identifies the leadership explicitly as "the leaders of the synagogue" (οἱ ἀρχισυνάγωγοι, 13:15), similar to the agonistic encounter between the apostles and the temple leadership in Acts 5:17. Presumably, then, Luke could have signaled the same here if he meant to specify the synagogue leaders in particular. Accordingly, "jealousy" in 13:45 is not to be interpreted in relation to a simple contest of honor between the Jewish leadership and the apostles. Those who demonstrated jealousy most likely included not simply the synagogue leaders but the synagogal Jews of Antioch collectively.

It is not difficult to envisage the matter that provoked their corporate jealousy. They were witnessing an increase of popular interest in the God of Israel without a corresponding regard for the ethnic dimension traditionally associated with worship of Israel's God. Seemingly, then, the Lukan narrative requires us to imagine that between the two gatherings of the Antiochene synagogue, the Christian message had circulated in one form or another within the city, meeting with popular interest. This interest was unfettered by a high regard for the synagogue, its traditions, and the people it prioritized.[23] Previously, Gentile God-fearers in Antioch had been welcome to involve themselves in synagogal piety and enrich their spirituality and way of life. But the parasitic presence of God-fearing Gentiles in the synagogue was not perceived as a threat to the identity of the ethnic group prioritized by that institution. Such was evidently not the case on this occasion, however, when throngs of Gentiles spilled out onto the streets outside the synagogue. At some point along the way, the universalistic penny had dropped, and the message of Paul and Barnabas was seen by the unbelieving synagogal Jews as endangering the salvific priority of the Jewish people.

Accordingly, "jealousy" in 13:45 is best interpreted as a defensiveness to guard one's possessions (i.e., divine favor on Israel). Granted, the Antiochene situation may well have involved the reduction of honor for the leaders of the synagogue, who had initially introduced Paul and Barnabas within the synagogue and then invited them back a second time. For these leaders, jealousy would have included the attempt to regain lost honor at Paul's expense. But this does not seem to be at the forefront of Luke's presentation. What he intends to depict by the word ζῆλος is the desire of synagogal Jews collectively to guard the privileges of their ethnic group over other ethnic groups. In essence, then, Luke unmasks the character induced by the Antiochene synagogue as a form of possessiveness.

Paul's encounters with the synagogue community in Pisidian Antioch, recounted in Acts 13, play a significant role in the development of the Lukan narrative. Those two encounters, separated in time by seven days, allow an important feature to come to light: the character of the synagogue community as protective of its perceived privileges. By extending the Antiochene narrative to cover an eight-day period, Luke is able to demonstrate that the critical issue at stake in the antagonism between Christianity and synagogal Judaism is the extension of salvation to Gentiles in a way that bypasses traditional forms of Judaism and that thereby decentralizes the ethnic group of the Jews. In the first Antiochene episode this feature is not explicit, and the response to Paul's sermon is the furthest thing from antagonism; only in the second Antiochene episode is this feature recognizable, and immediately the synagogal response

23. On the significance of the synagogue for preserving Jewish identity in the Diaspora, see J. M. G. Barclay, *Jews in the Mediterranean Diaspora: From Alexander to Trajan (323 BCE–117 CE)* (Edinburgh: T&T Clark, 1996), 26-27, 290, 416-17.

becomes marked out by a tendency to preserve jealously the salvific priority of the Jewish people.

There are places in the Lukan narrative, of course, where synagogal opposition arises against Paul without any direct mention of his controversial Gentile ministry. So in 18:5-17, as Paul preaches that Jesus is the Messiah, the Corinthian Jews have the same response as the Jews did in the second episode of the Pisidian Antioch narrative: they oppose (ἀντιτάσσειν) and malign (βλασφημεῖν) him (18:6). In this case one might think that Jewish opposition to Paul's message arises simply as a consequence of the identification of the Messiah as Jesus (cf. 9:22). But as in 13:23-39, that identification is not likely to be provocative enough to stir up Jewish public sentiment against Paul. What Luke has shown to be problematic among the synagogue communities is the offer of salvation to Gentiles in ways that bypass the expectations of mainstream forms of Judaism. Luke's readers are expected to recognize this feature in connection with synagogal opposition elsewhere, so that wherever the one is evident, so too the other is to be envisaged. Confirmation of this is found later in this same episode. Thus in 18:13 the accusation brought to Gallio against Paul by non-Christian Jewish opponents involves the charge that Paul is "persuading people to worship God contrary to the law," which must be a reference to Paul's nontraditional form of universalism.[24] Even here, then, synagogal opposition is shown to be motivated by a concern about ethnic privilege.

The same is likely to be the case in Acts 19. In 19:8 Luke states that Paul "spoke the truth boldly" (ἐπαρρησιάζετο) to those in the Ephesian synagogue for three months, "arguing persuasively" (διαλεγόμενος καὶ πείθων). Here the universalism of Christianity did not sever relations between Paul and the synagogue immediately. Nonetheless, even if the process in Acts 19 is not precisely the same as that evident in Acts 13, the end result is: "some were stubborn and refused to believe, speaking evil[25] of the Way before the [synagogue] assembly" (19:9). Luke has already made the root of this antagonism clear in repeated instances, and the reader is expected to attribute the same form of antagonism to the same character foible highlighted in Acts 13: "jealousy."

---

24. So also J. T. Sanders, *The Jews in Luke-Acts* (Philadelphia: Fortress, 1987), 275-76.

25. Κακολογοῦντες corresponds to βλασφημοῦντες in 13:45 (cf. 18:6), referring to the synagogal Jews.

Synagogal Jealousy in Lukan Perspective

In the ancient world this form of jealousy, wherein a person or group takes steps to protect what is perceived as rightfully belonging to them, would have been considered a natural component of the social codes of honor. But in the Lukan writings, this same form of jealousy is assessed differently. When translated into the economic terms that mark out much of Luke's Gospel, the concern to protect one's property, honor, or status is associated with a lack of generosity toward others. Luke's writings parade a generous God, with the Lukan Gospel establishing an "economic" corollary of this: a lifestyle of generosity for the benefit of others embodies and broadcasts the implementation of God's society. While Luke is not opposed to wealth per se, he is concerned that attitudes toward wealth be determined ultimately by an assiduous awareness of divine generosity.

This is clear, for instance, in Luke 19. When Zacchaeus the tax collector declares that he is giving half of his goods to the poor and repaying those he has defrauded four times the amount taken from them (19:8), Jesus pronounces that salvation has come to Zacchaeus's house (19:9) as part of Jesus' mission "to seek and save the lost" (ζητῆσαι καὶ σῶσαι τὸ ἀπολωλός, 19:10). So too the parable of the good Samaritan (Luke 10:29-37) commends one who used his resources to meet the immediate needs of another. This, we are told, is an example of one who shows mercy (ὁ ποιήσας τὸ ἔλεος, 10:37), and who therefore actively fulfills the command of 6:36: "Be merciful, even as your Father is merciful."

Such examples stand in stark contrast to that of the rich ruler, who imagined his riches as a means of benefiting himself (Luke 18:18-30). This devout and noble figure would have maintained patron-client relationships with an indefinite number of others lower on the socioeconomic ladder, providing them with tangible benefits. At the same time, however, the social conventions of patronage ensured that the patron would receive beneficial recompense in some form, perhaps only by means of his clients' public praise and adulation. The rich ruler's encounter with Jesus forces him to decide whether he is more concerned to win human or divine praise. He ultimately chooses to maintain an estimable reputation in the tangible society of his contemporaries rather than the somewhat elusive society of God. His riches may have served a beneficial function for others, but all the while they also served to enhance his own reputation; in the end he could not sever the connection between his generosity and the maintenance of his own stature.[26] In a sense the rich ruler hoards his social reputation, ensuring its promotion in the way that his resources were put to use. This kind of generosity stands in marked contrast to that of Zacchaeus or the good Samaritan, whose beneficence simply flowed from a character of generosity for the betterment of others in need.

The situation of the rich man in Luke 18 is, then, little different from that of the rich fool in the parable of Luke 12:16-21 who hoards his goods in barns and who revels in his self-sufficiency. There is no suggestion of generosity about this man, unlike the rich man of Luke 18, but in the end the two are shown to be in the same situation before God. Both in their respective ways involve the simple storing up of treasures for themselves. Neither, then, is "rich toward God" (εἰς θεὸν πλουτῶν, 12:21), who is the ultimate benefactor of all that is good.

Figures of this sort in the Lukan Gospel, I suggest, provide corollaries to the jealous Jews of Acts 13. The protective possessiveness demonstrated by (many) Jews in the Antiochene synagogue falls within the arena of a hoarding disposition that has already been negatively assessed in Luke's Gospel.[27] In Lukan perspective the synagogal form of universalism is much like the beneficence of the rich man of Luke 18; just as his riches served to benefit others and to promote himself, so too the synagogal Jews were content that the riches of Judaism should benefit others without compromising the primacy of Jewish people. In Luke's estimate, however, despite an outward appearance of generosity among synagogal Jews, the reality of the situation involved a hoarding character, similarly exemplified already in Luke's Gospel by the rich fool of Luke 12. An avaricious disposition concerned with the enhancement of status, stature, and security is exemplified in different forms by well-resourced men of the Lukan Gospel on the one hand and by the synagogal Jews of Acts 13 on the other. If, in Greco-Roman culture, protective "jealousy" would have been seen as the impulse of the honorable against the machinations of the envious, Luke

---

26. The issue is similar in Luke 14:12-14, where Jesus encourages generosity to be given not to those who bring benefit to oneself but to those who can provide no benefit at all.

27. The connection between moral character touched by God and the redefinition of purity boundaries is clear from Jesus' advice to the Pharisee who cleanses the outside but not the inside: "Give for alms those things which are within, and behold, anything is clean for you" (11:41).

assesses it altogether differently, placing it within the category of a world at odds with divine generosity.[28]

The "jealousy" highlighted by the Jews of Acts also stands in stark contrast to the attitude of Jesus, who preached "good news to the poor" (Luke 4:18). As the Gospel narrative makes clear, the phrase "the poor" (οἱ πτωχοί) frequently refers to those who are materially lacking or who are exposed to the harsh realities of life without the benefit of protective social structures. But Luke also suggestively extends the frame of reference to include those who are impoverished in their relationship to God. So the same Nazareth pericope wherein Jesus highlights the benefits of the gospel for the poor unfolds further to include a focus on Gentiles. In Luke 4:25-30 Jesus' ministry to "the poor" is likened to the ministries of Elijah and Elisha — prophets sent beyond the boundaries of Israel. This narrative feature remains largely undeveloped in the Lukan Gospel, but it comes into its own in the Acts narrative, where the divinely inspired generosity that had been depicted primarily in materialistic terms in the Gospel narrative now is depicted in ethnic terms in Acts. The encounter between Paul and the synagogal Jews of Antioch is a natural replication of Jesus' earlier encounter with the synagogal Jews of Nazareth, who shunned his proclamation of divine generosity to the materially and spiritually impoverished.

The Spread of Protective Jealousy among Synagogal Jews and of Christianity's Controversial Reputation

The Antiochene episode of Acts 13 plays a critical role in developing another significant strand in the Lukan narrative. According to Luke, Jewish antagonism to Christian universalism in Pisidian Antioch had an immediate effect in advancing the process whereby Christianity gained a dishonorable reputation among some of those at the upper echelons of society — "devout women of high social standing and prominent citizens of the city" (13:50). These holders of power and maintainers of social stability evidently came to perceive Christianity as a malignant societal cancer. If some of the elite of Pisidian Antioch held the view that Christians were a danger

---

28. Of course, an obvious embodiment of this form of divine generosity in the Acts narrative is the early community of believers in Jerusalem, whose members share possessions so that no one is in need (cf. 4:32-37).

to civic well-being, that perception is attributed by Luke to the fact that these leading citizens had themselves become pawns of some synagogal Jews (at least on this occasion): "the Jews incited" them. Something of this sort has already been highlighted in the passion narrative, where Roman officials who should have known better were duped by the machinations of some Palestinian Jews (cf. the intentions of certain Jews in Acts 23:12-15; 24:1-9; 25:1-3).

The Lukan narratives, then, indicate how miscarriages of justice ensue whenever self-interest is the driving force behind societal processes. In Acts this conviction animates at least six other episodes in which non-Christian Jews are featured as opponents of the Gentile mission. Thus in 14:1 Luke explains that "the same thing" (κατὰ τὸ αὐτό) that happened in Pisidian Antioch took place in Iconium as well. There "the unbelieving Jews stirred up the Gentiles and poisoned their minds" against the apostles, resulting in the attempt "to maltreat them and to stone them" (14:25), evidently because they were perceived to be destructive miscreants.

The same pattern is repeated in Luke's account of Paul and Barnabas in Lystra (14:8-20), with the arrival of certain Jews from Antioch and Iconium who are intent simply (it seems) to instigate a riot against Paul. The jealousy that had taken hold among the Jewish community in Antioch is now shown to be spreading to surrounding cities, resulting in the provocation of these cities against the Christian apostles as if they were degenerate malefactors corrupting society.

Similar is Luke's account in 17:4-9. After Paul had "persuaded" (πείθειν) some Thessalonian Jews and a great many of the devout (God-fearing) Gentiles, and even some leading women of the city, "the Jews became jealous, and with the help of some ruffians in the marketplaces they formed a mob and set the city in an uproar" (17:5). This resulted in accusations against Christians before the civic authorities, accusations involving breaches of social order and political orthodoxy (17:6-7). Consequently, Luke speaks of the city officials being "disturbed" (ταράσσεσθαι) by the spread of Christianity (17:8).

As was the case in Acts 14, so also in 17:10-15 Jewish opposition overflows from one city to another, with jealousy spreading from Thessalonica to Beroea. Beroean Jews had initially been "more receptive than those in Thessalonica, for they welcomed the message very eagerly" (17:11). Here many of them are converted, "including not a few Greek women and men of high standing" (17:12). But if things look initially promising, as they had in Pisidian Antioch in Acts 13, that promising scenario gives way to tragedy as some Jews from Thessalonica, still motivated by jealousy, stirred up trouble and incited the crowds against Paul and his companions (17:13).

Luke again highlights in Acts 18 that synagogal jealousy provoked civic turmoil in connection with Christian apostolic ministry. There the Corinthian Jews who oppose Paul's Gentile mission end up seeking to convince the proconsul of Achaia that the presence of Paul should worry one who defends the civic order (18:12-13).[29] The same occurs later in Acts 21, where "the Jews from Asia . . . stirred up all the crowd" (21:27) so that "all the city was aroused" in an attempt to kill Paul (21:30-31). From such disturbances the Roman tribune who arrests Paul mistakes him to be "the Egyptian who recently stirred up a revolt and led the four thousand men of the assassins out into the wilderness" (21:38).[30]

Throughout Luke's narrative in Acts, then, readers perceive the same scenario played out time and time again. Synagogal Jews, marked out by the impulse to preserve the salvific preeminence of the Jewish people, set in motion processes that result in Christianity acquiring an antisocial reputation among the civic authorities. This result is the organic outgrowth of the character deficiency of self-protective jealousy wherein privilege is hoarded. Luke capitalizes on this pattern frequently throughout his narrative, intent on indicting this form of jealousy (and primarily synagogal jealousy) as a principal cause of opposition to and defamation of the Christian movement. The trail of Jewish opposition to Christianity, and the antisocial reputation that became attached to Christianity in the process, is traced by Luke to an ignoble hoarding character taking hold of the synagogal community.[31]

29. That the charge against Paul is not couched in explicitly civic and political terms (as were those in 17:6-7 or 16:20-21) is not to say that there are no civic and political connotations to the charge. See, e.g., J. D. G. Dunn, *The Acts of the Apostles* (Narrative Commentaries; Valley Forge, Pa.: Trinity Press International, 1996), 244.

30. On the attraction of the wilderness for Jewish revolutionaries, see my "The Wilderness and Revolutionary Ferment in First-Century Palestine: A Response to D. R. Schwartz and J. Marcus," *JSJ* 29 (1998): 322-36. Schwartz's reply to me has force but, in my view, is not ultimately satisfactory; see D. R. Schwartz, "Whence the Voice? A Response to Bruce W. Longenecker," *JSJ* 31 (2000): 42-46. Surely the divine voice emerges from the heavenly realm, not the wilderness, as Schwartz contends.

31. I consider Luke to have had a nuanced view of the charge that Christianity is "turning the world upside down" (17:6) as a consequence of Christian proclamation of a king other than Caesar (17:7). What seems invalid in these claims is the connotation that

Non-Jewish Examples of a Fundamental Human Problem

To be sure, the impulse to protect or enhance one's interests in what is depicted as a selfish manner is not restricted in Acts to certain Jewish figures. It has other manifestations as well, realistically overflowing ethnic boundaries.

At least three episodes illustrate this. First, in Acts 16 Paul encounters the slave girl possessed by a spirit of divination; after an extended period of being greatly provoked by her, Paul exorcises the spirit from her (16:16-18).[32] Since her demonic state "brought her owners a great deal of money by fortune-telling" (16:16), it is not surprising to find her owners prosecuting Paul for having destroyed their profit-making enterprise. Embedded within the Lukan worldview, of course, is the conviction that the girl's personal well-being brought about by God is more important than the ill-won financial gain of her masters. Accordingly, the reader is expected to accept that the owners of the slave girl do not bear a legitimate grudge against Paul, their resentment arising simply from the fact that they can no longer advantage themselves at her expense. Predictably, this resentment then evolves further, with trumped-up charges being brought against Paul and Silas. These missionaries of Christ are accused of disturbing the city and advocating customs that are not lawful for Romans to adopt or observe (16:20-21).[33] With these trumped-up charges a massive public outcry

---

Christianity promotes societal ill-health; in Luke's view the challenges, criticisms, and adjustments that Christianity offers to society are dramatic indeed (thereby turning the world upside down). But that is different from Christianity being malevolent within society. Luke wants to portray the Christian movement as promoting the well-being of society, even if that society must at times undergo the painful process of renewal in order to be restored to health.

On the political implications of the Christian gospel within the Greco-Roman world, as depicted in Acts, see C. Burfeind, "Paulus *muß* nach Rom. Zur politischen Dimension der Apostelgeschichte," *NTS* 46 (2000): 75-91; see also other larger studies, such as G. E. Sterling, *Historiography and Self-Definition: Josephos, Luke-Acts and Apologetic Historiography* (NovTSup 64; Leiden: Brill, 1992); and P. F. Esler, *Community and Gospel in Luke-Acts: The Social and Political Motivations of Lucan Theology* (SNTSMS 57; Cambridge: Cambridge Univ. Press, 1987).

32. Presumably, since the exorcism does have financial implications for her owners, that Paul works the exorcism only after an extended period of provocation takes some of the sting out of what might be seen as a social transgression committed by Paul: depriving others of their source of income.

33. Although the charges are brought against Paul and Silas as Jews, the reader knows a more precise definition of their identity: Christian Jews.

follows, and once again Paul (along with Silas) is in the midst of a mob scene. Nonetheless, the reader is to see that this is simply the outcome of a process that originated in the deficient moral character of those who seek personal fulfillment by the exploitation of others. A sequence of events is initiated by a few social villains who are joined by others whose character is similarly configured. In contrast to this massive congregation of those who side with the exploiters of the needy, Paul is the agent of the God who gives generously to those in need.

Something similar is found in Acts 19. There we are told about a great Ephesian disturbance (lit. "no little disturbance," τάραχος οὐκ ὀλίγος, 19:23) in connection with Paul and the early Christian movement. The great Hellenistic cult of Artemis, based in Ephesus (the "temple keeper of the great Artemis," νεωκόρον οὖσαν τῆς μεγάλης Ἀρτέμιδος, 19:35), played an important cultural and economic role in the life of the city; pilgrims flocked there to worship this major goddess in her main temple, considered to be one of the seven wonders of the world. Demetrius, a silversmith, recognizes the economic implications of the Christian monotheistic message and denounces Paul as one who would undermine the whole economic substratum of the cult and the city.[34] Luke takes care to point out that Demetrius has a thriving business (19:24), from which he has made great wealth (19:25). While this in itself is not problematic, the narrative reveals Demetrius to be one who is concerned to maintain his wealth and prosperity at the expense of the Christian gospel of the generous God. As in Acts 16, so too here those of this ilk who instigate trouble against Christianity are joined by a much larger assembly of those who get caught up in the dynamics of the moment, working themselves up into a bizarre, undisciplined frenzy (19:28-29). That their madness is without proper foundation is made clear in 19:32, where there is no unanimity in their opinions, most being unsure of why they had assembled in the first place. A voice of common sense is then injected when the town clerk calms the throng by identifying their lack of any specific legal allegation against the apostles, who are thought to pose no threat to civic stability (19:35-40). That this is the case has already been implied by the mention that Paul's circle of Ephesian friends included

34. That Demetrius's suspicions are not unfounded is clear from the evidence of Pliny the Younger, who sixty years later indicates how Christianity has been a blight on the older established cults in Bithynia (*Epistulae* 10.96).

Asiarchs, who were among the socially elite, holding positions of high public office and serving as benefactors of their cities.[35]

As in Acts 16, so also here, then, the bearers of the Christian gospel find themselves on a collision course with those whose motivation is to excel in the acquisition of material goods. The collision that ensues involves Christian apostles in socially disruptive events with a reputation as instigators of sociopolitical insurgence. The reader, however, is invited to see past the surface of this now familiar pattern and recognize that a mischievous reputation has improperly been given to Christianity by those whose character is ultimately determined by the concern to promote themselves and to protect jealously their own interests.

Another important example of non-Jews demonstrating a selfish motive appears in Acts 24–25. There the Roman governor Felix is shown to want to exploit Paul's situation for his own financial gain, while simultaneously attempting to keep the Jews on his side (24:26-27; cf. 25:9). He seeks personal profit from both parties in the dispute, and as a consequence the case against Paul fails to reach its proper closure. If justice failed to be done in the early stages of the legal proceedings against Paul, this is not because his legal position was unclear, but because justice was prohibited by a Roman governor attempting to benefit from Paul's situation. As Agrippa articulates later, "This man could have been set free if he had not appealed to the emperor" (26:32); and as the narrative of Acts 24–25 makes clear, the reason why Paul had to appeal his case to the emperor was that justice was impeded by Felix, who sought to advance from Paul's misfortune.[36]

In at least three places (Acts 16, 19, and 24–25), then, Gentiles are shown to possess a character similar in its basic configuration to that of the jealous Jews depicted elsewhere in the narrative. Luke does not simply single out some non-Christian Jews as those who demonstrate a character wherein self-interest overrides concern for others; in his narrative non-

---

35. Some (e.g., S. J. Friesen, *Twice Neokoros: Ephesus, Asia and the Cult of the Flavian Imperial Family* [Leiden: Brill, 1993]) consider the Asiarchs to have been promoters of the imperial cult, which would make them strange bedfellows of Paul. The claim has not gone unchallenged; see, e.g., R. A. Kearsley, "The Asiarchs," in *The Book of Acts in Its Graeco-Roman Setting* (ed. D. W. J. Gill and C. Gempf; Book of Acts in Its First Century Setting 2; Grand Rapids: Eerdmans, 1994), 363-76.

36. The narrative also makes clear, however, that Paul's defense before the emperor is part of God's ultimate plan (27:24).

Christian Jews and non-Christian Gentiles alike are linked by means of this similarity in character. This kind of character flaw, like the Christian message itself, extends beyond the boundaries of any ethnic group.

Nonetheless, even with that said, it is also the case that, in the Lukan narrative, the Jews of jealous character are the ones who are primarily to blame for Christianity's bad name.[37] When Paul talks to the philosophers of the Athenian marketplace, for instance, they find him to propose a curious point of view, and some even believe, while others do not. But there is nothing here about jealousy, nor do the Athenian philosophers stir up trouble or denounce Paul as promoting an antisocial cancer. When the tribune Claudius Lysias rescues Paul from the Jewish ambush attempt, he sends a letter to the governor Felix (23:26-30), noting that certain Jews had seized Paul and unduly attempted to kill him, a Roman citizen. The implication of this is that they have been the social miscreants in this case; by contrast, Claudius has served the empire by protecting one of its citizens — "a citizen of an important city" (οὐκ ἀσήμου πόλεως πολίτης, 21:39), as Paul identifies himself. On balance, despite the fact that Jewish antisocial jealousy is simply one feature of a broader portrait of human degeneracy, it is nonetheless the feature that Luke is especially interested to parade.[38] (It is also, of course, a feature that needs careful historical, ethical, and theological consideration.)[39]

---

37. Cf. S. Cunningham, 'Through Many Tribulations': The Theology of Persecution in Luke-Acts (JSNTSup 142; Sheffield: Sheffield Academic Press, 1997), 247-51.

38. Cf. J. B. Tyson (Images of Judaism in Luke-Acts [Columbia: Univ. of South Carolina Press, 1992], 153): "For the most part, Jewish people [in the second half of the Acts narrative] take on the role of hostile unbelievers, and sometimes they are objects of ridicule and contempt." Many things need to be said to qualify such a statement, of course, and no one has worked harder than J. Jervell on precisely that front (see his The Unknown Paul [Minneapolis: Augsburg, 1984]; idem, Die Apostelgeschichte [KEK; Göttingen: Vandenhoeck & Ruprecht, 1998]). In the end, however, it is questionable whether such qualifications can assuage modern sensibilities with regard to Luke's portrait of the Jews and the synagogal form of their religion.

39. On this see C. A. Evans and D. A. Hagner, eds., Anti-Semitism and Early Christianity: Issues of Polemic and Faith (Minneapolis: Fortress, 1993); M. S. Taylor, Anti-Judaism and Early Christian Identity: A Critique of the Scholarly Consensus (Leiden: Brill, 1995); Anti-Judaism in Early Christianity, vol. 1, P. Richardson with D. Granskou, eds., Paul and the Gospels (Waterloo: Wilfrid Laurier Univ. Press, 1986); vol. 2, S. G. Wilson, ed., Separation and Polemic (Waterloo: Wilfrid Laurier Univ. Press, 1986); W. R. Farmer, ed., Anti-Judaism and the Gospels (Harrisburg, Pa.: Trinity Press International, 1999).

Moral Character and the Riches of Judaism
in the Lukan Narrative

N. R. Petersen writes concerning Acts: "the rejection of God's agents by God's people in connection with God's sanctuaries (synagogues and temple) is the plot device by which the movement of the narrative as a whole is motivated."[40] I have shown here that this "rejection . . . by God's people" is analyzed in the Lukan narrative in terms of moral identity, as demonstrated by social character. In this regard, then, the Acts narrative overlaps significantly with the interests of Luke's Gospel.

Furthermore, it is no doubt correct to say with Joel Green that the Christian dispute "with the Jewish people and with Jewish institutions in Acts is essentially hermeneutical: Who interprets the Scriptures faithfully?"[41] It also needs to be recognized, however, that in significant ways the hermeneutical issue is itself part of a larger issue concerning moral character. The faithful interpretation of the Scriptures is not simply a matter of exegetical accuracy and enlightenment, but involves the development of Christian character in conformity to the generosity of God.[42]

A comprehensive study of Luke's two volumes would, I believe, reveal that Luke depicts things Jewish in a curious double-natured way. On the one hand, he is convinced, and demonstrates in both his Gospel and Acts, that the religious heritage of the Jews is a rich and plentiful one. On the other hand, Luke shows repeatedly in Acts that a jealous protectionism has pervaded the institutions and character of a plenitude of non-Christian Jews. Their tendency to hoard the riches of their heritage generates their opposition to Christianity, with the frequent result that the reputation of Christianity has unnecessarily and illegitimately been associated with sociopolitical unrest. In Luke's view such charges are themselves the product of those whose character is all too often overtaken by the ignoble features worthy only of the underbelly of a healthy society.

These two strands in the Lukan narrative are not disparate and distinct but united by a common underlying theology of riches that has al-

---

40. N. R. Petersen, *Literary Criticism for New Testament Critics* (GBS; Philadelphia: Fortress, 1978), 83.

41. J. B. Green, "Acts of the Apostles," *DLNT* 18.

42. I found the same to be evident in Galatians; see my "Christian Character and Scriptural Interpretation," in *The Triumph of Abraham's God: The Transformation of Identity in Galatians* (Edinburgh: T&T Clark; Nashville: Abingdon, 1998), 162-71.

ready been established in the Gospel of Luke. The theology of possessions articulated in the Gospel on the level of personal identity and responsibility finds its extension and application in Acts on the level of national religious identity and responsibility. Luke's reader comes to see the Jews as those who are rich in religious piety and practice. Ancient readers would have had respect for such a tradition, and there is no indication that Luke thought this richness to be despicable. What is inappropriate to him is the way that, in his view, unbelieving Jews have a tendency to hoard the richness of Jewish piety and practice, especially in view of the offer of divine grace being extended to all through the Christian mission. Ironically, in attempting to preserve Judaism's rich treasures within traditional configurations of Jewish practice, these Jewish opponents of Christianity have, in Luke's view, relinquished their place within the legitimate boundaries of their ancestral religion. Conversely, Luke depicts the Christian movement as a force for the betterment of society, marked out by a character of staunch generosity in all arenas of life. In this way, Luke celebrates the Christian gospel and mission as the full flowering of the ancient religion of the Jews, and advertises a God whose generosity and sovereignty are interpenetrating characteristics.

Part III

EPISTLES

Philippians 1:28b, One More Time

Stephen E. Fowl

Introduction

It is a great privilege to contribute to a volume honoring Jerry Hawthorne. His teaching of Greek and his presence on the campus of Wheaton College influenced countless students over the course of his career. For those of us who went on to graduate school and to become teachers ourselves, Jerry stands as a model of the scholar/teacher — passionate about the subject matter, devoted to his students, engaged in Wheaton's mission, and yet never losing a proper perspective on himself.

In my contribution to this volume, I take up a discussion from Jerry's most influential writing, his commentary on Philippians.[1] In particular, I focus on the specific puzzles found in Phil 1:28.[2] I want to build on some of Jerry's suggestions about how to solve the obscurities in this passage in order to offer a reading of this verse in its broader context.

---

1. G. F. Hawthorne, *Philippians* (WBC 43; Waco: Word, 1983).

2. Hawthorne first laid out his position on this verse in a paper at the 1983 SNTS meeting in Canterbury, England (later published as "The Interpretation and Translation of Philippians 1:28b," *ExpTim* 95 [1983]: 80-81).

Setting the Stage: The Context of Philippians 1:27-30

Philippians 1:27-30 begins a section that forms the heart of the epistle. Immediately prior, in vv. 12-26, Paul has reflected on his own circumstances in prison. In these verses Paul provides the Philippians with news about himself and how he is faring in captivity. Specifically, in vv. 19-26 he claims that even though he would prefer to die, he will seek to live and remain with the Philippians (and his other congregations) because that is more beneficial to them. In doing this, Paul displays that disposition (i.e., seeking the benefit of others in the Lord) that he and other central characters in the epistle, such as Christ (2:6-11) and Timothy and Epaphroditus (2:18-30), also manifest to greater or lesser degrees.

Following that, Paul expresses his hope that he will soon hear from the Philippians about how they too are faring (1:27; 2:19). This in itself is not particularly remarkable. Within the genre we have come to know as the "letter of friendship," such sharing of news, commenting on received news, and requesting further news from the recipients is to be expected.[3] What is distinctive about Philippians in this regard is that in the course of sharing news about himself, Paul is also involved in a particularly theological endeavor. That is, Paul does not simply relate news to the Philippians. Rather, he narrates an account of his circumstances in prison in the light of his larger reading of God's economy of salvation. Paul's account is not simply about recent episodes in his life, but also about his life as an episode in the larger drama of God's saving purposes. Hence, despite what one might have expected, Paul argues that his imprisonment has actually worked to advance the gospel. Instead of despairing at his horrific conditions, he rejoices. By fitting his account within the larger story of God's activity Paul is able, using inference and analogy, to see how he should comport himself in his particular situation. As a result, he is able to be steadfast, rejoice in suffering, and find confidence in God's deliverance despite his current circumstances. Paul's ability to fit himself into the narrative of God's saving purpose forms in him the perspective to think and act in accordance with the gospel rather than in a manner that would seem

---

3. This point has been made convincingly by Stanley Stowers in *Letter Writing in Greco-Roman Antiquity* (LEC 5; Philadelphia: Westminster, 1986), 50-70; also see his "Friends and Enemies in the Politics of Heaven," in *Pauline Theology*, vol. 1 (ed. J. M. Bassler; Minneapolis: Fortress, 1991), 107-10; and L. C. A. Alexander, "Hellenistic Letter-Forms and the Structure of Philippians," *JSNT* 37 (1989): 87-101.

best to someone lacking this perspective. Moreover, it is precisely this ability and this type of formation that Paul displays for the Philippians and hopes that they will display as well.

The Text: Philippians 1:27-30

In 1:27-30 Paul shifts his attention from himself to the Philippians. Indeed, because he knows something of their circumstances, he offers an account of the Philippians' situation that shows the similarities between his circumstances and theirs. Hence in 1:30 Paul can make the crucial claim that the Philippians are engaged in the same struggle that he is. Further, because they are in the same struggle, they too should see their story in the light of the divine economy. Thus they should comport themselves in a manner similar to Paul.

Within this set of general concerns, Paul begins in 1:27 by urging the Philippians to order their common life in a manner worthy of the gospel of Christ. As is often observed, the verb πολιτεύεσθε in 1:27 is not the normal way Paul speaks about the conduct of believers. It would be much more common for him to use a verb like περιπατεῖν (cf. Rom 13:13; Eph 4:1; Col 1:10; 1 Thess 2:12; 4:12).[4] In this light, scholars argue that Paul must be doing something more than urging a particular pattern of individual behavior. The question is, What more does Paul mean by using πολιτεύεσθε? Raymond R. Brewer made the case that πολιτεύεσθε is a way of speaking about discharging one's obligations as a citizen. Brewer combined this account of πολιτεύεσθε with judgments about Philippi's status as a Roman colony with full legal standing to argue that Paul is urging the Philippians to continue to discharge their duties as citizens and residents of Philippi, while recognizing that their ultimate allegiance is to their heavenly πολίτευμα.[5]

The particular (and decisive) problem with this view is that, while Brewer has made a case that πολιτεύεσθε refers to discharging one's obligations as a member of a specific polity, it does not imply the particular polity represented by Rome. For example, E. C. Miller has shown that πολιτεύομαι is used widely in the LXX to refer to the practice of a Jewish way of

4. For other words Paul commonly uses in this regard see R. R. Brewer, "The Meaning of *Politeuesthe* in Philippians 1:27," *JBL* 73 (1954): 76-77.

5. See ibid., 82-83.

life (cf. Esth 8:12; 2 Macc 6:1; 11:25; 3 Macc 3:4; 4 Macc 2:8, 23; 4:23; 5:16). This is also the way the term is basically used in Josephus, *Vita* 12; *Let. Aris.* 31; and Acts 23:1.[6] As Markus Bockmuehl notes, however, in these particular contexts such a notion is clearly a *"politically relevant* act which in the context is distinguished from alternative lifestyles that might have been chosen."[7] In the case of Esther and 2 Maccabees this is particularly poignant since in each case Jews are under threat because of the ways they conduct themselves.

Hence, in using πολιτεύεσθε, Paul is speaking about the ordering of a group's polity or common life. What is clear, however, is that the standard against which this ordering takes place is not Rome or Jewish law — it is the gospel of Christ. Moreover, Philippi's distinctive position as a Roman colony with full legal status allows Paul's appeal to "live as a citizen worthy of the gospel of Christ" to stand both as a sharp contrast to the appeal of Roman citizenship and as an implicit appeal to recognize the implications of living as a citizen of the gospel.[8] "The rhetorical force of Paul's language is to play on the perceived desirability of citizenship in Roman society at Philippi, and to contrast against this the *Christian* vision of enfranchisement and belonging."[9] This seems especially clear in the light of 3:20, where Paul notes that the Philippians are citizens of a heavenly πολίτευμα. Taken in this light, there seems to be an implicit contrast here between Roman citizenship and being a citizen of the gospel of Christ. Bockmuehl recognizes this: "Paul interposes a counter-citizenship whose capital and seat of power are not earthly but heavenly, whose guarantor is not Nero but Christ."[10]

---

6. E. C. Miller Jr., "Πολιτεύεσθε in Philippians 1.27: Some Philological and Thematic Observations," *JSNT* 15 (1982): 86-96.

7. M. Bockmuehl, *The Epistle to the Philippians* (BNTC; London: A & C Black; Peabody, Mass.: Hendrickson, 1998), 97.

8. "Through the gospel which proclaims Christ as Savior, the Christian is made a citizen of the heavenly Jerusalem, a partner in a spiritual fellowship, a member of a new community, the Christian commonwealth, the Church. To live worthily of the gospel, then, also means that the Christian lives as a good citizen of this new state, governing his actions by the laws of this unique *politeuma* — righteousness, peace, faith, hope, love, mutuality, interdependence, good deeds, service to one another, worship of the living God, and so on" (Hawthorne, *Philippians,* 56).

9. Bockmuehl, *Philippians,* 98.

10. Ibid. Several commentators see Paul here arguing for a dual allegiance or citizenship (see, e.g., G. D. Fee, *Paul's Letter to the Philippians* [NICNT; Grand Rapids: Eerdmans, 1995], 162; P. T. O'Brien, *The Epistle to the Philippians* [NIGTC; Grand Rapids: Eerdmans,

As the rest of vv. 27-28 unfolds, it is clear that, for the Philippians, ordering their common life in a manner worthy of the gospel will require a set of practices in which they as a community will have to engage. They are to "stand in one spirit"; "with a single soul" they are to "strive together for the faith of the gospel"; and they are not to be intimidated by their opponents. We are not told directly who these opponents are, and it is important not to go beyond the evidence. From the claims in 1:29 it would appear that these opponents can inflict suffering on the Philippians. This would indicate that they are outside the church and thus different from those characters addressed in chapter 3.[11] In 1:30 the link Paul draws between his current struggle and the Philippians' would indicate that the Philippians, like Paul, are under pressure from imperial authorities because of their Christian confession. There is certainly a body of evidence indicating that Christianity was seen as a threat to political harmony and stability.[12] Moreover, in Acts 16:20 this is the charge brought against Paul in Philippi.[13] In addition, 2 Cor 8:1-2 suggests that Christians in Macedonia were being persecuted. All this would argue that the opponents in 1:28 are those from the local population who saw Christianity as a threat to the harmony and stability of this imperial outpost.[14]

1991], 147). This view requires further comment. Primarily, the dual citizenship view seems to underplay the contrast between Rome and Christ that Paul must bodily display for the Philippians. Remember, Paul is in a Roman prison for the sake of Christ (1:13). Further, the opponents of the Philippians mentioned in 1:28 would appear to be the Roman citizens of Philippi (see also Paul's claim in 1:30 that the Philippians are engaged in the same struggle as Paul). Clearly, Paul is not advocating violent opposition to the empire here. Nevertheless, he makes clear that the interests and aims of the church are different from and largely at variance with the interests and aims of the empire. On this issue see also the section on citizenship (πολιτεία) in G. W. Hansen, "Transformation of Relationships: Partnership, Citizenship, and Friendship in Philippi," in the present volume.

11. This goes against Hawthorne; cf. J.-F. Collange, *The Epistle of St. Paul to the Philippians* (trans. A. W. Heathcote; London: Epworth, 1979), 75; and W. Hendriksen, *New Testament Commentary: Exposition of Philippians* (Grand Rapids: Baker, 1962), 87, among others, who see the opponents in 1:28 as identical with those addressed in 3:2.

12. In addition to material in the NT, see, e.g., Origen, *Cels.* 5-7; and the narratives related in *The Acts of the Christian Martyrs* (ed. H. Musurillo; Oxford: Clarendon, 1972); see also R. L. Wilken, *The Christians as the Romans Saw Them* (New Haven: Yale Univ. Press, 1984).

13. On this passage see esp. B. W. Longenecker, "Moral Character and Divine Generosity: Acts 13:13-52 and the Narrative Dynamics of Luke-Acts," in the present volume.

14. See C. S. De Vos, *Church and Community Conflicts: The Relationships of the Thessalonian, Corinthian, and Philippian Churches with Their Wider Civic Communities*

The Puzzles of 1:28

At this point we come upon the problematic part of 1:28. The concluding phrase of this verse, ἥτις ἐστὶν αὐτοῖς ἔνδειξις ἀπωλείας, ὑμῶν[15] δὲ σωτηρίας, καὶ τοῦτο ἀπὸ θεοῦ, is obscure and has generated a variety of views. No one view stands head and shoulders above the rest. Indeed, all attempts to make sense of this verse end up having to supply words or concepts that are not directly expressed, but perhaps implied, in these two clauses.

Hawthorne argues that this clause contrasts two ways of evaluating the Philippians' steadfast unity in the face of opposition. To the opponents, it signals the Philippians' destruction. In reality, however, it testifies to the Philippians' salvation.[16] Subsequent commentators have tended either explicitly or implicitly to reject Hawthorne's views.[17] In what follows, however, I argue for the relative superiority of a version of Hawthorne's position. I largely focus my arguments against those commentators who lodge specific disagreements with Hawthorne. As will become clear, I do not think every aspect of Hawthorne's position is sustainable. Even so, the problematic elements in his position can be discarded or revised without loss to the overall force of his argument.

Recent commentators have devoted most of their attention to two central problems here. The first concerns the antecedent of ἥτις. The second concerns the nature of the destruction mentioned, and who is the object of that destruction. Several subsequent commentators seem to think that in rejecting Hawthorne's account of the antecedent of ἥτις they have undermined his overall position.[18] I will show that even adopting a differ-

---

(SBLDS 168; Atlanta: Scholars Press, 1999). This is also basically the position of Bockmuehl, *Philippians*, 100; Fee, *Philippians*, 167n.50; and O'Brien, *Philippians*, 153.

15. Some later MSS read ὑμῖν here. Though the evidence is against the originality of this variant, it does rightly capture the sense that the distinctions made in this verse are between ways of interpreting the sign and not between destruction and salvation. This is explicitly against F. W. Beare, *A Commentary on the Epistle to the Philippians* (BNTC; London: A & C Black, 1973), 68.

16. See Hawthorne, *Philippians*, 58-60.

17. For example, Fee, *Philippians*, 168n.53; O'Brien, *Philippians*, 154; and B. Witherington III, *Friendship and Finances in Philippi* (Valley Forge, Pa.: Trinity Press International, 1994), 53-54, all mention Hawthorne's views but reject them. Others, such as Bockmuehl, *Philippians*, 101, simply accept other interpretive options without so much as discussing Hawthorne's views.

18. See Fee, *Philippians*, 168n.53; and O'Brien, *Philippians*, 154.

ent view about ἥτις would not undermine Hawthorne's overall position. Moreover, I argue that a version of Hawthorne's position best fits the context of 1:27-30 and the larger context of the epistle as a whole.[19]

Most recent commentators argue — with some plausibility — that the feminine relative pronoun ἥτις takes its gender by attraction to ἔνδειξις.[20] Hawthorne argues that it is grammatically just as possible that the antecedent of ἥτις is τῇ πίστει in v. 27.[21] Grammatically, they agree in gender and number as they ought. I take it that the point would be that the Philippians' faith, which generates and sustains steadfast courage in the face of opponents, is a sign. Indeed, this is basically the way most commentators understand the clause even if they explain the grammar differently. Thus the sentence that begins in 1:27 with the demand that the Philippians order their common life in a manner worthy of the gospel then goes on, by means of the following participial phrases, to elaborate the specific practices Paul thinks are essential to this ordering. It is the Philippians' unified and steadfast faith in the face of opposition that is a sign to their opponents. Recent commentators, including Hawthorne, appear to take the verse roughly this way regardless of their views about the antecedent of ἥτις.[22] This would indicate that the rejection of Hawthorne's views on ἥτις by subsequent commentators is a red herring. The real issue concerns the following clause.

This clause indicates that the Philippians' steadfast faithfulness in the face of opposition is a sign. Based on the way Paul uses the term in Rom 3:25-26 and 2 Cor 8:24, here in Phil 1:28 ἔνδειξις is apparently to be understood as a concrete demonstration of a matter of fact.[23] The rest of the verse explains what type of sign it is and to whom it is directed.

19. Moreover, those commentators who explicitly reject Hawthorne's interpretation assume that his account depends on a reconstruction of 1:28b. I take it that the diagrams on p. 59 of his commentary lay out the conceptual, as well as the hypothetical original, structure of the verse. One could reject the latter without rejecting the former.

20. See, e.g., Fee, *Philippians*, 169n.53; and O'Brien, *Philippians*, 154. Also see the earlier commentaries of J. B. Lightfoot, *St. Paul's Epistle to the Philippians* (4th ed.; 1888; repr. Peabody, Mass.: Hendrickson, 1981), 106; and E. Lohmeyer, *Die Briefe an die Philipper, an die Kolosser, und an Philemon* (KEK; Göttingen: Vandenhoeck & Ruprecht, 1930), 76.

21. Hawthorne, *Philippians*, 58.

22. See Bockmuehl, *Philippians*, 101; Fee, *Philippians*, 168-69; O'Brien, *Philippians*, 154; Witherington, *Friendship*, 53-54.

23. Although Fee's preference for "omen" is well defended (*Philippians*, 168n.53), as is O'Brien's preference for "proof" (*Philippians*, 154), I think my account brings out what they want to do without the overtones either of something overly mysterious or of a logical proof.

The text is quite clear that, whatever else it is, the Philippians' stead-fast adherence to their faith is a sign of destruction to their opponents. What sort of destruction is this, and who is destroyed? Recent commenta-tors tend to try to answer this question by focusing on the nature of de-struction signified by ἀπωλεία.[24] This, in part, is driven by concerns about the use of σωτηρία in the subsequent clause. The common way in which Paul (and the Bible generally) uses these terms is to refer to eternal damna-tion and eschatological salvation.[25] But Hawthorne and Collange argue that here these words are used "with less than such ultimate meanings (cf. Matt. 26:8; Phil. 1:19)."[26] In this respect, the weight of the linguistic evi-dence is against Hawthorne. This, however, may not be as decisive as some think.[27] To show this it is important to shift attention for a moment. In-stead of focusing on the nature of the destruction mentioned here, we need to clarify who is the object of this destruction. By focusing on this question I think we can get an answer to the nature of the destruction (and the salvation) mentioned here that does not go against the bulk of the lin-guistic evidence.

The majority of the recent commentators and recent English transla-tions take it that Paul is claiming here that the Philippians' steadfast faith in the face of opposition is a concrete manifestation to their opponents of the opponents' destruction.[28] However, the syntax of this clause neither demands nor indicates this. Moreover, such a reading makes it much more difficult to make sense of the clause.

What is problematic here is that the common way of taking 1:28b as-serts that the faithfulness of the Philippian Christians in the face of perse-cution is a sign to their opponents of the opponents' destruction. How ex-actly do the opponents recognize this sign? Of the modern commentators, F. W. Beare at least treats this as a serious interpretive problem. As a result he comes up with an account of how the Philippians' behavior would have,

24. See Bockmuehl, *Philippians*, 101-2; Fee, *Philippians*, 168-69n.53; O'Brien, *Philip-pians*, 155-57.

25. See in particular the pairing of the verbal forms of these two words in 1 Cor 1:18. See also the survey of different passages in O'Brien, *Philippians*, 156-57.

26. Hawthorne (*Philippians*, 60) also cites 1 Cor 5:5. See also Collange, *Philippians*, 75.

27. For example, Fee, *Philippians*, 169n.53.

28. See Bockmuehl, *Philippians*, 101; Fee, *Philippians*, 168; Hendriksen, *Philippians*, 89; O'Brien, *Philippians*, 156-57; Witherington, *Friendship*, 51. In addition, the RSV, NRSV, NEB, CEV, and NAB are just some of the English versions that translate the verse this way.

at least subliminally, affected the opponents' psyches.[29] While Beare is to be commended for addressing what appears to be a serious weakness in this position, his is not a very persuasive solution. In particular, his allusion to Paul's own role as persecutor tells against rather than for his explanation. As Paul notes explicitly in Phil 3:4-11, he took his role as persecutor of Christians to be a mark of virtue, a concrete manifestation of his commitment to Judaism. He was sinfully misguided in this perception, but there is no evidence that he suffered from the turmoil in his psyche that Beare ascribes to such people. Indeed, Paul notes that as to the righteousness found in the law he was blameless (3:6).[30]

The difficulties that arise if one assumes that the sign for the opponents is a sign of their own destruction do not arise if we follow Hawthorne's view that the Philippians' steadfastness in the face of opposition is a sign to the opponents of the Philippians' destruction.[31] If the Philippians remain steadfast in their faith in the face of opposition from pagans who see Christianity as a threat to the empire, or at least to the harmony and stability of Philippi, then the opponents will not characterize the Philippians' attitude as steadfast courage. Rather it will be a mark of stubbornness, a stubbornness that will result in their justifiable punishment at the hands of imperial authorities.

This view is hardly idiosyncratic. There are numerous occasions in Scripture when the enemies of the faithful take the persecution, misfortune, or death of the so-called faithful as a sign that God has rejected these people (e.g., Ps 22; 41:4-12 [MT 5-13]; Isa 36; 52:13–53:12; and esp. Job). This, of course, raises questions about whether the faith and practice of such people were "faithful" at all. The most obvious example of this is the way Jesus' opponents evaluate the crucifixion (see Matt 26:32-44 par.). In addition, there are numerous occasions when the faithfulness of the people of God is a sign to them of their enemies' demise (e.g., Exod 14:13-14; Josh 4–6; 1 Sam 17, etc.). What is manifestly clear is that steadfast fidelity in the

---

29. See Beare, *Philippians*, 68. Hendriksen speaks of the opponents' "dim awareness" of their destruction (*Philippians*, 89).

30. O'Brien (*Philippians*, 155) rejects Beare's psychological speculations by claiming that αὐτοῖς is a dative of reference that shows that the "sign" is a sign of the opponents' destruction whether they recognize it or not. This is not really an argument, but an arbitrary assertion.

31. In a sense the ὑμῶν serves double duty, pointing back to ἀπωλείας and forward to σωτηρίας.

face of persecution is often evaluated one way by the persecutors and another way by the faithful.

The stories of Christian martyrs also reflect this, as they often relate the position held by those who put Christians to death. The unwillingness of Christians to apostatize is viewed as irrational, impious, superstitious, willful, and worthy of death.[32] It is a concrete manifestation to the opponents of the Christians' impending destruction, a destruction that would have entailed not only physical death but also the judgment of the gods.[33]

Paul, however, asserts that the Philippians' fidelity to the gospel in the face of opposition results in their salvation. While the Philippians' steadfast unity in the midst of persecution is a sign to the persecutors of the Philippians' destruction, such fidelity is rather a concrete manifestation of their salvation. That is, from the Philippian Christians' perspective, steadfast adherence to the faith is a concrete manifestation of their salvation to those who are able to interpret the economy of God's salvation properly. In 1:28 Paul is displaying two competing conceptions of the result of the Philippians' adhering to their faith in the ways Paul admonishes. To the opponents, it is willful flaunting of Roman authority and anticipates the Christians' imminent destruction. In reality, it marks the salvation of the Christians.[34] On this account, debates about whether the destruction/ salvation pairing here refers to the temporal or eternal realm simply miss the point. The opponents view the Philippians' physical destruction as testimony to their eternal perdition. For Paul and the Philippians, their steadfastness demonstrates their salvation, whether they live or die. It is simply the way they magnify Christ in their bodies (cf. 1:20). The final clause in this verse, καὶ τοῦτο ἀπὸ θεοῦ, works to offer divine authorization for the perspective Paul is advocating. Of course, God's authorization of this perspective is laid out more fully in the account of God's dealing with Christ in 2:6-11.[35]

---

32. See the paradigmatic account of the death of Marcellus of Tangier in the *Acta Marcelli* (Musurillo, *Acts of the Christian Martyrs,* 250-59).

33. For a discussion of Roman attitudes toward the early Christians see Wilken, *Christians as the Romans Saw Them,* esp. chap. 3.

34. As Hawthorne notes (*Philippians,* 60), the real contrast here is between two different perceptions of the Philippians' behavior.

35. On the opening lines of this passage, see G. F. Hawthorne, "In the Form of God and Equal with God (Philippians 2:6)," in *Where Christology Began: Essays on Philippians 2* (ed. R. P. Martin and B. J. Dodd; Louisville: Westminster John Knox, 1998), 96-110.

In addition to avoiding unconvincing explanations of how the opponents come to recognize their own damnation in the Philippians' behavior, this account of 1:28b fits with a general pattern of Paul's argument thus far. Opponents of the gospel always misperceive the difficult circumstances in which Christians find themselves. In 1:12-26 Paul relates how his circumstances have worked to advance, rather than frustrate, the gospel. Those who seek to increase Paul's tribulation ironically work to advance the gospel and lead Paul to rejoice (1:17-18). Those seeking to secure political harmony and stability by destroying Christians provide an occasion for Christians to demonstrate their salvation and the grace they have been given to suffer for Christ (1:28-29).

Further, in chapter 3 Paul relates for the Philippians his own dramatic change of perspective. While Paul never says it in these words, it is precisely this christologically dense, ironic perspective that he seeks to form in the Philippians. It is only with this perspective that one could even consider being a friend rather than an enemy of the cross (3:20). This is because one learns that, despite the signs to the contrary, the cross of Christ does not signify God's destruction of Jesus; rather, it is a concrete manifestation of salvation.

What becomes clear here is that any acts of faithfulness such as Paul argues for in 1:27-30, which might lead to persecution and even death, will always result in competing evaluations of those very acts of steadfast fidelity. Further, the differences in these competing evaluations cannot simply be resolved when one party is subdued by the other. As Stanley Hauerwas notes,

> Rome could kill Christians but they could not victimize them. The martyrs could go to their death confident that the story to which their killers were trying to subject them — that is, the story of victimization — was not the true story of their death. To Rome, Christians dying for their faith, for their refusal to obey Caesar, was an irrational act. For the martyrs, their dying was part of a story that Rome could not acknowledge and remain in power as Rome.[36]

---

36. S. Hauerwas, *After Christendom?* (Nashville: Abingdon, 1991), 38.

Conclusion and Further Issues

Thus far I have argued that the best way to account for the obscurities of 1:28b is to adopt a version of Hawthorne's view. This view reads this clause as asserting that the Philippians' steadfast faith in the face of opposition is a sign, but it is a sign that can be read two ways. The opponents will take it as a sign of the Philippians' imminent destruction. To the Philippians, however, it is a sign from God of their salvation. This reading has numerous conceptual antecedents in Scripture. Moreover, this reading fits best with both the immediate context of 1:27-30 and with the larger aims of the epistle.

This reading of 1:28b in light of the larger aims of Philippians shifts the terms of the interpretive dispute regarding the nature of the salvation Paul talks about here. Recent commentators have argued back and forth about whether σωτηρία here refers to the eternal salvation of souls or deliverance from persecution.[37] While those opting for "salvation" as the eternal salvation of individual souls would seem to have the better argument, this way of putting the matter tends to separate the spiritual and the political in unhelpful ways. While the Philippians have no reason to think that their common steadfast adherence to the gospel in the face of persecution will lead to the cessation of their troubles (esp. in the light of Paul's comments in 1:29), the salvation Paul talks about cannot really be understood apart from the material presence of a community of faithful believers who can remember and narrate the stories of the martyrs as stories of salvation rather than destruction. Again, Hauerwas explains, "Rome does not get to tell the story of our lives, but rather the church claims to be the triumphant political community that knows the truth of our existence better than Rome. The church — exactly because it does not seek to rule through violence, though it necessarily manifests God's rule — triumphs by remembering the victory of the Lamb through the witness of the martyrs."[38]

For those familiar with the interpretation of Philippians in the twentieth century, this reading of 1:28b may well conjure up the specter of Ernst Lohmeyer's widely rejected attempt to interpret the entire epistle as a manual of martyrdom.[39] Surprisingly, while Lohmeyer did seem to find refer-

---

37. See, e.g., those listed in nn. 24 and 25 above.
38. Hauerwas, *After Christendom?* 38.
39. See Lohmeyer, *Philipper.*

ences to martyrdom under almost every exegetical stone, he reads 1:28b in the way that most modern commentators have.[40]

In offering this reading of 1:28b I am not attempting to resurrect Lohmeyer's overall position. Philippians is not explicitly a manual of martyrdom. Nevertheless, one of the aims of the epistle is to display and to help form habits of perception, attention, and action necessary for life as a faithful Christian in a world often hostile to Christianity. If this is so, then it is also fair to claim that such habits are those necessary for forming people capable of being martyrs. It is important to remember that very early in the life of the church, Christians recognized that being a martyr is not an end in itself. Steadfast obedience and fidelity, such as Paul calls for in 1:27 and elsewhere, are the proper ends of Christian living. Whether faithful Christians become martyrs is largely out of their hands. It depends, rather, on the acts and responses of a hostile world. Philippians, then, is not directly about martyrdom. It is about the habits and dispositions needed to be a people capable of offering their lives back to God in the face of intense hostility with martyrdom as a possible consequence. In 1:28b Paul simply reminds the Philippians that manifesting these habits and dispositions in the face of opposition will always be misread by those who persecute the faithful. Nevertheless, such habits and dispositions are concrete material demonstrations of God's ultimate salvation.

---

40. See ibid., 76-77.

Transformation of Relationships:
Partnership, Citizenship, and Friendship in Philippi

G. Walter Hansen

Gerald Hawthorne observes that one purpose for Paul's letter to the Philippians was "to correct division within their ranks." Since Paul was aware that "the fellowship was fractured, not by doctrinal but by personal differences," his letter "encourages them to unity."[1] Professor Hawthorne has fulfilled the same purpose in his life: his influence on all he taught always strengthened friendships in Christ. With gratitude I dedicate this chapter to him with the hope that it will also promote unity in the church.

The topic of social relationships in the Pauline churches has generated extensive research, most of it subsequent to the publication of Hawthorne's commentary on Philippians (1983).[2] My purpose here is to build on the solid foundation of Hawthorne's work by interacting with some recent discussion of the social relationships of Philippian Christians. My work is organized around three of Paul's focal points: partnership (κοινωνία), citizenship (πολιτεία), and friendship (φιλία). Paul not only used but also radically transformed the contemporary concepts of partnership, citizenship, and friendship in order to rebuild the fractured fellowship of the church.

---

1. G. F. Hawthorne, *Philippians* (WBC 43; Waco: Word, 1983), xlviii.
2. For a review of research and bibliography see D. J. Tidball, "Social Setting of Mission Churches," *DPL* 883-92; S. C. Barton, "Social-Scientific Approaches to Paul," *DPL* 892-900.

Partnership — κοινωνία

Paul's use of the term "partnership" (κοινωνία) has been compared to two types of Roman partnerships: *societas,* a joint venture by consensus; and *communio,* common ownership.[3]

Societas: *A Joint Venture by Consensus*

A good place to enter the discussion of partnership is J. Paul Sampley's work, *Pauline Partnership in Christ.* Sampley claims that Paul described his relationship with the Philippian Christians in terms of a "*societas,* the Roman legal contract of consensual partnership."[4] Unlike a *societas* of family members that was established merely on the basis of direct lineage, a consensual *societas* was voluntarily set up by partners committed to a common goal. Persons of different social strata could become equal partners with one another in a consensual partnership. In keeping with the origins of *societas* in the family unit, partners considered themselves to be in a quasi-brotherly relationship. To establish this contractual relationship it was not necessary to have witnesses or a written document; a simple agreement was adequate. The *societas* continued as long as the agreement of its members was sustained. But disunity among the partners or a breach of trust could result in a court suit, a verdict of *infamia,* and a termination of the partnership.[5]

To substantiate his claim that Paul used the Roman concept of *societas* to depict his relationship with the Philippians, Sampley sets forth three lines of evidence. First, Paul's reference to the gift he had received from the Philippians (4:10-18) is stated in "commercial technical terms."[6] His phrase "I have received full payment" (4:18) is a commercial technical term used in a formal receipt to indicate payment received for work done

3. My partner, Simon Gathercole, has provided much of the research material for this section. For an expanded version of this section, see our book, G. W. Hansen and S. J. Gathercole, *Support the Progress of the Gospel: Christians as Partners and Stewards* (Grand Rapids: Eerdmans, forthcoming).

4. J. P. Sampley, *Pauline Partnership in Christ: Christian Community and Commitment in Light of Roman Law* (Philadelphia: Fortress, 1980), 51.

5. Ibid., 11-20.

6. Ibid., 53.

on behalf of a partnership.[7] Paul's commendation of their partnership with him in the "arrangement of giving and receiving" (4:15) is another instance of Paul's appropriation of the commercial language of bookkeeping used within a partnership. Paul's reference to the Philippians' "gift" (4:17) in response to his "need" (4:16) would be better understood if we interpreted "gift" as a *payment* for services rendered on behalf of the partnership and "need" as a *request* for remuneration legally due to Paul as the Philippians' partner in *societas*.[8]

Second, Roman citizens in the Roman colony of Philippi would have been familiar with the Roman institution of *societas*. In that context they would have interpreted Paul's use of κοινωνία in combination with commercial terminology to mean "the consensual partnership that in Roman law came to be known as *societas*."[9] As a result, they would have considered themselves as equal partners with Paul in a contractual relationship for the purpose of preaching the gospel.[10]

Third, Paul's frequent use of the verb φρονεῖν ("to think, set one's mind on, be minded") indicates that he had the Roman institution of consensual partnership in mind.[11] For Roman law stipulated that the contractual relationship of *societas* was binding only so long as the partners were in agreement, "of the same mind," regarding the terms and purposes of the partnership. The Roman legal traditions codified by Gaius stated that "a partnership *(societas)* lasts as long as the parties remain of the same mind *(in eodem sensu)*."[12] No wonder then that Paul called on all the Philippians to be "of the same mind" (2:2) and pleaded with the two women in disagreement to be "of the same mind" (4:2), since disagreement could terminate the partnership.[13]

Sampley's work provoked severe criticism. Greg Horsley insists that "Sampley's argument, attributing to κοινωνία and related words the same force as *societas* in its technical Roman legal context, is philologically un-

---

7. All translations are mine, unless otherwise indicated.

8. Sampley, *Pauline Partnership*, 54.

9. Ibid., 60.

10. Ibid., 61.

11. BAGD 866; Phil 1:7; 2:2 (twice); 2:5; 3:15 (twice); 3:19; 4:2, 10 (twice).

12. Sampley, *Pauline Partnership*, 15.

13. Ibid., 62-65; see also G. F. Hawthorne, "The Imitation of Christ: Discipleship in Philippians," in *Patterns of Discipleship in the New Testament* (ed. R. N. Longenecker; McMaster New Testament Studies; Grand Rapids: Eerdmans, 1996), 176.

sound."[14] Gerald Peterman points out that there is no evidence "that κοινωνία was used by Greek speakers as a label for the Roman association of *societas*."[15] Horsley also questions whether Paul's readers would have equated τὸ αὐτὸ φρονεῖν ("to think the same thing") with the technical, legal phrase *in eodem sensu*.[16] These criticisms demonstrate that Sampley pushed his argument too far by claiming that κοινωνία was used by Paul with the specialized, technical sense of the Roman institution of *societas*, a legally binding consensual partnership. Yet, despite this judgment, Horsley is willing to allow that "there are some points of overlap, undoubtedly," and that "Paul is applying a metaphor."[17] If we look for "some points of overlap" between Paul's use of κοινωνία and the Roman partnership of *societas*, we find four significant parallels: (1) the consensual nature of a partnership, (2) the goals of a partnership, (3) the equality of partners, and (4) the danger of disagreement between partners.

(1) Partnership was distinguished from patronage especially by its consensual nature. Whereas patronage was solicited by the prospective client and entailed obligations for both the patron and the client, partnership was a voluntary agreement to pursue a joint venture. Consensual partnership was also distinguished from the older, hereditary form of partnership by its voluntary nature.[18]

Paul emphasizes that his partnership with the Philippians was a voluntary association. His account of the history of the Philippians' support provides a record of unsolicited gifts (4:10-18). Paul explicitly denies any solicitation: "not that I sought the gift" (οὐχ ὅτι ἐπιζητῶ τὸ δόμα, 4:17). Yet he expresses his joy because his partners renewed their concern for him (4:10), and he commends them for demonstrating their concern by volunteering to provide support for him during his imprisonment (4:14). All their gifts from the early days of their partnership and throughout Paul's travels after he left Philippi had been a unique expression among all the Pauline churches of freely giving to support Paul's proclamation of the

---

14. G. H. R. Horsley, *New Documents Illustrating Early Christianity,* vol. 3, *A Review of the Greek Inscriptions and Papyri Published in 1978* (North Ryde: Macquarie University, 1983), 19.

15. G. W. Peterman, *Paul's Gift from Philippi: Conventions of Gift-exchange and Christian Giving* (SNTSMS 92; Cambridge: Cambridge Univ. Press, 1997), 125.

16. Horsley, *New Documents,* 3:19.

17. Ibid.

18. Sampley, *Pauline Partnership,* 12-13.

gospel (4:15-16). The entire account of the Philippians' support omits any reference to solicitation or obligation.

(2) Partnerships were established to achieve a specific goal. Roman legal texts list a number of purposes: joint ownership and management of a farm, pearl selling, cloak making, banking, maintaining a watercourse, horse selling, and teaching grammar.[19] The following example describes a partnership between Victor, a landowner, and Asianus, a builder: "Victor and Asianus had agreed that monuments should be erected with the exertions and skill of Asianus on land purchased with Victor's money. They would then be sold. Victor would recover his money with the addition of an agreed sum, and Asianus would get the rest in recognition of the hard work he had put into the partnership."[20]

Paul's thanksgiving for "partnership in the gospel" (1:5) points to a joint venture shared by Paul and the Philippians. In the context of Paul's focus on "defending and confirming the gospel" (ἐν τῇ ἀπολογίᾳ καὶ βεβαιώσει τοῦ εὐαγγελίου, 1:7) and his report of the circumstances that "served the advance of the gospel" (εἰς προκοπὴν τοῦ εὐαγγελίου ἐλήλυθεν, 1:12), "partnership in the gospel" must mean active participation with Paul in the propagation of the gospel message. The Philippians actively participated in the joint venture for the advance of the gospel by their prayers for Paul in his affliction (1:19), their suffering for their faith in Christ in the face of opposition (1:27-30), their radiant witness (2:15-16), the mission of Epaphroditus on their behalf to care for Paul's needs (2:25-30), and their financial support of Paul (4:10-18).

(3) Persons from different strata of society could become equal partners within a partnership. Even slaves who had no legal standing under Roman law were recognized as full partners with other persons of high social standing.[21]

Paul and the Philippians had equal standing in the partnership. Though Paul is clearly the founder and mentor of this community, he does not emphasize his apostolic authority as in other letters. In fact, Paul introduces himself and Timothy as "slaves of Christ Jesus" (δοῦλοι Χριστοῦ Ἰησοῦ, 1:1) and Epaphroditus as the Philippians' apostle (ὑμῶν δὲ ἀπόστο-

---

19. Justinian, *Digesta* 17.2.39-71.

20. Justinian, *Digesta* 17.2.52.7. Translation of T. Mommsen, P. Krueger, and A. Watson, *The Digest of Justinian* (4 vols.; Philadelphia: Univ. of Pennsylvania Press, 1985).

21. Sampley, *Pauline Partnership*, 17.

λον, 2:25). Paul's condemnation of selfish ambition and vain conceit and his appeal for humility are especially fitting in a letter written to strengthen a partnership of equal partners.

(4) Since a partnership was based on personal consensus, unresolved conflict between partners could easily lead to the termination of the partnership. Reinhard Zimmerman asserts that "if there were problems that could no longer be resolved in an amicable manner, the cooperation between the partners had lost its gravitational centre."[22]

Paul's partnership with the Philippians was endangered by disagreement. The theme of discord is prominent in this letter. The most explicit evidence of internal strife is Paul's specific appeal for the two influential women, Euodia and Syntyche, "to agree with each other in the Lord" (τὸ αὐτὸ φρονεῖν ἐν κυρίῳ, 4:2). Paul gives special recognition to "these women who have contended at my side in the cause of the gospel" (αἵτινες ἐν τῷ εὐαγγελίῳ συνήθλησάν μοι, 4:3); they were Paul's "fellow workers" (συνέργαι, 4:3). These women were clearly significant leaders in the partnership for the gospel. Paul names these two women, perhaps because their dispute gravely endangered the unity of the church and, hence, the future of the partnership with Paul.

Davorin Peterlin speculates that these two women were divided over support for Paul.[23] One of them withdrew her support and led her house church to follow her anti-Pauline position. This disagreement over Paul was the outcome of a conflict caused by different views on suffering and perfectionism. One group within the church viewed suffering as a sign of failure and developed perfectionist tendencies. This group, perhaps led by one of the women named in the text, viewed Paul's imprisonment as a failure to fulfill his mission. Hence any further support of Paul would not be a wise investment. As attractive as Peterlin's hypothesis is in many respects (e.g., it seems to provide plausible explanations for discord in the church), it suffers from a lack of clear evidence. Conflict within the church was certainly a problem Paul addressed. Conflict between the church and Paul is not so clearly indicated.

Another direct indication of disunity in the church is given in Paul's

22. R. Zimmerman, *The Law of Obligations: Roman Foundations of the Civilian Tradition* (Cape Town: Juta, 1990), 457.

23. D. Peterlin, *Paul's Letter to the Philippians in the Light of Disunity in the Church* (NovTSup 79; Leiden: Brill, 1995), 101-32.

instruction to "do everything without complaining or arguing" (πάντα ποιεῖτε χωρὶς γογγυσμῶν καὶ διαλογισμῶν, 2:14). This language echoes descriptions of Israel in the wilderness (Exod 15:24; 16:2, 7-9).[24] The complaining attitude of the Philippian Christians against their leaders paralleled the complaining by the Israelites against Moses.[25] Such divisive conduct fostered discord within the Philippian community and undermined the ability of the partnership to advance the gospel.

The problem of rivalry in the church is also mirrored in Paul's command to "do nothing out of selfish ambition or vainglory" (μηδὲν κατ' ἐριθείαν μηδὲ κατὰ κενοδοξίαν, 2:3). As we shall see in the following section on citizenship, the terms ἐριθεία and κενοδοξία have political overtones and refer to political discord. These terms point to political competition and factionalism in the Philippian church.

All of this evidence for discord in the church is a backdrop to Paul's appeals for unity: "Stand firm in one spirit, striving together with one soul" (στήκετε ἐν ἑνὶ πνεύματι, μιᾷ ψυχῇ συναθλοῦντες, 1:27); "Make my joy complete by being like-minded, having the same love, being one in spirit and purpose" (πληρώσατέ μου τὴν χαρὰν ἵνα τὸ αὐτὸ φρονῆτε, τὴν αὐτὴν ἀγάπην ἔχοντες, σύμψυχοι, τὸ ἓν φρονοῦντες, 2:2). The repetition of the appeal to "be like-minded" or, more literally, "think the same" (τὸ αὐτὸ φρονῆτε . . . τὸ ἓν φρονοῦντες . . . τὸ αὐτὸ φρονεῖν) in 2:2 and 4:2 highlights Paul's main concern. His desire that the Philippians will experience reconciliation, reunion, and harmony in their community is directly linked to his concern for the health of their partnership. Without unity there would be no future for the partnership.

These four parallels between Paul's use of κοινωνία and the Roman partnership of *societas* build a good foundation for understanding Paul's use of the metaphor of a joint venture by consensus for his relationship with the Philippians. True, we cannot be certain that Paul used κοινωνία as a technical, legal term referring to the Roman *societas*. Yet Paul's description of the partnership for the advance of the gospel (κοινωνία εἰς τὸ εὐαγγέλιον, 1:5) certainly sounds like a Roman *societas*: it was a voluntary association of equal partners in a joint venture for a specific goal. But Paul

24. P. T. O'Brien, *The Epistle to the Philippians: A Commentary on the Greek Text* (NIGTC; Grand Rapids: Eerdmans, 1991), 290-91.

25. M. Silva (*Philippians* [BECNT; Grand Rapids: Baker, 1992], 144n.80) suggests that the unusual reference to "overseers and deacons" (1:1) might be caused by this problem of complaints against leaders.

transformed the contemporary concept of a consensual business partnership in two significant ways.

First, the partnership is not merely between two parties (Paul and the Philippians) but triangular — it involves God, Paul, and the Philippians. God is the founder and guarantor of this partnership. After Paul declares his joy in his partnership with the Philippians (1:4-5), he expresses confidence that the partnership will last because God, who began the good work of the partnership in them, will carry it on to completion until the day of Jesus Christ (1:6). Of course, Paul's reference to the good work of God may be applied to the comprehensive work of salvation and the new creation. But Hawthorne is right to insist that this application is secondary to the primary, specific reference that Paul has in mind.[26] Paul connects the "good work" of God (1:6) directly to the "partnership in the gospel" (1:5). True, Phil 1:6 is widely interpreted as a basis for personal confidence: God began the work of salvation in me, and he will complete that work in me. But as true as that individualistic application of the text is, it misses the primary, corporate reference: God began the good work of the joint venture of advancing the gospel, and he will complete that work. Paul also underscores this confidence in the divine work as the basis for human work in 2:12-13. Here again, Hawthorne leads us in the right direction by interpreting 2:12 as an exhortation "not to individual but to corporate action, to cooperative effort in the common life together as a community."[27] In the context Paul speaks out against selfish ambition, looking out only for individual personal interests (2:3-4), and complaining and arguing (2:14). These attitudes have destroyed the unity of the church. Instead, the church should pursue unity (2:2) by humble service for one another (2:3-4), just as Christ Jesus took the form of a servant and humbled himself (2:5-8). So Paul's exhortation to the Philippians to "work out your salvation" (2:12) would most naturally be understood by them to be a call to work together for the unity of the church through humble service. Such work is empowered by God's work (2:13). The joint venture of the Philippians is really God's venture.

Second, Paul transforms the nature of the joint venture because the triangular nature of the partnership — God, Paul, and the Philippians — changes the expectations of reciprocity. In the Roman world social reci-

26. Hawthorne, *Philippians*, 21-20.
27. Ibid., 98.

procity would obligate the recipient of gifts to express gratitude by return-ing gifts.[28] If there was no reciprocal return, then the recipient changed status from a partner to a client.[29] But in Paul's view of his partnership with the Philippians, such expectations of reciprocity had to include God in the equation. Since God was in this partnership, Paul expected God to reciprocate and reward all gifts. The Philippians had met Paul's needs by their gifts (4:10-18). Now Paul tells them, "God will meet all your needs according to his glorious riches in Christ Jesus" (4:19). Since God had recip-rocated the gifts of the Philippians to Paul, Paul was under no obligation to do so. Thus a true partnership could be maintained even though there was no reciprocity on the human level.

Paul's use of the concept of *societas,* a joint venture by consensus, as a metaphor to describe his relationship with the Philippians points to his appreciation for their voluntary association with him in his mission to proclaim the gospel. He transforms the nature of this relationship by ex-pressing his confidence that his mission is, in reality, God's mission.

Communio: *Common Ownership*

For Paul the gravitational center for partnership was life in Christ. His ap-peal for unity was based on the common experience of life in Christ. "En-couragement from being united with Christ" (παράκλησις ἐν Χριστῷ) mo-tivated "being like-minded, having the same love, and being one in spirit and purpose" (2:1-2). The experience of life in Christ was realized by "fel-lowship with the Spirit" (κοινωνία πνεύματος, 2:1). Here Paul uses κοινωνία in the sense of *communio.* The *communio* of the Spirit motivated and em-powered the *societas,* the joint venture to proclaim the gospel. In other

---

28. See Peterman, *Paul's Gift,* 51-89.

29. By way of contrast to this partnership, see, e.g., the following on patron-client re-lationships: in Josephus cf. P. Spilsbury, "God and Israel in Josephus: A Patron-Client Rela-tionship," in *Understanding Josephus* (ed. S. Mason; JSPSup 32; Sheffield: Sheffield Academic Press, 1998), 172-91; and M. Strangelove, "Patron-Client Dynamics in Flavius Josephus' *Vita*: A Cross-disciplinary Analysis" (Ph.D. diss., Univ. of Ottawa, 1991); in the NT cf. D. A. DeSilva, "Exchanging Favor for Wrath: Apostasy in Hebrews and Patron-Client Relation-ships," *JBL* 115 (1996): 91-116; and H. Moxnes, "Patron-Client Relations and the New Com-munity in Luke-Acts," in *The Social World of Luke-Acts* (ed. J. H. Neyrey; Peabody, Mass.: Hendrickson, 1991), 241-68.

words the relationship of a joint venture *(societas)* is rooted in the relationship of *communio.*

Horsley asserts that "the true equivalent for κοινων- is *communis/ communitas.*"[30] While his restriction of the multivalent term κοινωνία to this one meaning is too reductionistic, it is true that the Latin versions of the NT normally translate κοινωνία with the term *communio.*[31] *Communio* was a partnership on the basis of common ownership of property either by joint purchase, inheritance, or gift. In a case of common ownership as a result of gift or inheritance, owners had not voluntarily entered into a joint venture as in *societas.* In such a case *communio* was a nonconsensual association and in this way differed from a *societas.* Common ownership did not mean that each partner owned part of the property, but that each partner was part owner of the whole property. A papyrus survives from 140 C.E. recording exactly this sort of ownership: "From Philiscus's plot of land, twelve shares from the eighteen common and undivided shares, in accordance with the partnership."[32]

What then were the rights of the part owner over his property in general, and over his particular share? These rights depended on the nature of the object: "the use of a bath, a colonnade, or a square is entire to each several person (for the use by others does not mean I use it less)." However, Justinian's *Digesta* goes on, "in the case of a hired or borrowed vehicle I have in effect a share of its use, because I cannot be everywhere the vehicle goes."[33] As for one's share, one could dispose of it at will, unlike in the partnership contract. With regard to profits drawn from common property, the *Digesta* gives the example of what proportion of fruit one is entitled to from shared land. The legal position is that the produce that a co-owner is entitled to is in proportion to the land, irrespective of who did the sowing.[34]

---

30. Horsley, *New Documents,* 3:19.

31. In all 19 instances of κοινωνία in the NT, the standard Latin translation is *communio,* except in 2 Cor 6:14, where κοινωνία is translated *societas.*

32. *P. Flor.* 41: εκ του φιλισκου κληρου αρουρας δε καδου απο κοινων και αδιαιρετων αρουρων ιη κατα κοινωνιαν . . . (from Hermopolis Magna), *Papiri greco-egizii. Papiri Fiorentini,* 3 vols. (ed. G. Vitelli and D. Comparetti; Supplementi Filologico-Storici ai Monumenti Antichi; Milan: U. Hoepli, 1906-1915). No breathings or accents are given in this edition.

33. Justinian, *Digesta* 13.6.5.15 (Ulpian citing Celsus the Younger). Translation of Mommsen, Krueger, and Watson.

34. Justinian, *Digesta* 22.1.25 (Julianus).

By God's grace believers in Christ were given not land but the Spirit. They had been placed by grace not in a house but in Christ. The *communio* of the Spirit and of life in Christ motivated and empowered the *societas,* the joint venture to proclaim the gospel. As partners of God's grace (1:7), the Philippian Christians were given a common ownership of the Spirit (2:1). It may seem odd to speak of owning the Spirit. But it is the best way to understand what Paul has in mind. In the grammatical construction of the phrase "partnership in the Spirit" (κοινωνία πνεύματος, 2:1), the genitive case of πνεύματος denotes the property held in common by the partnership. Perhaps an analogy may help. In the division of the land between the twelve tribes of Israel, the Levites were told that they were not given an inheritance of land because the Lord was their inheritance (Deut 10:9). Likewise, God has given the Spirit to the new people of God in Christ. The phrase "partnership in the Spirit" emphasizes the corporate rather than the individual experience of possessing the Spirit: all believers share together in the common gift of the Spirit. What all believers have in common is their life in the Spirit. This *communio,* this partnership in the Spirit, is the basis for "being like-minded (τὸ αὐτὸ φρονῆτε), having the same love, being one in Spirit" (2:2).

Partnership in the Spirit involves union with Christ. Paul's autobiographical statements offer a paradigmatic view of life in Christ: "I want to know Christ and the power of his resurrection and the fellowship of his sufferings" (τοῦ γνῶναι αὐτὸν καὶ τὴν δύναμιν τῆς ἀναστάσεως αὐτοῦ καὶ [τὴν] κοινωνίαν [τῶν] παθημάτων αὐτοῦ, 3:10). Paul was expressing his desire for continuous participation in the resurrection power of Christ and the sufferings of Christ rather than merely his recollection of his first encounter with Christ, who died and rose again for him. Thus we can take his statement here as a description of the entire process of being conformed to Christ throughout the whole of life rather than as a reference to the inaugural experience of identification with the death and resurrection of Christ in baptism.

The polarity of life in Christ joins together the experience of his resurrection power and participation in his sufferings. Here we see "participation" (κοινωνίαν) used to denote both the solidarity of all believers and the communion of human and divine. Participation in the sufferings of Christ cannot be seen as an individualistic enterprise reserved only for heroic martyrs like Paul. Paul told all Philippian Christians, "It has been granted to you on behalf of Christ not only to believe on him, but also to suffer for him, since you are going through the same struggle you saw I had, and now hear that I still have" (1:29-30). All believers are joined together as one in the participation in his sufferings, and this participation recapitulates and extends the life of Christ. The pattern of the life of Christ is reproduced in the life of all believers. As Christ emptied himself and humbled himself and was obedient unto death (2:7-8), so Paul emptied himself and humbled himself when he considered all his privileges as dung (3:7-8) and poured out his life like a drink offering (2:17). And so all believers are to humble themselves (2:3) and be obedient (2:12) and thus show their identification with Christ. Suffering is not meaningless; it is the sign of participation in the sufferings of Christ. Suffering is not in vain; it prefaces vindication.[35] Christ suffered and was vindicated (2:6-11). Paul suffered and anticipated vindication with Christ (3:14).

Citizenship — πολιτεία

A major question in the interpretation of Paul's command to "live worthily as citizens" (ἀξίως . . . πολιτεύεσθε, 1:27) is whether Paul is referring to Roman citizenship or heavenly citizenship.[36] According to Timothy Geoffrion, "Paul does not call the Philippians to live as good Roman citizens (against Brewer); rather he urges them to think in terms of what it means to be good citizens in the civil context and then apply that construct to their identity as Christians."[37] Geoffrion builds his position on Paul's explicit reference in 3:20 to "the Philippians' Christian identity as citizens of a heavenly commonwealth."[38] The opposite position is taken by Bruce Winter, who argues that Paul's focus in Phil 1:27 is "the civic responsibility of Christians in the public place."[39] Winter asserts that "Paul's use of a cog-

---

35. See L. G. Bloomquist, *The Function of Suffering in Philippians* (JSNTSup 78; Sheffield: JSOT Press, 1993), 196.

36. On this question see also S. E. Fowl, "Philippians 1:28b, One More Time," in the present volume.

37. T. C. Geoffrion, *The Rhetorical Purpose and the Political and Military Character of Philippians: A Call to Stand Firm* (Lewiston, N.Y.: Mellen Biblical Press, 1993), 48. For his reference to Brewer, see R. R. Brewer, "The Meaning of πολιτεύεσθε in Phil 1:27," *JBL* 73 (1954): 76-83.

38. Geoffrion, *Rhetorical Purpose*, 48.

39. B. W. Winter, *Seek the Welfare of the City: Christians as Benefactors and Citizens* (Grand Rapids: Eerdmans, 1994), 85.

nate in Phil. 3:20 does not influence the translation of the verb in 1:27."[40] A synthesis of both positions gives us a full picture. If we interpret "live as citizens" (1:27) in its context (1:27–2:18) and "commonwealth" (3:20) in its context (3:2-21), we will see that Paul is referring to the dual citizenship of the Philippians. Hawthorne steers us in the right direction by showing how Paul speaks of living as "a good citizen of an earthly state" and "as a good citizen of this new state," the heavenly commonwealth.[41] First, Paul appeals to the Philippians' sense of the civic responsibility of Roman citizens (1:27). Then he gives them the perspective of citizens of the commonwealth in heaven (3:20).

Roman Citizenship

Paul's call to unity — "stand firm in one spirit, striving together with one soul for the faith of the gospel" (στήκετε ἐν ἑνὶ πνεύματι, μιᾷ ψυχῇ συναθλοῦντες τῇ πίστει τοῦ εὐαγγελίου, 1:27b) — begins with the summons to "live as citizens in a manner worthy of the gospel of Christ" (Μόνον ἀξίως τοῦ εὐαγγελίου τοῦ Χριστοῦ πολιτεύεσθε, 1:27a).[42] This emphasis on good citizenship is unusual in the Pauline corpus. As many have observed in the interpretation of this phrase, the pride of Roman citizenship in Philippi, a Roman colony, probably inspired this emphasis.[43] Drawing on this civic pride, Paul advises the Philippians that good citizenship demands unity in the church. Conversely, disunity in their church association discredits the Christian witness of Roman citizens. Since non-Christian citizens of Philippi already oppose the gospel of Christ (1:28),[44] it is crucial to validate the witness to the gospel by unity in the church.

This close connection between harmonious relationships in the church and an effective witness in the public square is also the focus of 2:14-16. "Complaining and grumbling" against one another in the church

---

40. Ibid., 103n.45.

41. Hawthorne, *Philippians,* 56.

42. The political connotation of πολιτεύεσθε is omitted by major English versions: RSV, NRSV, NASB, NIV.

43. See R. P. Martin, *The Epistle of Paul to the Philippians* (TNTC; Grand Rapids: Eerdmans, 1959), 83: "Philippi, as a Roman colony, was intensely proud of its privileges."

44. See O'Brien (*Philippians,* 153) for support of the position that the opposition described in 1:28 comes from the citizens of Philippi outside the church.

must cease (2:14) in order to live as God's blameless children in the midst of a depraved generation (2:15), to "shine like stars in the world" (2:15). Thus Paul begins and ends this section of exhortation (1:27–2:18) with an appeal to Christians to strengthen their witness as citizens in the public domain by seeking unity in the private domain of their association as a church. As Winter points out, a theme of this section is the civic responsibility of Christians, which includes their responsibility to work for unity in their Christian community.[45]

Paul's appeal for the two quarreling women in the church to "agree with each other" (4:2) is directly related to his appeal for Roman citizens to "stand firm in one spirit" (1:27). His instruction to these women in the church to live in unity tells Christians how to fulfill their duties in the state. This interplay between Paul's concern for unity in the church and his exhortation to live as good citizens of the state builds on the same interrelationships as Aristotle describes in the opening section of his *Politica*.

Aristotle declares that the most supreme of all partnerships is the one that aims at the supreme of all goods and that "this is the partnership entitled the state, the political association" (αὕτη δ' ἐστὶν ἡ καλουμένη πόλις καὶ κοινωνία ἡ πολιτική).[46] The state as the supreme partnership is composed of the smaller partnerships of households and villages. Several households make a village; several villages make a state. Since the state is the goal of these smaller partnerships, it is the chief good.[47] Thus Aristotle's discussion of the ideal state and of the duties of citizenship necessarily includes a discussion of the ethics of family life and the education of children and women. "For since every household is part of a state, and these relationships are part of the household, and the excellence of the part must have regard to that of the whole, it is necessary that the education both of the children and of the women should be carried on."[48]

Of course, the Roman state was not the ideal state, the supreme partnership, or the goal of all partnerships from Paul's perspective. The goal of Paul's partnership with the Philippians was the advance of the gospel in the Roman state, and that goal was jeopardized by the disunity of Roman citizens in the church.

---

45. Winter, *Seek the Welfare*, 85.

46. Aristotle, *Pol.* 1.1.1. Translation of H. Rackham, *Aristotle, Politics* (LCL; Cambridge: Harvard Univ. Press, 1944).

47. Aristotle, *Pol.* 1.1.1-8.

48. Aristotle, *Pol.* 1.5.12. Rackham's translation.

The way that Paul connects his directive to be good citizens with his call for unity in the church (1:27) runs parallel to the concerns of Plutarch and Dio Chrysostom, two of Paul's near contemporaries.[49] Plutarch advises a young man entering politics how to handle the problem of discord in the public arena. The highest calling of a politician is "to see to it in advance that factional discord shall never arise" and "to instil concord and friendship in those who dwell together with him and to remove strifes, discords, and all enmity."[50] Plutarch warns that discord in the public sphere is not always caused by public disputes, "but frequently differences arising from private affairs and offenses pass thence into public life."[51]

Similarly, Dio Chrysostom frequently expresses his concern for the negative impact of discord on political life and his desire to encourage concord.[52] Ultimately, only the gods can promote unity and remove disunity in the life of a city. So Dio invokes their help, "that from this day forth they may implant in this city a yearning for itself, a passionate love, a singleness of purpose, a unity of wish and thought; and, on the other hand, that they may cast out strife and contentiousness and jealousy, so that this city may be numbered among the most prosperous and the noblest for all time to come."[53]

Paul begins his letter to the Philippians with his prayer report: "And this is my prayer: that your love may abound more and more in knowledge and depth of insight" (1:9). In the middle of his exhortations to remove discord and build unity, he expresses his confidence in God: "who works in you to will and to act according to his good purpose" (2:13).

Dio claims the struggle to be first, above all the rest, as the chief cause for discord. This ambition to occupy first place comes from vainglory, according to Dio: it "has come to be regarded as a foolish thing even in private individuals, and we ourselves deride and loathe, and end by pitying, those persons above all who do not know wherein false glory differs from the genuine."[54]

---

49. See Winter, *Seek the Welfare*, 86-93.

50. Plutarch, *Praec. ger. rei publ.* 824C-D. Translation of H. N. Fowler, *Plutarch's Moralia*, vol. 10 (LCL; Cambridge: Harvard Univ. Press, 1936).

51. Plutarch, *Praec. ger. rei publ.* 825A. Fowler's translation.

52. Winter, *Seek the Welfare*, 89.

53. Dio Chrysostom, *Or.* 39.8. Translation of H. Lamar Crosby, *Dio Chrysostom*, vol. 4 (LCL; Cambridge: Harvard Univ. Press, 1946).

54. Dio Chrysostom, *Or.* 38.28-29. Crosby's translation.

Paul, likewise, admonishes his readers to "do nothing out of selfish ambition or vainglory" (2:3). Rather than seeking only to advance themselves they should advance the interests of others (2:4). The way of Christ, who did not take advantage of first place but took the place of a servant, sets forth the exemplar for all relationships.

Heavenly Citizenship

Paul lifts the Philippians to a higher level of citizenship than Roman citizenship by his assertion that "our commonwealth (πολίτευμα) is in heaven" (3:20). This declaration needs to be understood in the context of Paul's reevaluation of his former status in the Jewish community (3:4-11). All of his excellent credentials and achievements as a Hebrew of Hebrews and a Pharisee he considers as rubbish in comparison to gaining Christ, being found in Christ, and knowing Christ. Paul sets forth this reevaluation immediately after warning his readers to be on guard against the persuasive tactics of the Jewish Christian Judaizers.[55] His readers were evidently being tempted to join the Jewish community. The theological argument of the Judaizers may have been that identification with the Jewish people through circumcision and obedience to the law would be the only way for Gentile Christians to be fully included in the people of God. But Paul overthrows their theological argument by setting forth a complete reversal of titles. Names that the Jews applied to Gentiles are now applied to the Judaizers: "dogs, evil workers, mutilators of the flesh" (3:2). And the name that the Jews claimed for themselves is applied to his Gentile converts: "For we are the circumcision" (3:3). This Jewish title for the true people of God is claimed by Paul for those "who worship by the Spirit of God and who glory in Christ Jesus" (3:3).

Gentile Christians would also have been especially tempted by the political argument for membership in the Jewish community in Philippi. When they became Christians, they withdrew from their civic obligation to worship Roman gods and to participate in the imperial cult. Loyal citizens of Philippi would have taken their confession that Jesus is Lord as a

---

55. See M. Tellbe, "The Sociological Factors behind Philippians 3.1-11 and the Conflict at Philippi," *JSNT* 55 (1994): 99-100; R. Jewett, "Conflicting Movements in the Early Church as Reflected in Philippians," *NovT* 12 (1970): 382-87.

seditious rejection of the lordship of Caesar. No wonder then that Paul spoke so clearly about the opposition and suffering that the Philippian Christians would face for their faith in Christ (1:28-30). But all the opposition and persecution for their withdrawal from the imperial cult of Philippi could have been averted by joining the Jewish community. A Jewish community, sometimes referred to as a Jewish "commonwealth" (πολίτευμα),[56] was exempt from participation in the imperial cult. In fact, the Jewish community was granted protection by the Roman state to practice their own religion. By joining the Jewish community (πολίτευμα), the Gentile converts could have enjoyed the same freedom to withdraw from the religious functions of the city and to practice their new religion. "Join our commonwealth and you will be safe," argued the Judaizers. But their political argument receives the same response as their theological argument: Paul again turns the tables on them. First, Jewish judgments against Gentiles are applied to the Judaizers: "their destiny is destruction, their god is their stomach, and their glory is their shame. Their mind is on earthly things" (3:19). Then the title that the Jewish people claimed for their community (πολίτευμα) is applied with a transformed meaning to the Christian community. The Christian commonwealth is not merely an earthly state that provides protection in a hostile world. Instead "our commonwealth (πολίτευμα) is in heaven" (3:20).[57]

Since the Philippian Christians have their citizenship in the heavenly πολίτευμα, they are not to find their safety by joining the earthly Jewish πολίτευμα.[58] As Mikael Tellbe puts it, "it is not in keeping with knowing Christ to seek identity with the Jewish community as a means of mitigating the conflict and escaping suffering."[59] Knowing Christ involves "sharing in his sufferings, becoming like him in his death" (3:10). True followers of

---

56. See Tellbe, "Sociological Factors," 116n.72; A. T. Lincoln, *Paradise Now and Not Yet: Studies in the Role of the Heavenly Dimension in Paul's Thought with Special Reference to His Eschatology* (SNTSMS 43; Cambridge: Cambridge Univ. Press, 1981), 98-100.

57. Tellbe, "Sociological Factors," 118: "Paul's references to the true circumcision (Phil. 3.3) and the heavenly πολίτευμα (3.20) may thus reverse positions that were ascribed to the Jewish community." Cf. Lincoln's argument (*Paradise*, 97) that 3:20 echoes the Jewish claim to heavenly citizenship; this is based on a questionable mirror reading of the text and a few references from Philo.

58. Note the contrast between earthly and heavenly in Phil 3:19-20: "Their mind is on earthly things. But our commonwealth is in heaven."

59. Tellbe, "Sociological Factors," 119-20.

Christ do not seek to escape the sufferings of identification with Christ by political means; they endure this suffering by the "power of his resurrection" (3:10) with the hope "to attain to the resurrection from the dead" (3:11).

Paul sets forth both present and future aspects of the commonwealth in heaven.[60] Believers are already enjoying the reality of the common-wealth in heaven by their union with Christ. Believers are also eagerly ex-pecting the future consummation of salvation when the Savior will come from heaven. Then the Lord Jesus Christ "will transform our lowly bodies so that they will be like his glorious body" (3:21). Now we experience the "body of our humiliation" (τὸ σῶμα τῆς ταπεινώσεως ἡμῶν); then he will transform our body to "be like his glorious body" (σύμμορφον τῷ σώματι τῆς δόξης αὐτοῦ, 3:21).

Thus Paul transforms the relationships of the Philippian believers by prescribing how to express their dual citizenship. To live as Roman citizens in a manner worthy of the gospel they must be united in their Christian community; their witness as Roman citizens must not be negated by dis-unity in the church. As heavenly citizens they must be identified with the Lord of their commonwealth in heaven; their present suffering as heavenly citizens cannot be mitigated by identification with the Jewish common-wealth.

Allegiance to the Lord Jesus is the basis of unity among heavenly citi-zens. That unity confirms their witness in the world where they live as Ro-man citizens. But that allegiance to the Lord Jesus also causes them to suf-fer persecution where Roman citizens pledge allegiance to Lord Caesar. So Roman citizens who are also citizens of the commonwealth in heaven "ea-gerly await a Savior from there, the Lord Jesus Christ" (3:20). That com-mon hope is the basis for Paul's exhortation to his friends to "stand firm in the Lord" (4:1; cf. 1:27) and to "agree with each other in the Lord" (4:2; cf. 2:2). Dual citizenship in Rome and in the heavenly commonwealth re-quires and inspires harmonious friendship in the church.

Friendship — φιλία

Paul used such terms as "community" (κοινωνία), "thinking the same thing" (τὸ αὐτὸ φρονεῖν), and being of "one soul" (μία ψυχή) to describe

60. See Lincoln, *Paradise*, 101-3.

"partnership" and "citizenship." But the meaning of these terms cannot be restricted to the semantic fields of economic or political language. As L. Michael White points out, the language of partnership and that of citizenship have a "common social grounding in the technical language of friendship (φιλία)."[61] Classical authors from Aristotle to Plutarch depicted various economic and political associations in terms of the larger category of friendship language.[62] "All friendship," says Aristotle, "involves community," and "friendship appears to be the bond of the state."[63] In Philippians Paul uses friendship language in ways remarkably similar to classical essays on friendship in the Greco-Roman world.[64]

John Fitzgerald suggests that "throughout Philippians Paul is seeking to elevate the Philippians' understanding of friendship and place it on a higher plane."[65] Paul's aim, as expressed in his opening prayer, is that their "love may abound more and more in knowledge and depth of insight" (1:9). In his closing exhortation (4:8-9), two commands define two ways to elevate friendship: (a) "think" about virtue; and (b) "practice" Paul's example.

Thinking about Virtue

Paul seeks to establish virtue as the basis of his friendship with the Philippians by listing eight virtues in 4:8: "whatever is true, whatever is noble, whatever is right, whatever is pure, whatever is lovely, whatever is admirable — if there is any virtue (ἀρετή) and anything praiseworthy — think about such things." According to Aristotle, "the perfect form of friendship is that between the good, and those who resemble each other in virtue."[66]

---

61. L. M. White, "Morality between Two Worlds: A Paradigm of Friendship in Philippians," in *Greeks, Romans, and Christians: Essays in Honor of Abraham J. Malherbe* (ed. D. L. Balch, E. Ferguson, and W. A. Meeks; Minneapolis: Fortress, 1990), 211.

62. Ibid., 212.

63. Respectively, Ἐν κοινωνίᾳ μὲν οὖν πᾶσα φιλία ἐστίν, *Eth. nic.* 8.12.1; ἔοικε δὲ καὶ τὰς πόλεις συνέχειν ἡ φιλία, *Eth. nic.* 8.1.4.

64. See J. T. Fitzgerald, "Philippians in the Light of Some Ancient Discussions of Friendship," in *Friendship, Flattery, and Frankness of Speech: Studies on Friendship in the New Testament World* (ed. J. T. Fitzgerald; NovTSup 82; Leiden: Brill, 1996), 141-56.

65. Ibid., 157.

66. Aristotle, *Eth. nic.* 8.3.6: Τελεία δ᾽ ἐστὶν ἡ τῶν ἀγαθῶν φιλία καὶ κατ᾽ ἀρετὴν ὁμοίων. Translation of H. Rackham, *Aristotle, The Nicomachean Ethics* (LCL; Cambridge: Harvard Univ. Press, 1934).

Since "virtue is a permanent quality,"[67] friendships based on virtue are permanent. Cicero also points to virtue as the priority of true friendship: "let this be ordained as the first law of friendship: Ask of friends only what is honourable; do for friends only what is honourable."[68]

Two types of inferior friendship described by Aristotle are friendship based on utility and friendship based on pleasure.[69] Friends who look only for some benefit to be gained from their friendship have a friendship of utility. Friends who enjoy each other only because they enjoy the pleasure of witty people have a friendship of pleasure. In these types of friendship, friends do not love each other for being what they are in themselves but for some benefit or pleasure to be gained through the friendship. Since utility and pleasure change with time, "friendships of this kind are easily broken off, in the event of the parties themselves changing, for if no longer pleasant or useful to each other, they cease to love each other."[70]

The Philippians were apparently in danger of basing their friendships on utilitarian self-interest. Paul counsels them, "each of you should look not only to your own interests" (2:4). He warns them against "complaining and arguing" (2:14). According to Aristotle, "complaints and recriminations occur solely or chiefly in friendships of utility, as is to be expected."[71] Furthermore, Paul did not want the Philippians to view his acceptance of their financial support as evidence that their friendship with him was based on the benefit he enjoyed. True, their friendship was useful to Paul for financial support in their partnership for the advance of the gospel. But to guard against viewing their friendship in terms of utility, Paul directs them to "think" about virtue as the basis of their friendship (4:8).[72]

Paul seems eager to correct any conception that he had utilitarian motives for his friendship with the Philippians. He insists on his self-sufficiency: "I have learned to be self-sufficient whatever the circumstances" (ἐγὼ γὰρ ἔμαθον ἐν οἷς εἰμι αὐτάρκης εἶναι, 4:11). He was not looking to his friends with self-interest, depending on them to meet his

---

67. Aristotle, *Eth. nic.* 8.3.6: ἡ δ' ἀρετὴ μόνιμον. Rackham's translation.
68. Cicero, *Amic.* 13.44. Translation of W. A. Falconer, *Cicero, De Senectute, De Amicitia, De Divinatione* (LCL; Cambridge: Harvard Univ. Press, 1923).
69. Aristotle, *Eth. nic.* 8.3.1-5.
70. Aristotle, *Eth. nic.* 8.3.3. Rackham's translation.
71. Aristotle, *Eth. nic.* 8.13.2. Rackham's translation.
72. See Fitzgerald, "Philippians," 157-60.

needs. Friendship based on need often received severe criticism in the ancient discussions of friendship. True friendship is expressed by one who is "self-sufficient" or "content" (αὐτάρκης).[73] According to Cicero, "it is far from being true that friendship is cultivated because of need; rather, it is cultivated by those who are most abundantly blessed with wealth and power and especially with virtue, which is man's best defence; by those least in need of another's help; and by those most generous and most given to acts of kindness."[74] Moreover, Cicero asserts, "to the extent that a man relies upon himself and so is fortified by virtue and wisdom that he is dependent on no one and considers all his possessions to be within himself, in that degree is he most conspicuous for seeking out and cherishing friendships."[75]

Paul, of course, stresses that his self-sufficiency was really empowered by Christ: "I can do everything through him who gives me strength" (4:13). Christ's empowerment gives independence from a utilitarian focus in friendship. Even though gifts can be given and received as an expression of true friendship, there is no dependence on friends to meet needs. For as Paul assures the Philippians themselves, "My God will meet all your needs according to his glorious riches in Christ Jesus" (4:19).

When personal needs are met by dependence on God, there is the freedom to develop permanent friendships. If friends are viewed only as a resource for meeting personal needs, they will no longer be friends if they cannot meet those needs or if those needs are already met. Friendships of utility and pleasure do not outlast the benefits or pleasures received from the friend. But friendships of virtue are permanent because virtuous persons keep growing in virtue and love their friends in and for themselves.[76]

Practicing Selfless Love

By calling his readers to think about the list of virtues in 4:8, Paul is obviously elevating his friendship with the Philippians to the level of a friend-

73. See A. J. Malherbe, "Paul's Self-Sufficiency (Philippians 4:11)," in *Friendship, Flattery,* ed. Fitzgerald, 124-39.

74. Cicero, *Amic.* 14.51. Falconer's translation.

75. Cicero, *Amic.* 9.30. Falconer's translation.

76. Cf. S. Stern-Gillet, *Aristotle's Philosophy of Friendship* (Albany: SUNY Press, 1995), 66-67.

ship of virtue. But thinking about a common list of Hellenistic virtues is not the final goal of friendship. Paul connects the command to think with the command to practice: "Whatever you have learned or received or heard from me, or seen in me, put into practice" (4:9). Hence the virtues are to be defined in light of the paradigm presented by Paul. What the Philippians learned, received, heard, and saw in their association with Paul was the message of Christ in word and act. Throughout his letter to the Philippians, Paul emphasizes that his preoccupation is preaching and living the gospel message. Even in a Roman prison, all that matters is the progress of the gospel (1:12-14).

When Paul summarizes the message of Christ in the famous Christ-hymn, he stresses the self-giving and self-humbling love of Christ: "he emptied himself . . . he humbled himself" (2:7-8).[77] Christ did not take advantage of his position of equality with God (2:5-6), but emptied and humbled himself to take the place of a slave and die on the cross (2:7-8). As a result of his voluntary humiliation, God exalted and honored him (2:9-11). White asserts rightly that Paul has used the Christ-hymn to present "a new moral paradigm. The model of selflessness, the willingness to give up one's own status and share another's troubles, is the ultimate sign of true friendship."[78] Set as it is in a section of the letter regarding social relations, the hymn guides the reader to "adopt towards one another, in your mutual relations, the same attitude which was found in Christ Jesus" (2:5).[79]

Stephen Fowl's helpful work on the function of Phil 2:6-11 explains how the hymn presents an *exemplar* to the Philippians. As an exemplar, the hymn does not present a one-to-one relationship between the behavior of Christ and the Philippians' situation. The hymn is not a step-by-step pattern for the imitation of Christ. "If the Philippians are to let the events presented in vv. 6-11 guide their common life, they will have to draw an anal-

---

77. On this hymn see O. Hofius, *Der Christushymnus Philipper 2,6-11* (2d ed.; WUNT 17; Tübingen: Mohr [Siebeck], 1991); R. P. Martin, *Carmen Christi: Philippians ii.5-11 in Recent Interpretation and in the Setting of Early Christian Worship* (SNTSMS 4; Cambridge: Cambridge Univ. Press, 1967; repr. with updated preface and bibliography [Grand Rapids: Eerdmans, 1983]; repr. with updated preface and bibliography as *A Hymn of Christ* [Downers Grove, Ill.: InterVarsity Press, 1997]).

78. White, "Morality," 212; cf. Hawthorne, "Imitation," 163-79.

79. This is C. F. D. Moule's translation in "Further Reflexions on Philippians 2:5-11," in *Apostolic History and the Gospel: Biblical and Historical Essays Presented to F. F. Bruce* (ed. W. W. Gasque and R. P. Martin; Grand Rapids: Eerdmans, 1970), 265.

ogy from the events in vv. 6-11 to their situation."[80] To draw an analogy requires an understanding of the similarities and differences between the narration of the Christ-event in 2:6-11 and the situation faced by the Philippians. Thus v. 5 is a call "to apply to their communal life the precedent that is theirs by virtue of the fact that they are in Christ."[81]

This interpretation of the Christ-hymn as an exemplar transcends the false dichotomy of the debate between the ethical and the kerygmatic readings of the hymn. On the one hand, the verbal parallels between the moral instruction to the Philippians and the narration of the Christ-event stress the ethical implications. Believers are exhorted to "do nothing from selfish ambition or conceit, but in humility regard others as better than yourselves" (2:3) just as Christ "did not regard equality with God as something to be exploited, but emptied himself . . . and being found in human form he humbled himself" (2:6-8).[82] On the other hand, the narration of the incarnation, crucifixion, exaltation, and universal lordship of Christ infinitely surpasses a mere ethical model that can be imitated by any human behavior. As an exemplar, the hymn presents the story of Christ in ways that are somewhat parallel to and yet vastly different from the story of the church. Thus, as Peter O'Brien suggests, "it is better to speak of Paul's ethics as having to do with 'conformity' to Christ's likeness rather than an 'imitation' of his example."[83]

Conformity to Christ's precedent for true friendship is the plot of Paul's own story in chapter 3. As a result of his conversion, he did not regard his exalted status, all his credentials and achievements, as something to be exploited, but as garbage (3:4-9). Thus in his own way "he emptied himself . . . and humbled himself" by his identification with Christ. Paul sought to share in Christ's sufferings and be *conformed* to his death (3:10) with the anticipation of also being *conformed* to the glorious resurrected body of Christ (3:11, 21). All of the self-emptying and humbling in Paul's story was for the purpose of pouring out his life as a sacrifice on behalf of

---

80. S. E. Fowl, *The Story of Christ in the Ethics of Paul: An Analysis of the Function of the Hymnic Material in the Pauline Corpus* (JSNTSup 36; Sheffield: Sheffield Academic Press, 1990), 92.

81. Ibid., 92.

82. On this see esp. G. F. Hawthorne, "In the Form of God and Equal with God (Philippians 2:6)," in *Where Christology Began: Essays on Philippians 2* (ed. R. P. Martin and B. J. Dodd; Louisville: Westminster John Knox, 1998), 96-110.

83. O'Brien, *Philippians*, 262.

his friends, the Philippians (2:17). His story serves as an exemplar, a precedent, for them. Hence he urges them to "join with others in following my example" and to "take note of those who live according to the pattern we gave you" (3:17).

Two of those especially noted by Paul for their pattern of selfless love are Timothy and Epaphroditus. Timothy is distinguished for having a genuine interest in the welfare of others, quite unlike so many who "are looking out for their own interests" (2:20-21). Epaphroditus "almost died for the work of Christ, risking his own life" to serve others (2:30). Selfless love is demonstrated by this willingness to risk one's own life in the interests of one's friends. In this way is the gospel proclaimed: not merely by word, but also by sacrificial giving of oneself. For that was the story of Christ, "who emptied himself by taking the form of a slave" (2:7). All who are in Christ will express, as Paul did, the "affection of Christ" (1:8) for their friends.

Conclusion

Hawthorne directs us to consider the parallels between John 13:3-17 and Phil 2:6-11.[84] Both texts portray Jesus setting aside his divine glory to give himself in humble, self-sacrificing service (John 13:4-5; Phil 2:6-8). Both texts refer to the subsequent exaltation of Jesus as Lord (John 13:13; Phil 2:9-11). And both texts explicitly call the community to follow the Lord Jesus by demonstrating his kind of humble service (John 13:14-17; Phil 2:1-5). In the context of the same upper room discourse in John, Jesus calls his disciples his friends (φίλοι, 15:14-15) and challenges them: "Greater love has no one than this, to lay down one's life for one's friends" (15:13). Friendship (φιλία) in Christ is demonstrated and developed in the work of partnership (κοινωνία), in the public square of citizenship (πολιτεία), and above all in selfless love supremely expressed and always empowered by Christ.

---

84. Hawthorne, *Philippians*, 78, and "Imitation," 170-71.

Ephesus and the Literary Setting of Philippians

Frank S. Thielman

Those of us who made our first, halting attempts at exegesis under Jerry Hawthorne's kind but exacting eye know how unwilling he is to accept the status quo at face value — to swallow traditional assumptions simply because they have always been presupposed. It came as no surprise, therefore, when, in his 1983 commentary on Philippians, Jerry broke with scholarly convention and argued that Paul wrote the letter not from Rome or Ephesus but from Caesarea.[1] Although relatively rare, the position was old, going back at least to Heinrich Eberhard Gottlob Paulus in 1799, and had some distinguished advocates, including Ernst Lohmeyer and J. A. T. Robinson.[2]

Hawthorne argued his case with characteristic care, but scholarly debate remains focused on two alternatives for the provenance of Philippians: Rome or Ephesus. Rome has been the well-established tradition at least since the second century for what have seemed like obvious reasons. Paul was imprisoned in a praetorium when he wrote the letter (1:13), and, as Chrysostom says, in Paul's time that is what Caesar's palace was

---

1. G. F. Hawthorne, *Philippians* (WBC 43; Waco: Word, 1983), xli-xliv.

2. Paulus suggested this idea in his 1799 *Osterprogramm* at Jena entitled "De tempore scriptae prioris ad Timotheum atque ad Philippenses epistolae Paulinae." See also E. Lohmeyer, *Die Briefe an die Philipper, an die Kolosser, und an Philemon* (8th ed.; KEK; Göttingen: Vandenhoeck & Ruprecht, 1930), 3; J. A. T. Robinson, *Redating the New Testament* (Philadelphia: Westminster, 1976), 60-61.

called.[3] What better place to find "Caesar's household" (4:22), moreover, than in Rome?

At the end of the nineteenth century, however, Ephesus began to emerge as a serious rival to the dominant position.[4] Apparently already in 1894 Paul Feine was suggesting to his students in the Protestant faculty at Vienna that linguistically and theologically Philippians belonged with the older letters of Paul, letters that came from the period of his struggle with Judaizing Christianity.[5] In 1897 Adolf Deissmann incorporated into his lectures to students in the theological seminary at Herborn the thesis that Colossians, Philemon, and Ephesians were written from Ephesus.[6] Then, in 1908, in *Licht vom Osten,* Deissmann claimed that the question of Philippians' provenance ought to be reopened since evidence from inscriptions and papyri revealed that the expressions "praetorium" and "Caesar's household" should not limit the answer to Rome. In a note he commented that documentary evidence existed for the presence of Caesar's slaves in Ephesus.[7]

3. John Chrysostom, *Hom. Phil.* 2. In the introduction to his homilies on Philippians he says similarly that Paul calls "the palace of Nero a 'praetorium.'" This is apparently not correct, since the common term for Caesar's palace in Rome during Paul's time seems to have been *palatium.* On this see J. B. Lightfoot, *St. Paul's Epistle to the Philippians* (4th ed.; London: Macmillan, 1896), 100-101; and Lohmeyer, *Philipper,* 41n.5. Lightfoot and other advocates of the Roman hypothesis since his time have argued that the term *praetorium* refers not to Caesar's palace, however, but to a body of men — the praetorian guard — that was the emperor's personal body guard and therefore stationed in Rome. See Lightfoot, *Philippians,* 101-4.

4. For brief histories of the scholarly discussion about the provenance of Philippians, see P. Feine, *Die Abfassung des Philipperbriefes in Ephesus mit einer Anlage über Röm. 16,3-20 als Epheserbrief* (Gütersloh: Bertelsmann, 1916), 7-13; W. Michaelis, *Die Gefangenschaft des Paulus in Ephesus und das Itinerar des Timotheus: Untersuchungen zur Chronologie des Paulus und der Paulusbriefe* (Gütersloh: Bertelsmann, 1925), 1-8; W. Michaelis, *Einleitung in das Neue Testament: Die Entstehung, Sammlung und Überlieferung der Schriften des Neuen Testaments* (Bern: Buchhandlung der Evangelischen Gesellschaft, 1946), 205-6; G. S. Duncan, *St. Paul's Ephesian Ministry: A Reconstruction with Special Reference to the Ephesian Origin of the Imprisonment Epistles* (New York: Scribner's, 1930), 59-65.

5. Feine, *Abfassung des Philipperbriefes,* 12-13. On Feine's career see R. Morgan, "Feine, Paul," *DBI* 1:388.

6. See Deissmann's comment on this, in response to a reviewer, in the 1909 edition of *Licht vom Osten: Das Neue Testament und die neuendeckten Texte der hellenistisch-römischen Welt* (3d ed.; Tübingen: Mohr [Siebeck], 1909), 171n.1; ET: *Light from the Ancient East* (trans. L. R. M. Strachan; repr. Grand Rapids: Baker, 1965), 237n.1.

7. A. Deissmann, *Licht vom Osten: Das Neue Testament und die neuendeckten Texte der hellenistisch-römischen Welt* (Tübingen: Mohr [Siebeck], 1908), 166; ET: *Light,* 238n.3.

Meanwhile, in 1900 Heinrich Lisco produced an extraordinary book in which he argued not only that Philippians was written from Ephesus but that all the captivity epistles, including 2 Timothy, came from an imprisonment there and were produced within a few weeks.[8] The book was widely, and perhaps justly, ignored, but Deissmann's weighty support for reopening the question appears to have exercised an enormous influence.[9] After 1908, scholarly studies began appearing in quick succession advocating an Ephesian provenance for Philippians, all mentioning Deissmann, and some speaking specifically of his influence. Martin Albertz argued the position in 1910; Feine included it in his *Einleitung in das Neue Testament* in 1913 and dedicated a book to the subject in 1916.[10] Wilhelm Michaelis argued for it in 1925, and George S. Duncan in 1930.[11]

A hundred years later, however, at least among English-speaking commentators, interest in Ephesus is waning. The commentaries by Bruce, Silva, O'Brien, Witherington, Fee, and Bockmuehl all opt for Rome, and none but O'Brien even considers Ephesus a serious rival.[12] The sentiments of Moisés Silva are representative:

Deissmann fully embraced the thesis that Philippians was written from Ephesus in "Zur ephesinischen Gefangenschaft des Apostels Paulus" (in *Anatolian Studies Presented to Sir William Ramsay* [ed. W. H. Buckler and W. M. Calder; Manchester: Manchester Univ. Press, 1923], 122), and this conviction was then incorporated into the 4th ed. (1923) of *Licht vom Osten* (the basis of the ET). The phrase οἱ ἐκ τῆς καίσαρος οἰκίας refers to slaves and freed slaves who served the emperor either as part of his entourage of personal attendants in Rome or as part of the more widely dispersed group of servants who supervised his financial affairs. Both groups were proud of the status that their work in the emperor's service accorded them, and they often added to their names an abbreviation showing that they were slaves or freedmen of the emperor. See P. R. C. Weaver, *Familia Caesaris: A Social Study of the Emperor's Freedmen and Slaves* (Cambridge: Cambridge Univ. Press, 1972), 1-8.

8. H. Lisco, *Vincula Sanctorum: Ein Beitrag zur Erklärung der Gefangenschaftsbriefe des Apostels Paulus* (Berlin: F. Schneider, 1900).

9. See the summaries and critiques of Lisco's book in M. Albertz, "Über die Abfassung des Philipperbriefs des Paulus zu Ephesus," *TSK* 83 (1910): 555-56; Michaelis, *Gefangenschaft des Paulus,* 1; and Duncan, *St. Paul's Ephesian Ministry,* 59-61. Deissmann was careful to distance himself from Lisco and wanted readers to know that although he published his ideas later than Lisco, he had developed them independently. See the 1909 edition of *Licht vom Osten,* 171n.1; ET: *Light,* 237n.1; and "Zur ephesinischen Gefangenschaft," 122.

10. Albertz, "Über die Abfassung"; P. Feine, *Einleitung in das Neue Testament* (Leipzig: Quelle & Meyer, 1913), 50-52; idem, *Abfassung des Philipperbriefes* (1916), 12-13.

11. Michaelis, *Gefangenschaft des Paulus;* Duncan, *St. Paul's Ephesian Ministry.*

12. F. F. Bruce, *Philippians* (Good News Commentary; San Francisco: Harper & Row,

We have no positive evidence either for an imprisonment of Paul in Ephesus or for the presence of a praetorian guard in a senatorial province. . . . To be sure, no one disputes the likelihood that Paul may have been imprisoned during his lengthy stay in that city; and the possibility that a praetorian guard could have been stationed in Ephesus must be left open. One must wonder, however, how much weight can be placed on a theory that builds possibility upon likelihood.[13]

This sentiment is understandable in light of the way the case for Ephesus has been argued, particularly by Lisco in Germany and by several English-speaking advocates since his time. Many elements of that case are specious and ought to be rejected. Once rejected, however, they should not be allowed to taint the persuasive literary case that can be made for placing Philippians 3, and therefore the rest of the letter, in close proximity to Galatians on one hand and 1 Corinthians on the other. This literary affinity of Philippians 3 with Paul's earlier correspondence convinced Feine by 1894 that Philippians was written earlier than Paul's Roman imprisonment. After Deissmann helped Feine to overcome his doubts about locating "Caesar's household" in Ephesus, these affinities became for Feine a major reason for preferring Ephesus as the provenance of the letter.[14] The literary argument was also critical to the case of Albertz in 1910.[15] This argument for Ephesus remains the most persuasive way to make the case. In subsequent years it has unfortunately been obscured by a fog of less plausible arguments against Rome and for Ephesus.

1983); M. Silva, *Philippians* (BECNT; Grand Rapids: Baker, 1992); P. T. O'Brien, *The Epistle to the Philippians* (NIGTC; Grand Rapids: Eerdmans, 1991); B. Witherington III, *Friendship and Finances in Philippi: The Letter of Paul to the Philippians* (Valley Forge, Pa.: Trinity Press International, 1994); G. D. Fee, *Paul's Letter to the Philippians* (NICNT; Grand Rapids: Eerdmans, 1995); M. Bockmuehl, *The Epistle to the Philippians* (BNTC; Peabody, Mass.: Hendrickson, 1998). Continental commentators on the letter lean just as decidedly in favor of Ephesus. See, e.g., J. Gnilka, *Der Philipperbrief* (HTKNT; Freiburg: Herder, 1976); J.-F. Collange, *The Epistle of Saint Paul to the Philippians* (trans. A. W. Heathcote; London: Epworth, 1979); U. Müller, *Der Brief des Paulus an die Philipper* (THKNT 11/I; Leipzig: Evangelische Verlagsanstalt, 1993).

13. Silva, *Philippians,* 8-9.

14. See Feine, *Abfassung des Philipperbriefes,* 12-43.

15. Albertz, "Über die Abfassung," 563-66, 583-93. This does not mean that the details of Feine's or Albertz's arguments are always convincing, but that the method they followed is sound.

Specious Arguments against Rome

The most commonly advanced argument against a Roman origin for Philippians is the distance between Rome and Philippi. The argument claims that the distance between the two cities was too great to accommodate the four journeys between Paul and the Philippians that had already taken place and the three others that Paul envisions.[16] All of this traveling, the argument goes, demands that we bring Paul and the Philippians closer together than a Roman imprisonment will allow.

As advocates of a Roman provenance often point out in their defense, however, the number of journeys envisioned in Philippians, particularly the number surrounding Epaphroditus's illness, have been exaggerated. It is not necessary to think that Epaphroditus became ill after arriving at Paul's location, that word then made its way to Philippi about the illness, and that the Philippians sent word back that they were worried. As Paul A. Holloway has recently pointed out, Paul's praise of Epaphroditus's willingness to risk his life to deliver the Philippians' gift (2:29-30) implies that Epaphroditus became ill on his way to Paul and heroically pressed on with his assignment, undeterred by this adversity.[17] We can easily imagine a traveling companion or sympathetic passerby taking word of Epaphroditus's illness back to Philippi, and then Epaphroditus assuming that the church would be worried about him when they got the news.

The difficulty of travel in the ancient world has also been exaggerated. Great weight has been placed on the enormous distance between Philippi and Rome. The journey — "370 [miles] from Philippi to Dyracchium, 100 across the Adriatic from Dyracchium to Brundisium, and 360 from Brundisium to Rome" — would take a month, it is said.[18] But why should this be

---

16. See, e.g., C. R. Bowen, "Are Paul's Prison Letters from Ephesus?" *AJT* 24 (1920): 112-35; Deissmann, "Zur ephesinischen Gefangenschaft," 123-26; G. S. Duncan, "A New Setting for St. Paul's Epistle to the Philippians," *ExpTim* 43 (1931-32): 9; P. Benoit, *Les épîtres de Saint Paul aux Philippiens, à Philémon, aux Colossiens, aux Éphésiens* (3d ed.; Paris: Cerf, 1959), 12; Gnilka, *Der Philipperbrief*, 21; Collange, *Philippians*, 16; H. Koester, *Introduction to the New Testament* (2 vols.; Berlin and New York: de Gruyter, 1982), 2:131; Müller, *An die Philipper*, 16-17.

17. P. A. Holloway, *Consolation in Philippians: Philosophical Sources and Rhetorical Strategy* (SNTSMS 112; Cambridge: Cambridge University Press, 2001), 25-26.

18. Bowen, "Ephesus?" 125. Bowen's figures come from Lightfoot, who was himself a proponent not only of the Roman provenance of the letter but also of dating the letter early in Paul's imprisonment there. Lightfoot is correctly unimpressed by the hindrances that dis-

the route? Lionel Casson, in his engaging study of travel in the ancient world, observes that between May and October, when the skies were generally clear and the Etesian winds from the north were steady, "the voyage from Rome to Corinth or back involved both fair and foul winds and consequently took between one and two weeks."[19] The trip from Corinth to Philippi would not have been arduous. As for traveling conditions in general,

> the first two centuries of the Christian Era were halcyon days for a traveller. He could make his way from the shores of the Euphrates to the border between England and Scotland without crossing a foreign frontier, always within the bounds of one government's jurisdiction. A purseful of Roman coins was the only kind of cash he had to carry; they were accepted or could be changed everywhere. He could sail through any waters without fear of pirates, thanks to the emperor's patrol squadrons. A planned network of good roads gave him access to all major centres, and the through routes were policed well enough for him to ride them with relatively little fear of bandits. He needed only two languages: Greek would take him from Mesopotamia to Yugoslavia, Latin from Yugoslavia to Britain. Wherever he went, he was under the protection of a well-organized, efficient legal system.[20]

In light of all this, it is difficult to understand the gravity with which the death sentence is pronounced upon a Roman provenance for the letter in the name of distance. Silva's bluntness is fully justified. This argument, he says, "should be dropped from further consideration."[21]

In addition to the argument from distance, opponents of a Roman provenance for Philippians frequently mention the letter's statements about Paul's travel plans. Such arguments usually take two forms. One

---

tance poses to his position and observes: "The sea route was more uncertain: but under favourable circumstances would be quicker than the journey by land, whether the course was by the gulf of Corinth or round the promontory of Malea" (Lightfoot, *Philippians*, 38n.1).

19. L. Casson, *Travel in the Ancient World* (Baltimore: Johns Hopkins Univ. Press, 1994), 152. Casson does not say how he arrives at this figure, but in his account of *Ships and Seamanship in the Ancient World* (Baltimore: Johns Hopkins Univ. Press, 1995), 284n.56 and 290n.87, he observes that Apollonius sailed from Corinth to Puteoli in four and a half days under favorable conditions and from Puteoli to Ostia with unfavorable winds in two and a half. The total trip, therefore, took a week. See Philostratus, *Vit. Apoll.* 7.10, 16.

20. Casson, *Travel in the Ancient World*, 122.

21. Silva, *Philippians*, 7. Cf. Bockmuehl, *Philippians*, 32.

form focuses on Paul's future relationship with the Philippians, and specifically on his comment that he hopes to see the Philippians soon (1:24-25; 2:24). By the time Paul wrote Romans, it is pointed out, he felt that he had completed his work in the east and planned to shift his efforts to Spain (Rom 15:23-24, 28).[22] This argument has little merit, however, since we know from Paul's letters that he sometimes changed his stated plans. He was notorious for this in Corinth (cf. 1 Cor 16:5-7 with 2 Cor 1:15-24); and, if Philemon was written from a Roman imprisonment, we have evidence that Paul abandoned his plan to travel from Rome to Spain and intended to go back to the east instead (Phlm 22).

The second form of this argument focuses on Paul's past relationship with the Philippians. The letter gives the impression, it is said, that at the time of writing Paul had not visited the church since its founding (1:30; 4:15-16); yet, if the letter were from Rome, he would have been in Philippi at least once since then (Acts 20:1-6). It is difficult to see, however, why Paul's claim that the Philippians are now enduring the same struggle they saw him endure in Philippi (1:30) and his reference to their generosity in the early days of his ministry in Macedonia (4:15-16) should imply that he has not visited the city since that time. Paul may have looked back to the founding moment of the church, skipping over other visits, because the circumstances of that initial visit paralleled his concerns in the letter: to console the Philippians in the midst of their suffering and to thank them for their gift. The impression that one scholar receives from these statements, then, will be countered by another scholar's failure to see the point, and so this argument too can carry little weight.[23]

With these arguments against the traditional position before them, it is no wonder that many recent commentators have remained unconvinced that they should abandon the ancient ascription of this letter to a Roman imprisonment. Some arguments in favor of Ephesus have proved no less attractive, and again for good reason.

---

22. See, e.g., Deissmann, "Zur ephesinischen Gefangenschaft," 127; Bowen, "Ephesus?" 122-23; Duncan, "Setting," 8-9; Müller, *An die Philipper*, 17.

23. These texts are sometimes coupled with 2:12, 22-24, and 1:26, but again the claim that they imply a single past visit to Philippi is subjective. They indicate only a past relationship, not the number of times that Paul has visited the Philippians. See Gnilka, *Philipperbrief*, 20; Müller, *An die Philipper*, 16. C. J. Roetzel ("Philippians, Letter to the," *DBI* 2:281) claims that Paul speaks of making a second visit in the letter, but Paul is not this explicit. He only says that he will come πάλιν πρὸς ὑμᾶς (1:26).

Specious Arguments in Favor of Ephesus

Advocates of Ephesus have often damaged their case with illogical argumentation and faulty historical method. Three kinds of problems are particularly prevalent.

First, although arguments that Philippians *could* have been written from Ephesus are not arguments that it *was* written from that place, they are sometimes presented this way. Thus arguments that Paul may have been imprisoned in Ephesus, that a contingent of the praetorian guard may have been stationed there, and that "Caesar's household" may refer to Caesar's civil servants outside of Rome are sometimes said to "support" the view that Paul was in Ephesus when he wrote.[24] They do not support the view, but they do allow it; and if they allow Ephesus, they certainly allow Caesarea also. Indeed, if the presence of the right civic and legal conditions for the production of Philippians counts in favor of one provenance over another, then Hawthorne is right to prefer Caesarea — we have explicit literary evidence from within a few decades of Paul's letter not only that Caesarea had a praetorium, but that Paul was imprisoned there (Acts 23:35).[25]

Second, advocates of Ephesus have frequently tried to buttress their case with unreliable historical data or implausible historical reconstructions. For example, in an effort to supply evidence that Paul was imprisoned in Ephesus, advocates of this hypothesis have frequently taken Paul's claim that he "fought with wild beasts in Ephesus" (1 Cor 15:32) literally. The memory of this incident, they sometimes claim, is preserved in apocryphal tales of Paul's adventures with the lions in the Ephesian arena from the *Acts of Paul* (2d century), Hippolytus (3d century), and Nicephorus Callistus Xanthopoulos (14th century).[26] It is true that the *Acts of Paul*, upon which both Hippolytus and Nicephorus Callistus depend, speaks of an Ephesian imprisonment, but this romance also records a cordial conversation between Paul

---

24. See, e.g., R. P. Martin, *Philippians* (NCB; Grand Rapids: Eerdmans, 1980), 48, 51.

25. See Hawthorne, *Philippians*, xli; and the comments of F. F. Bruce, "St. Paul in Macedonia 3: The Philippian Correspondence," *BJRL* 63 (1980-81): 264.

26. Lisco, *Vincula Sanctorum*, 2; Bowen, "Ephesus?" 120-21. Hippolytus (*Comm. Dan.* 3.29) does not mention Ephesus, but since he says that a lion was loosed upon Paul and lay down at his feet, he appears to have knowledge of the story about Paul's Ephesian adventures in the *Acts of Paul*. Nicephorus Callistus recounts the tale in his *Historia Ecclesiastica* 2.25 (PG 145:822).

and the beast with whom he fought — they were, it turns out, old friends. The *Acts of Paul* also informs us that the city ruler Hieronymous, apparently in his frustration at the lion's unwillingness to kill Paul, sent "many beasts" into the arena to finish the job, and archers to slay the uncooperative lion. A miraculous hailstorm ended the spectacle, and Hieronymous, painfully injured on the ear by a hailstone, cried out to God for help. None of this inspires confidence in the historical value of these sources.[27]

As Abraham J. Malherbe has demonstrated, Paul's reference to fighting with wild beasts in Ephesus is a convention of moral philosophy, not to be taken literally.[28] The mistake of taking the reference literally, as the entertaining fiction of the *Acts of Paul,* Hippolytus, and Nicephorus Callistus reveals, goes back centuries. These castles are constructed in thin air, however, and arguing from them that early Christians knew of an actual Pauline imprisonment in Ephesus is risky business indeed. It is no wonder that those who have studied such arguments in preparing their commentaries on Philippians have fled for refuge to Rome or Caesarea.

In an effort to propose a plausible Ephesian setting for Philippians, more than one author has created a virtual historical novel. Duncan, for example, constructs an elaborate series of events to explain how Paul landed in an Ephesian prison on capital charges. The Ephesian Jews, he says, may have charged Paul with temple robbery since Jewish Christians were probably no longer enthusiastic about sending their annual contributions to the Jerusalem temple. This was an offense of great seriousness because, as Josephus tells us, the right of Jews to make the annual temple offering was guaranteed in Ephesus by a special edict (*Ant.* 16.6.4 §§167-68). The cry went up to throw Paul to the beasts (1 Cor 15:32), and although Paul was finally acquitted and set at liberty, he had been made a prisoner (Phil 1:13) and his life threatened (1:18b-26). What is the evidence for all

---

27. See the "Acts of Paul," in E. Hennecke, *New Testament Apocrypha* (ed. W. Schneemelcher; trans. ed. R. McL. Wilson; 2 vols.; Philadelphia: Westminster, 1963-65), 2:372-73.

28. A. J. Malherbe, "The Beasts at Ephesus," *JBL* 87 (1968): 71-80. Contrast Albertz, "Über die Abfassung," 558; Bowen, "Ephesus?" 115 (who claims that the expression is "almost certainly to be taken literally"); Duncan, "Setting," 8. G. D. Fee (*The First Epistle to the Corinthians* [NICNT; Grand Rapids: Eerdmans, 1987], 770-71) wonders how Paul could have lived to tell about the experience if the expression is literal. Perhaps, suggests Albertz ("Über die Abfassung," 558), the beasts refused to eat Paul. Although an advocate of an Ephesian imprisonment, Gnilka (*Philipperbrief,* 22) correctly denies that 1 Cor 15:32 should be used to support this view.

this? In Acts 19:37 the town clerk dismisses a charge of temple robbery against Paul. This is a slender thread indeed from which to hang such a complicated web of events.[29]

Third, advocates of Ephesus often build their case on top of other hypothetical reconstructions that, although accepted by some scholars, must remain uncertain. Several champions of the Ephesian hypothesis believe that Romans 16 was originally sent to Ephesus and that Paul's references in that passage to Prisca and Aquila, who "laid their own necks down for my life" (16:4), and to Andronicus and Junia "my fellow prisoners" (16:7) support an Ephesian imprisonment for Paul.[30] Some believe that Philippians is a composite document and that the multiplication of letters from Paul to Philippi demands a location for Paul that was geographically closer to the recipients than Rome will allow.[31] John Ferguson observes that the so-called hymn in Phil 2:6-11 shares some lexical and conceptual similarity with the Fourth Gospel. Relying on the hypothesis that John's Gospel originated in Ephesus, he then claims that Philippians was probably written in Ephesus, where the author of the Fourth Gospel and Paul had access to the same hymn.[32] As hypothesis is placed upon hypothesis, the student of Philippians who reads this literature begins to have the uneasy feeling that he or she has entered a house of cards.

Although these arguments are nearly always mixed with more plausible reasons for preferring Ephesus, they are so far-fetched and so faulty from the perspective of historical method that they seem to have tainted the whole case for Ephesus in the eyes of those who prefer Rome or Caesarea. As Richard I. Pervo has said in a different connection, "Granted that all is possible, the task of the historian is . . . to elucidate what seems most probable."[33] Advocates of an Ephesian provenance for Philippians

---

29. Duncan, *St. Paul's Ephesian Ministry,* 26-46; Duncan, "Setting," 8.

30. See, e.g., Bowen, "Ephesus?" 115; Duncan, *St. Paul's Ephesian Ministry,* 68. Albertz ("Über die Abfassung," 562) and Müller (*An die Philipper,* 19-20) correctly point out that even if Rom 16 was sent to Rome the reference to Prisca and Aquila risking their necks for Paul may be relevant since this may have happened in Ephesus (cf. 2 Cor 1:8-10). Cf. Duncan, *St. Paul's Ephesian Ministry.*

31. Collange, *Philippians,* 16-17.

32. J. Ferguson, "Philippians, John and the Traditions of Ephesus," *ExpTim* 83 (1971): 85-87.

33. R. I. Pervo, review of B. Witherington III, *The Acts of the Apostles: A Socio-Rhetorical Commentary,* JBL 118 (1999): 366.

have too often settled for what is possible but improbable. Evidence exists, however, that makes an Ephesian provenance for the letter probable.

Literary Evidence for Ephesus from Philippians 3

Philippians 3 has posed several literary puzzles for interpreters, but two stand out as particularly vexing. First, is Paul attacking a threat that is present among the Philippians at the time he writes? Second, why does he attack two apparently incompatible tendencies: an error that places emphasis on the Jewish law (3:2) and an error that seems opposed to common ethical restrictions (3:18-19)?

A Present Threat?

The first puzzle originates from Paul's suddenly strident tone in 3:2, halfway through one of his more placid letters. "Well, my brothers and sisters, rejoice in the Lord," he says; "to write the same things to you is not irksome for me, and is safe for you" (3:1). Then suddenly, "Watch out for the curs! Watch out for the criminals! Watch out for the cutters!" (βλέπετε τοὺς κύνας, βλέπετε τοὺς κακοὺς ἐργάτας, βλέπετε τὴν κατατομήν, 3:2). The rhetoric is so heated that many interpreters simply assume Paul is speaking of a threat present in Philippi.[34] Others have recognized that the tone of Philippians generally differs from the tone of letters in which Paul is opposing an active threat from false teachers.[35] This second view of the passage is probably correct. When Paul remembers the Philippians in prayer, he is thankful and joyful (1:3-4). They are his partners in the grace that God had given to him (1:5, 7; 4:14-16), his joy and crown (4:1). In letters where Paul faces active opposition to his ministry and gospel, however, the strident tone is scattered throughout the letter. The best example of this is Galatians (Gal 1:6-9; 3:1; 4:11, 15-16; 5:7; 6:17), but 1 Corinthians (1 Cor 3:1-4; 4:8, 18; 6:5a; 11:17) and 2 Corinthians (2 Cor 3:1; 5:12; 11:19-20; 12:1, 20-21; 13:1-10) show the same tendency.

Those who hold this second view, however, must explain why Paul's

---

34. See, e.g., M. R. Vincent, *A Critical and Exegetical Commentary on the Epistles to the Philippians and to Philemon* (ICC; Edinburgh: T&T Clark, 1897), 92-93; Silva, *Philippians*, 4, 173; and the survey of scholarship on this issue in Fee, *Philippians*, 290n.18.

35. See, e.g., Bruce, *Philippians*, 79; Fee, *Philippians*, 289-90.

tone shifts at 3:2. Many have concluded that 3:2 reveals an editorial seam in the letter and that chapter 3 is part of a separate letter to Philippi written at a time when Judaizers threatened the church there. The threat was not present when the other one or two letters of which Philippians is composed were written, and so the change in tone is fully understandable.[36] For those who hold the more probable position that Philippians is a unified document, the change in tone is more difficult to explain, particularly if the document is thought to originate from Rome. Lightfoot thought that when Paul reached the end of chapter 2 in the composition of the letter he became aware that Judaizers in Rome had hatched some fresh plot to annoy him.[37] Others have tried to explain the triple βλέπετε of 3:2 not as a strong warning but as an admonition to "consider" the bad example of the Jews, arguing that when βλέπειν is used as a warning it is always followed by μή or ἀπό.[38] Still others believe that the Judaizers were a persistent irritant to Paul over many years, and that he issues a general warning to the Philippians against these tiresome enemies of the gospel. "Such people have been 'dogging' him for over a decade," says Fee; "he has long ago had it to the bellyful with these 'servants of Satan.'"[39]

None of this works very well. It is unclear why Paul would swat in Philippi a mosquito that was buzzing around his head in Rome. Moreover, the threefold repetition of βλέπετε and the alliteration in κ (κύνας . . . κακούς . . . κατατομήν) are powerful rhetorical features and make it likely that βλέπετε is a verb of warning in 3:2, despite the deviation from customary usage.[40]

Most importantly, it is improbable that Paul, writing from Rome

36. See the survey of partition theories in L. Bormann, *Philippi: Stadt und Christengemeinde zur Zeit des Paulus* (NovTSup 78; Leiden: Brill, 1995), 108-18; and the cogent case for the letter's unity in Holloway, *Consolation*, 7-33.

37. Lightfoot, *Philippians*, 69-70; cf. A. Plummer, *A Commentary on St. Paul's Epistle to the Philippians* (London: Robert Scott Roxburghe House, 1919), 68.

38. G. B. Caird, *Paul's Letters from Prison* (Oxford: Oxford Univ. Press, 1976), 132-33; Hawthorne, *Philippians*, 124-25. Both Caird and Hawthorne rely on G. D. Kilpatrick, "ΒΛΕΠΕΤΕ Philippians 3₂," in *In Memoriam Paul Kahle* (ed. M. Black and G. Fohrer; BZAW 103; Berlin: Töpelmann, 1968), 146-48. Kilpatrick draws no conclusions about the identity of Paul's opponents in Phil 3. He argues only that βλέπετε must mean "see, look at, consider," rather than "beware of," since "there is no example of βλέπειν used with the accusative demonstrably with the meaning 'beware of'" (147).

39. Fee, *Philippians*, 294-95. Cf. Bruce, *Philippians*, 79.

40. See Silva, *Philippians*, 172.

around 62 C.E., would resurrect the Judaizers whom he had battled years earlier in Galatia and issue a warning about them to the Philippians.[41] There is no basis for the claim that the Judaizers had been "'dogging' him for over a decade" other than the supposition that Philippians was written from Rome. The other epistles written from Paul's first Roman imprisonment (Colossians, Philemon, and Ephesians) betray no concern over Judaizers, and this has always been an embarrassment for adherents of the Roman provenance of Philippians.[42] Indeed, prior to Paul's Roman imprisonment he had smoothed over tensions between himself and Jewish Christians in Jerusalem (Acts 21:17-26). The Jewish opposition to Paul at this point in his work originated with unbelieving Jews, not with Judaizing Christians.[43]

Two Errors or One?

The second puzzle — why Paul attacks nomism in 3:2 and antinomianism in 3:18-19 — has yielded a bewildering array of explanations. Does Paul attack a single enemy, either Jews, Jewish Gnostics, Jewish Christian Gnostics, or Jewish Christians? Or does he attack two separate enemies, Jews or Jewish Christians on the one hand, and some variety of antinomian Christians on the other?[44]

41. Fee (*Philippians,* 37) dates the letter toward the end of Paul's Roman imprisonment and believes that the imprisonment itself occurred between 60 and 62 C.E.

42. Scholars who consider Colossians, Philemon, and Ephesians authentic usually separate them from Philippians chronologically by placing them at the opposite end of Paul's Roman imprisonment. See the discussion in Lightfoot, *Philippians,* 30-46. Many scholars attribute Colossians and Ephesians to a pseudepigrapher. The unusual compositional style and theological emphases of these letters unite them with one another but separate them from Paul's undisputed correspondence. On the hypothesis that Colossians, Philemon, and Ephesians comprise a unique trilogy of authentic Pauline correspondence from his Roman house imprisonment, however, it is easy to see why they resemble one another stylistically and theologically but stand apart from Paul's other letters.

43. Assuming that Paul is ultimately responsible for the Pastorals, he does mention the threatening presence of "people from the circumcision" in Titus 1:10. These false teachers, however, are not likely to be Galatian-style Judaizers. Like the false teachers censured in 1 Tim 1:3-7, they are probably Jews with gnostic tendencies. On this see F. Thielman, *Paul and the Law: A Contextual Approach* (Downers Grove, Ill.: InterVarsity Press, 1994), 230-33.

44. See the survey of approaches in J. J. Gunther, *St. Paul's Opponents and Their Background: A Study of Apocalyptic and Jewish Sectarian Teachings* (NovTSup 35; Leiden: Brill, 1973), 2.

The notion that Paul is attacking a single enemy in both passages fails to do justice to Paul's description of his opponents in each passage. The strident tone of 3:2, the focus on circumcision in 3:2b-3a, and the concern with confidence in the flesh in 3:3b-4 bear a striking similarity to Paul's concerns in Galatians, making a reference to Jewish Christian "agitators" like those in Galatians probable.[45] Paul's warning in 3:18-19, however, seems ill suited to his Judaizing opponents. Although they could certainly be described as "enemies of the cross of Christ" (v. 18; cf. Gal 5:11; 6:12), he would not describe them as worshiping their belly and glorying in their shame. These terms most naturally refer to self-indulgence in matters of food and sex.[46] The Judaizers had many faults, but teaching this approach to life (περιπατεῖν, 3:18) was not among them.

To whom, then, do these epithets refer? Among those who believe that Paul is writing from Rome, the answer to this question is vague. Lightfoot claims that Paul spoke against those who perverted his gospel into a license for sin.[47] Plummer wonders whether Paul had encountered antinomian teaching in Rome and wanted to warn the Philippians of it.[48] Fee believes that Paul may be warning the Philippians of itinerant Christians who are teaching self-indulgence and whose presence in Philippi from time to time was assured by the city's prominent position on the Via Egnatia.[49]

45. Paul's tone in Galatians is strident (Gal 1:6; 3:1; 4:12, 21; 5:4, 10, 12; 6:12-13). The Galatian agitators' chief demand was for circumcision (2:3; 5:2, 6, 11; 6:12-13, 15). Paul associates the Galatian agitators' "other gospel" with "the flesh" (3:3; 4:23, 29; 6:12-13). Arguments that in Philippians Paul is referring to Jews generally, or to Jewish Gnostics, have not persuaded most scholars.

46. To find here a biting reference to dietary laws and circumcision of the *membrum virile* goes far beyond the evidence for two reasons. First, no one has produced convincing literary analogies for such uses of κοιλία and αἰσχύνη. On this see Fee, *Philippians*, 371n.36 and 372n.39. Second, although we can imagine Paul saying that glorying in circumcision was shameful (if that meant placing justifying confidence in the procedure), he would not say that by glorying in circumcision the Judaizers were glorying in something of which they should instead be ashamed. For Paul, circumcision itself was either an *adiaphoron* (Gal 5:6; 6:15; 1 Cor 7:19) or something of positive value (Rom 4:11). On the other hand, making a god of one's belly would be a natural way to refer to self-indulgence in matters of food, and in Rom 1:20-25 Paul connects inappropriate sexual gratification with shame. See Fee, *Philippians*, 372, 373n.43.

47. Lightfoot, *Philippians*, 70, 151, 154-55.

48. Plummer, *Philippians*, 82.

49. Fee, *Philippians*, 366.

A Literary Solution

By locating Philippians late in Paul's Ephesian ministry, however, one can offer a plausible solution to both puzzles. When Paul wrote 3:2-11, his conflict with Judaizers in Galatia was still fresh in his mind. The agitators had not yet traveled to Philippi, but in case they had plans to go there, Paul warned the Philippians against them in 3:2-3 and then reminded them in 3:4-11 of his conversion from the kind of trust in the Mosaic law that the Judaizers were advocating. Paul had told them the story of his conversion before (τὰ αὐτὰ γράφειν ὑμῖν ἐμοὶ μὲν οὐκ ὀκνηρόν), but in light of the Galatians' near capitulation to this error, the account was worth repeating (ὑμῖν δὲ ἀσφαλές, 3:1).

Paul's conversion story inevitably stressed the abandonment of the former objects of his confidence in order that he might gain Christ (3:8), be found in him (3:9), know him (3:10), and, like him, attain the resurrection of the dead (3:11). But, with sweat still on his brow from wrestling with the Corinthians, Paul is eager that nothing he has said here should be misinterpreted to mean that he has already been perfected (οὐχ ὅτι ἤδη . . . τετελείωμαι, 3:12). The Corinthians had been puffed up (1 Cor 4:6, 8, 18-19) and proud of their "knowledge" (8:1-3), apparently despising Paul's "foolish" message of the cross (1:18–2:5). In light of this, Paul had to inform them that they were not among the mature (ἐν τοῖς τελείοις) but were still babes in Christ, fleshly rather than spiritual (2:6; 3:1-3).

Their spiritual immaturity was also apparent in their approach to food and sex. Some of the upper-class Corinthian youth had reached the period of life after adulthood but before marriage when, by Roman custom, they were free to live self-indulgently. Like their compatriots, they saw nothing wrong during this period of life in participating in the unholy trinity of eating, drinking, and sex at cultic meals sponsored by civic leaders (1 Cor 6:12-20; 8:10; 10:7-10; 15:32-33).[50] "Everything is permitted to me" (6:12) and "food for the stomach (τῇ κοιλίᾳ) — the stomach (ἡ κοιλία) for food" (6:13) were their watchwords. The sanctity of the church generally had reached such a low ebb that its members were taking pride in a scan-

---

50. Here I follow the reconstruction of the Corinthian situation offered in B. W. Winter, *After Paul Left Corinth: The Influence of Secular Ethics and Social Change* (Grand Rapids: Eerdmans, 2001), 86-93. I am grateful to Dr. Winter for allowing me to see an early draft of this work. See also A. Booth, "The Age for Reclining and Its Attendant Perils," in *Dining in a Classical Context* (ed. W. J. Slater; Ann Arbor: Univ. of Michigan Press, 1991), 105-20.

dalous sexual aberration, intolerable even among unbelieving Gentiles. "Ought you not rather be ashamed (ἐπενθήσατε)?" Paul told them (5:1-2). Unless they took steps toward church discipline and personal discipline, he said, they would not inherit God's kingdom (6:9).

Paul's warning to the Philippians, who were themselves steeped in Roman culture, reads like a condensed version of all this. He had often told them to avoid these kinds of errors, but when he wrote the letter, his advice took on special urgency: "For, as I have often told you and now say weeping, many live as enemies of the cross of Christ. Their end is destruction. Their god is the belly (ἡ κοιλία), and their glory is their shame (τῇ αἰσχύνῃ). Their mind is on earthly things" (Phil 3:18-19).

Paul's antidote to these false notions recalls the argument of 1 Cor 15:42-49. There Paul had opposed the Corinthian view that because the body will not be resurrected it ought to be indulged (15:29-34). Against this Paul had said that the mortal bodies of believers, fashioned like Adam's body from the dust of the earth, would undergo a transformation in the future to become like the heavenly body of the resurrected Jesus. This transformation, he had said, ought to be an incentive to avoid immoral behavior: "And even as we have borne the image of the man of dust, so let us bear the image of the man of heaven" (15:49).[51] In Philippians Paul followed the same strategy. We can avoid imitating the example of those whose minds dwell on earthly things, he said, by thinking about our heavenly citizenship and the Savior who rules over our heavenly πολίτευμα: "For our homeland exists in heaven, whence we also await a Savior — the Lord Jesus Christ, who will transform the body of our humility to make it like his glorious body, according to the effective work of the one who is also able to subject all things to him" (Phil 3:20-21). Acting like the Roman citizens of Philippi would lead to destruction. The common view in that context was that the body was mortal and ought therefore to be indulged. If the Philippians lived as citizens of the heavenly realm, however, and remembered that their bodies were immortal, they would avoid the error that the culture around them made. The Corinthian Christians had fallen into this trap, and Paul wanted the Philippians to escape the Corinthians' mistake.

51. Here I accept the aorist hortatory subjunctive φορέσωμεν rather than the future indicative φορέσομεν in NA²⁷. The subjunctive is clearly the right reading on external grounds, and once the ethical thrust of the chapter is understood (15:10, 30-34, 58), internal criteria support it as well. On the text-critical element of the question see Fee, First Corinthians, 794-95.

Philippians 3, then, makes sense if it was written around the time of Galatians and 1 Corinthians. Since 1 Corinthians definitely originated in Ephesus (16:8), and many scholars believe that Galatians comes from Ephesus also, Philippians was perhaps written from that city as well.[52]

A Fatal Objection?

F. F. Bruce, one of the staunchest defenders of the Roman provenance of Philippians, conceded that an Ephesian imprisonment for Paul was "highly probable."[53] He also believed that Philippians 3 was best understood as an attack on Galatian-style Judaizers on one hand and Corinthian-style antinomians on the other.[54] In addition, he was willing to say, as advocates of the Ephesian provenance of Philippians had pointed out for decades, that "Caesar's household" was scattered throughout the empire.[55] The fatal objection to locating the composition of the letter in Ephesus, he said, was Paul's "use of the loanword *praetorium*" in 1:13. Paul's transcription of this Latin term into Greek, Bruce argued, reveals that the apostle was giving the word its technical sense. It means either the headquarters of the praetorian guard or, by extension, the praetorian guard itself, and "there is no known instance of its use for the headquarters of a proconsul, the governor of a senatorial province, such as Asia was at this time."[56]

Advocates of Ephesus have commonly cited in their favor epigraphic evidence that places praetorians in Ephesus around the time of Paul, and

---

52. On the Ephesian provenance of Galatians see, e.g., the second-century Marcionite prologue, "hos apostolus revocat ad fidem veritatis scribens eis ab Epheso"; M.-J. Lagrange, *Saint Paul épître aux Galates* (2d ed.; Ebib; Paris: LeCoffre, 1925), xxvii-xxviii; A. Wikenhauser, *New Testament Introduction* (trans. J. Cunningham; New York: Herder & Herder, 1958), 380; E. F. Harrison, *Introduction to the New Testament* (Grand Rapids: Eerdmans, 1964), 263; Koester, *Introduction,* 2:123-26; H. Schlier, *Der Brief an die Galater* (6th ed.; KEK; Göttingen: Vandenhoeck & Ruprecht, 1989), 18; F. J. Matera, *Galatians* (SP; Collegeville, Minn.: Liturgical Press, 1992), 24-26; J. Murphy-O'Connor, *Paul: A Critical Life* (Oxford: Oxford Univ. Press, 1996), 180-82. This does not mean, however, that Paul wrote Galatians to North rather than to South Galatia. See M. Silva, *Explorations in Exegetical Method: Galatians as a Test Case* (Grand Rapids: Baker, 1996), 131-32.

53. Bruce, "St. Paul in Macedonia," 263.

54. Bruce, *Philippians,* 78-79, 104-5.

55. Bruce, "St. Paul in Macedonia," 265. See n. 7 above.

56. Ibid., 263.

Bruce has pointed out in response that the relevant inscriptions speak of a single, former praetorian now working as a policeman on a road near the city.[57] This evidence, he concludes, is irrelevant.

Bruce may be right about the inscriptional evidence for the presence of praetorians in Ephesus, but it is difficult to see why we should limit Paul's use of πραιτώριον to its technical, legal meaning. The term could certainly refer to "the headquarters of a provincial governor," and Cicero, for example, uses it twice to describe the palace of the corrupt Verres, Roman proconsul of Sicily (Ver. 4.65; 5.106).[58] It could also lose all of its military connotations and signify simply "a large mansion or palace."[59] Paul may have preferred πραιτώριον to the Greek term βασίλειον simply to give his language a Roman ring, appropriate to the Roman colony to which he was writing. He at least seems to have done this in 4:15, where he calls the Philippians Φιλιππήσιοι, virtually transcribing the Latin name for the colony's residents, Philippenses, into Greek and adding the Greek masculine plural suffix. Paul surely knew that the normal way to write "Philippians" in Greek was Φιλιππεῖς.[60] The best guess about Paul's reason for formulating such an unusual word is that he was aware of the Roman character of the city and wanted to refer to his readers by their Roman name.[61] In the same way, in 1:13 he may have wanted to use a common Latin word for the governor's headquarters when he spoke of the progress of the gospel in the

57. Ibid., 263n.3; Fee, Philippians, 35n.86. See CIL 3.6065, 7135, 7136.

58. See Oxford Latin Dictionary (ed. P. G. W. Glare; Oxford: Oxford Univ. Press, 1982), s.v. "praetorium." In 4.65 Verres, intent on stealing an enormous bejewelled lampstand from a visiting Syrian prince, asks that it be brought to him so that he can admire it. The unsuspecting prince orders his servants to take the lampstand "in praetorium" and never gets it back. In 5.106 Verres hurries "e praetorio," eager to hatch another evil plot. It is true that Verres was a "praetor," and served prior to the restructuring of the government of the provinces under Julius Caesar and Augustus when Rome's territories were divided into imperial and senatorial provinces. Still, the word appears to have been used prior to Paul's time for a proconsul's headquarters, and Paul probably felt no compulsion to observe fine political distinctions.

59. Oxford Latin Dictionary, s.v. "praetorium." The term's other meanings are "a general's headquarters building or tent," "a meeting of officers at the general's headquarters," "a rest-house for travelling magistrates, etc.," or "the imperial bodyguard."

60. This is the way "Philippians" is spelled in Greek inscriptions from the period. The spelling Φιλιππήσιοι, on the other hand, appears in neither literature nor inscriptions prior to Paul's time. See P. Pilhofer, Philippi (2 vols.; WUNT 87 and 119; Tübingen: Mohr [Siebeck], 1995, 2000), 1:116-17.

61. Pilhofer, Philippi, 1:117.

place of his imprisonment, and the common term *praetorium* could have easily come to mind.[62] Paul's use of this term for the place of his imprisonment should not, therefore, impede the argument that he wrote from Ephesus.

Conclusion

When Paul Feine, in 1894, and later Martin Albertz, in 1910, argued that Philippians belonged with Paul's early correspondence, they had already taken the most important methodological step that advocates for the Ephesian provenance of Philippians can make. The battles that Paul fights in Philippians 3 are the battles of Galatians and 1 Corinthians, not those that he undertook in Colossians, Philemon, and Ephesians during his Roman imprisonment. This is where the case for Ephesus needs to be made, and both Feine and Albertz were wise to see this. Since their time, the case for Ephesus has followed less plausible methods, and many commentators at the close of the century have been understandably impatient with the improbable proposals of its advocates. Provided that the case is made on the basis of the literary evidence, however, the Ephesian origin for Philippians is not only possible but historically probable.[63]

62. It is sometimes said that Paul must be referring to the praetorian guard when he uses the term πραιτώριον, since he couples πραιτώριον with the phrase τοῖς λοιποῖς πᾶσιν, obviously referring to people. The sense would then be, "among the whole praetorian guard and everyone else." See Lightfoot, *Philippians*, 99-104, esp. 102, for the classic case, followed by many others. But Chrysostom, who read the letter in his native tongue, believed that Paul gave the word a local meaning: both those who worked in the praetorium and others elsewhere in the city had heard that Paul was in chains for Christ (*Hom. Phil.* 2).

63. If Philippians was written from Ephesus after Galatians and 1 Corinthians, then Paul probably wrote it during the summer of 55 after Timothy had returned from the visit to Corinth that Paul describes in 1 Cor 4:17 and 16:10-11 (cf. Acts 19:22), and after the sorrowful visit and the tearful letter of 2 Cor 2:1-4. The imprisonment from which Philippians was written, then, would be "the affliction we experienced in Asia" of 2 Cor 1:8-11. In Philippians Paul plans to send Timothy on a quick round trip to Philippi so that Paul and the Philippians might be cheered by news of each other (2:19), and he hopes eventually to come to Philippi himself (2:24; cf. 2 Cor 2:12-13; Acts 20:1). Timothy would naturally accompany him on this journey, and 2 Cor 1:1 reveals that he did so. For a similar understanding of these events, see V. P. Furnish, *II Corinthians* (AB 32A; Garden City, N.Y.: Doubleday, 1984), 42, 104-5.

The Meaning of Ἀπείραστος Revisited

Peter H. Davids

Introduction

One of the more curious words in the Epistle of James is ἀπείραστος in 1:13: μηδεὶς πειραζόμενος λεγέτω ὅτι Ἀπὸ θεοῦ πειράζομαι· ὁ γὰρ θεὸς ἀπείραστός ἐστιν κακῶν, πειράζει δὲ αὐτὸς οὐδένα (traditionally translated: "No one, when tempted, should say, 'I am being tempted by God'; for God *cannot be tempted* by evil and he himself tempts no one").[1] One of the problems with the term in this verse is that it is otherwise relatively rare. In an earlier article,[2] I could locate only a few other occurrences of the term in Greek literature (Pseudo-Ignatius, *Philippians* 11; Clement of Alexandria, *Stromata* 7.12; *Acts of John* 57, 90; Philodemus, *Volumnia Rhetorica* 1; Dorothei Abottis, *Epistolae ad Diversos* 5; John of Damascus, *De Fide Orthodoxa* 3; Maximus Confessor, *Quaestiones ad Thalassium epist.* 258;[3]

---

1. Quoted from the NRSV. One impetus for the present discussion is that at least three major English translations (NIV, NRSV, NLT) have appeared since my original work was completed (see below); none of them has chosen to follow the suggested translation. Thus reexamination is appropriate to see if the original conclusions can indeed be supported or whether I missed something in the original article.

2. This essay is a follow-up to "The Meaning of ἀπείραστος in James i.13," *NTS* 24 (1978): 386-92.

3. The textual issue here is whether ἀπείραστος or ἀπείρατος is to be read. *TLG* takes the latter reading, so this reference will not show up in a *TLG* search.

Alciphron, *Letters to Farmers* 35 [2.35.3.6]; Gregory of Nazianzus, *Epistles* 214), all significantly later than James.[4] Thus many have supposed that James may have coined the term by analogy with ἀπείρατος to fit with his repeated use of the πειράζω/πειρασμός root.

As pointed out in my previous work, the phrase including ἀπείραστος has been variously rendered by commentators and translators: (1) "God cannot be tempted" (i.e., solicited to evil),[5] (2) "God is inexperienced in evil," or (3) "God should not be tested by evil people." It was this last translation that I defended in the previous article. Yet because these multiple translations by reputable scholars are all grammatically possible, the text clearly presents a number of issues. First, there is always the possibility that James or an early copyist has misspelled the more common ἀπείρατος; that is also a possibility in any of the later uses of ἀπείραστος, although this study will show that to be less likely in the case of Christian literature.[6] Second, there is the need to make sense of the logic of the text itself. This includes not only the vocabulary, for the meanings of both ἀπείραστος and κακῶν (neuter or masculine plural; "evil" or "evil people"?) are disputed, but also the grammar: a charge (which might logically flow from strong views of divine sovereignty) one is *not* to make about God, followed by γάρ and a statement about God (that includes a negated verbal noun), plus the mild adversative δέ and a statement about what God does *not* do. Many translations and interpretations of the verse either fail to give the text any transparent logic or turn the text into a tautology. Why is this phrase a reason that God is not testing a person, and why does

---

4. Also possibly Josephus, *B.J.* 7.8.1 §262, depending on the reading of the text. In this case ἀπείραστος would be the more difficult reading due to Josephus's choices elsewhere, although *TLG* does not include the possibility of this term appearing in Josephus. If this reading were accepted, Josephus, writing relatively close to the time James was composed, would reveal a wider use of the term in James's world.

5. Cf. L&N 1:776, §88.309: "pertaining to not being able to be tempted — 'unable to be tempted, one who cannot be tempted.' ὁ γὰρ θεὸς ἀπείραστός ἐστιν κακῶν 'God cannot be tempted by evil' Jas 1.13. There may be some difficulties involved in rendering the passive expression in Jas 1.13, but it is often possible to restructure this as an active expression with an indefinite person made the subject, for example, 'no one can tempt God to do what is bad.' It is also possible to shift the meaning slightly in terms of desire or will and thus say 'God would never want to do what is evil.'"

6. My argument is that the term is probably original in James because this would explain the prevalence of the term in later Christian literature and its comparative absence in non-Christian Greek literature.

the idea that God never tests follow from it? Third, the text should be meaningful within some first-century social-rhetorical context. The most likely context is that of the Jewish wisdom tradition; Ben Sira expresses the sense of our text well:

> Do not say, "It was the Lord's doing that I fell away";
>   for he does not do what he hates.
> Do not say, "It was he who led me astray";
>   for he has no need of the sinful.
> The Lord hates all abominations;
>   such things are not loved by those who fear him.
>
> (Sir 15:11-13 NRSV)

Within this wisdom tradition, we need to pay special attention to Jewish teaching on testing, since the previous verse (Jas 1:12) as well as 1:2-4 speaks of πειρασμόν or πειρασμοῖς.[7] That is, James surely knows of Abraham as the man who endured testing and received God's commendation, and of Israel in the wilderness as the classic example of failure under testing (for they continually put God to the test).[8] Finally, 1:13 is pointing toward an explanation of the true source of failure under testing in 1:13-15 — the power of desire. This does not appear to appeal to the Stoic idea of ἀπαθεία, or absence of desire, but is more a development of the Jewish idea of יֵצֶר, or the need to keep desire, which is cre-

---

7. On the Jewish testing tradition see B. Gerhardsson, *The Testing of God's Son* (ConBNT 2/1; Lund: Gleerup, 1966), 25-35. Specifically, there is the OT theme of God testing his people (never the other nations) and the theme of his people failing the test by testing God. The theme of God testing human beings is reinterpreted, starting in Chronicles and continuing in *Jubilees*, as Satan becomes the agent of testing and God recedes into the background. The theme of people failing the test by testing God gets amplified, with the roots of testing God connected to desire and/or the divided heart; the latter finds its roots in such texts as Ps 78:18 but is expanded in later texts, including the Dead Sea Scrolls. See further Gerhardsson, 48-51; P. H. Davids, "Themes in the Epistle of James That Are Judaistic in Character" (Ph.D. diss., Univ. of Manchester, 1974), 120-50.

8. Given the socialization of all converts to Christianity, this would be probable no matter what the background of the author of James. However, he clearly shows that he knows the Abraham narrative in 2:21, and uses it in a way that shows his awareness of Jewish midrashic expansions on the narrative. See P. H. Davids, "Tradition and Citation in the Epistle of James," in *Scripture, Tradition, and Interpretation: Essays Presented to Everett F. Harrison* (ed. W. W. Gasque and W. S. LaSor; Grand Rapids: Eerdmans, 1978), 113-16.

ated by God but is by nature without boundaries, under control rather than being controlled by it.[9]

Out of these considerations came the suggestion, first put forward without support by Friedrich Spitta, that the critical phrase in James should be translated "God ought not to be tested by evil people."[10] According to Moulton, this translation fits the range of meanings of verbal adjectives ending in -τος.[11] That is, these adjectives (which can be passive in meaning as well as active and intransitive) can express not only capability or possibility but also suitability. Furthermore, this translation satisfies the logic of the passage. That is, the reason why James commands one not to accuse God of putting him or her to the test is supplied, introduced by γάρ. This reason comes in two parts separated by the mild adversative conjunction δέ: (a) you should not put God to the test, and (b) God does not test people. Finally, this translation fits well with the Jewish testing tradition in that failure of the test in the Hebrew Scriptures is frequently shown by one testing God, that is, by accusing God or by demanding that God act in a certain manner,[12] and in that the Abrahamic narrative was interpreted in the first century to say that God tests no one.

My goal in this present work is to reexamine these conclusions in the light of the wider evidence that is available for the use of ἀπείραστος, especially that provided by the *Thesaurus linguae graecae (TLG)* project. Through a search of this database one finds not only the uses of the term

9. See P. H. Davids, *The Epistle of James* (NIGTC; Grand Rapids: Eerdmans, 1982), 35-38, and the literature cited there.

10. F. Spitta, "Der Brief des Jakobus," in *Zur Geschichte und Litteratur des Urchristentums* (3 vols.; Göttingen: Vandenhoeck & Ruprecht, 1893-1907), 2:33: "Gott werde von Bösen versucht und durch solches Versuchtwerden gekränkt, er selbst aber versuche keinen."

11. J. H. Moulton, *A Grammar of New Testament Greek*, vol. 1, *Prolegomena* (3d ed.; Edinburgh: T&T Clark, 1908), 221-22. Cf. H. W. Smyth, *Greek Grammar* (Cambridge: Harvard Univ. Press, 1956), 157, §472; 343, §1488.

12. There is almost a complete identity between the Hebrew and the Greek πειρασ-root. See J. H. Korn, *ΠΕΙΡΑΣΜΟΣ: Die Versuchung des Gläubigen in der griechischen Bibel* (BWANT 72; Stuttgart: Kohlhammer, 1937), who discusses the few possible exceptions on pp. 6-7. That testing God indicates failure in the test is seen classically in Num 14:22 (the Israelites are those who "have tested me these ten times and have not obeyed my voice") and Deut 6:16 ("Do not put the LORD your God to the test, as you tested him at Massah"); but this also appears elsewhere, e.g., Deut 9:22-24; Ps 78:18-20; 95:8-9. Isa 7:12 shows a use of this same theology, but in this case to justify a lack of trust in God. Judg 6:9 indicates that Gideon fears God may become angry with him for his repeated testing of God (and the testing itself may be a way in which the author indicates the low state of Israel's spirituality).

cited above, but also no less than 58 other instances of the term, making a total of 67 uses, of which 64 fall within the period from the third century B.C.E. to the fourth century C.E.

A similar search of the related terms ἀπείρατος and ἀπείρητος[13] is also indicative in that one discovers that both of these terms appear earlier than ἀπείραστος. For example, ἀπείρατος appears four times in Pindar in the sixth century B.C.E. and also in Demosthenes and Demandes in the fourth century,[14] while ἀπείρητος shows up several times in Homer.[15] Even more interesting is that while, starting in the first century C.E., ἀπείραστος appears almost exclusively in medical or Christian literature, ἀπείρατος and ἀπείρητος, which are more common during this period (187 occurrences compared to 66 for their close cousin), rarely appear in either type of literature until the fourth century C.E.[16] When they do appear, they often appear in different types of literature. For example, ἀπείρητος is found in apologetic literature of the second and third centuries (e.g., Melito and Theophilus), but the same author will use different terminology in nonapologetic literature. Origen uses ἀπείρητος in *Contra Celsum* but ἀπείρατος in *Scholia in Apocalypsem* and ἀπείραστος in *Fragmenta in Psalmos 1–150* (plus quotes our James passage in both *Selecta in Exodum* and *Adnotationes in Exodum*).[17] A similar distinction occurs in Clement of Alexandria, although two of the three terms appear in his *Stromata*.[18] One must conclude that while these terms are close enough that they may have been confused at times due to scribal errors, that they are common in different bodies of literature and are kept separate by the few authors who use two or more of them indicates that they had distinct semantic fields.[19]

---

13. These will normally be handled together, since the former is the Doric form of the latter, although by the 1st century C.E. they appear to have separated in meaning.

14. Pindar, *Ol.* 8.61; 11.18; *Nem.* 1.23; *Isthm.* 3/4.48; Demosthenes, *Cor.* 249.8; Demades, *Fragmenta* 87,12.2.

15. Homer, *Il.* 12.304; 17.41; *Od.* 2.170; *Hymni Homerici* H5 133.

16. Interestingly enough, LSJ (183 s.v. ἀπείρατος or ἀπείρητος, adjacent entries) seems to make the term that appears later the original term, claiming to find it in Heliodorus with the meaning "pure" or "chaste" and hence "inexperienced" (or "untested"). LSJ does not list a reference, and a search of *TLG* failed to turn up any such occurrence.

17. For example, Origen, *Cels.* 1.36.19; 5.48.33; *Schol. Apoc.* 35.1.

18. Clement of Alexandria, *Paed.* 2.9.78.1.1; 3.11.59.2.7; *Strom.* 1.1.10.1.1; *Protr.* 10.91.1.3.

19. The meaning of ἀπείρατος and ἀπείρητος will not be discussed further, for they are outside the scope of this article and do not occur in NT literature, although they would indeed make an interesting study on their own.

First-Century and Earlier Usage:
An Earlier Use Than James?

Returning to the focus of our study, most interesting among the occurrences of ἀπείραστος is that, unlike ἀπείρατος and ἀπείρητος, only one occurrence *may* come before James, that is, Chrysippus Philosophus, *Fragmenta moralia* 639.2: μὴν σοφὸν ὄντα ἐνάρξεσθαι τοῦ κυνισμοῦ. The actual fragment reads, οὗτος ἡμῖν, αὐστηρὸς οὐκ εἰς τὸ ἀδιάφθορον μόνον, ἀλλὰ καὶ εἰς τὸ ἀπείραστον. οὐδαμῇ γὰρ ἐνδόσιμον οὐδὲ ἁλώσιμον ἡδονῇ τε καὶ λύπῃ τὴν ψυχὴν παρίστησιν· δικαστής, ἐὰν ὁ λόγος καλῇ, ἀκλινὴς γενόμενος, μηδ' ὁτιοῦν τοῖς πάθεσι ("Whence he is always mild and meek, accessible, affable, long-suffering, grateful, endued with a good conscience. Such a man is rigid, not alone so as not to be corrupted, but so as *not to be tempted* [or 'put to the test']. For he never exposes his soul to submission, or capture at the hands of Pleasure and Pain. If the Word, who is Judge, call; he, having grown inflexible, and not indulging a whit the passions, walks unswervingly where justice advises him to go").[20] It is clear in this passage that ἀπείραστον means "not to be tested/tempted," showing its character as a verbal noun. Its use here raises two questions. The first is whether it actually antedates James, since this reference in Chrysippus is known only through a quotation in later Christian literature (which strongly prefers ἀπείραστος over ἀπείρατος) and since Chrysippus also appears to use ἀπείρατος (*Fragmenta logica et physica* 298a, frg. 3.20). The second question is whether the Stoic sense (i.e., that the passions per se, such as pleasure and pain, are what test the person) was always inherent in the word, or whether that sense also comes from the later Christian author.

Second- and Third-Century Usage,
Christian and Secular

After James we find two occurrences of ἀπείραστος in the first and early second century.[21] There is a secular use in Onasander Tacticus, *Strategicus*

20. Cited by Clement of Alexandria, *Strom.* 7.7. English translations of the ante-Nicene fathers are from A. Roberts and J. Donaldson, eds., *The Ante-Nicene Fathers* (repr. Grand Rapids: Eerdmans, 1969), unless otherwise noted.

21. While Ignatius was martyred under Trajan (98-117 C.E.), only the original form of his letters would necessarily date to this period. This quotation is from spurious letters or

22.3.2: ἄλλως τε καὶ ἐν αὐτοῖς τοῖς δεινοῖς ἐπιφάνειαι πολεμίων ἀπειράστων ἐκπλήττουσι τὰς ψυχάς· προλαμβάνουσαι γάρ τι χεῖρον, οὗ πείσονται, φοβερώτερον ("Especially with respect to those fearful ones does the appearance of *untested* enemies frighten the souls, for anticipating the worst, they are not persuaded, being more fearful"). There is also a Christian use in Ignatius, *Epistulae interpolatae et epistulae suppositiciae* 5.11.1.2: Εἰ τοίνυν σὺ πάτημα τῶν ποδῶν τοῦ κυρίου, πῶς πειράζεις τὸν ἀπείραστον, ἐπιλαθόμενος τοῦ νομοθέτου παρακελευομένου, ὅτι οὐκ ἐκπειράσεις κύριον τὸν θεόν σου, ἀλλὰ καὶ τολμᾷς . . . ("If, then, you [Satan] are trampled down by the feet of the Lord, how, having tested the *untestable*, [will you] escape notice of the lawgiver who gave the command, 'You will not put the Lord your God to the test,' but you even dare . . .").[22] These two uses show an interesting breadth in the semantic field of our term. Onasander's context demands a meaning such as "untested" or "untried," that is, enemies whose capabilities in battle are unknown. The Ignatius quotation would make no sense with such a meaning, but rather demands that the term mean either "untestable/untemptable" (i.e., God cannot be moved by Satanic testing) or the preferred meaning of "the one who ought not to be tested," which fits very well with the quotation of Deut 6:16 (LXX) that follows this statement.

Moving on we come to Clement of Alexandria, where we find two uses, namely the citation of Chrysippus (which we now put into its fuller context in the translation) in *Stromata* 7.7.45: οὗτος ἡμῖν ⟨ὁ⟩ αὐστηρὸς οὐκ εἰς τὸ ἀδιάφθορον μόνον, ἀλλὰ καὶ εἰς τὸ ἀπείραστον οὐδαμῆ γὰρ ἐνδόσιμον οὐδὲ ἁλώσιμον ἡδονῇ τε καὶ λύπῃ τὴν ψυχὴν παρίστησιν, δικαστής ("Whence he [our Gnostic] is always mild and meek, accessible,

---

letters that, although originally genuine, contain significant amounts of interpolation. It is believed that the Ignatian epistles, including the spurious ones, were interpolated in the 4th century (so C. C. Richardson, *Early Christian Fathers* [New York: Macmillan, 1970], 81); thus this quotation may well be from the 4th century. However, the *Tendenz* of these interpolations was in support of a diluted form of Arianism, whereas this quotation appears to speak of Jesus as "the Lord your God." Is this, then, 4th-century or genuine material from Ignatius? It is included here because it does not appear to fit with 4th-century uses of ἀπείραστος, but it is recognized that it may really stem from a later period.

22. Cf. Ps.-Ignatius, *Phil.* 11: "If, therefore, thou art trodden down under the feet of the Lord, how dost thou tempt Him that cannot be tempted, forgetting that precept of the lawgiver, 'Thou shalt not tempt the Lord thy God?' Yea, thou even darest, most accursed one, to appropriate the works of God to thyself, and to declare that the dominion over these was delivered to thee." As noted above, the dating of this quotation is problematic.

affable, long-suffering, grateful, endued with a good conscience. Such a man is rigid, not alone so as not to be corrupted, but so as *not to be tempted*. For he never exposes his soul to submission, or capture at the hands of Pleasure and Pain. If the Word, who is Judge, call; he, having grown inflexible, and not indulging a whit the passions, walks unswervingly where justice advises him to go"); and *Stromata* 7.12.70: ἀγάπης, καὶ πάσης κατεξανιστάμενος πείρας τῆς διὰ τέκνων καὶ γυναικὸς οἰκετῶν τε καὶ κτημάτων προσφερομένης. τῷ δὲ ἀοίκῳ τὰ πολλὰ εἶναι συμβέβηκεν ἀπειράστῳ. μόνου γοῦν ἑαυτοῦ κηδόμενος ἡττᾶται πρὸς τοῦ ἀπολειπομένου μὲν κατὰ τὴν ἑαυτοῦ σωτηρίαν, περιττεύοντος δὲ ἐν τῇ κατὰ τὸν βίον οἰκονομίᾳ, εἰκόνα ἀτεχνῶς ("For having become perfect, he has the apostles for examples; and one is not really shown to be a man in the choice of single life; but he surpasses men, who, disciplined by marriage, procreation of children, and care for the house, without pleasure or pain, in his solicitude for the house has been inseparable from God's love, and withstood all temptation arising through children, and wife, and domestics, and possessions. But he that has no family is in a great degree *free of temptation* [or 'untested']. Caring, then, for himself alone, he is surpassed by him who is inferior, as far as his own personal salvation is concerned, but who is superior in the conduct of life, preserving certainly, in his care for the truth, a minute image").

Again we find a breadth of meaning, here within a single author. In Clement's quotation of Chrysippus the meaning of the term must be something like "unable to be tempted" in that it indicates a person whom the normal human passions cannot even entice, much less corrupt, while in the second use of the term the sense of "able" is absent. Instead, we find a sense more like that in Onasander: the person without a family is "untested" or "untempted" in that he or she has never faced those tests/temptations that normal family life brings and thus could not develop the virtue that results from withstanding those tests.

The secular references from this same period all come from Galen. In each of the four references we find similar meanings. That is, in *De simplicium medicamentorum temperamentis ac facultatibus* 12.260.12 we discover that Galen did not want to venture into the "untested" (or possibly "untestable"; οὐκ ἐδόκει μοι καλῶς ἔχειν ἐπί τι τῶν ἀπειράστων ἀφικνεῖσθαι). Likewise, rather than using untested raw material one should work from what has already been tested (ἀπό τινος ὡρισμένης ἀρχῆς ἐπὶ τὴν ἀπείραστον ὕλην μεταβαίνειν σε χρή, παρὰ τοῦ προπεπειραμένου μαθόντα τὰς ἐν αὐτοῖς ὑπεροχάς, 12.281.2). In *De compositione medicamentorum per genera* 7.13.459.14 he points out that necessity may force one to try rash experiments using untested treatments (ἀλλ' ὅπερ ἔφην, ἀνάγκη καταλαμβάνει πολλάκις ἡμᾶς, ὡς καὶ τοῖς ἀπειράστοις αὐτοσχεδιάζοντας χρῆσθαι), but in *In Hippocratis aphorismos commentarii* 7.17b.354.3 he states that it is not safe to test the untested upon the human body (and that it may even kill the person; ἐπ' ἀνθρωπείου δὲ σώματος πειρᾶσθαι τῶν ἀπειράστων οὐκ ἀσφαλές). Wise as this advice is (may medical researchers and physicians today take note!), it shows us that in medical literature ἀπείραστος meant "untested."[23] That is not a meaning that would fit in James, for the context at least demands that God be viewed as untestable rather than simply untested.[24]

There are also two passages in *Acts of John*, 57 and 90. Here we are coming into an uncertain time period. While it was first mentioned by Eusebius, we cannot be sure how early the *Acts of John* existed, although certainly before 300 C.E. *TLG* classifies the work in the second century, which is defended

---

23. This same usage is found in Ps.-Galen, *Introductio seu medicus* 14.679.2, where he divides treatments into those having been tested and those untested (καὶ ἱστορίᾳ τῇ τῶν προπεπειραμένων καὶ τῇ τοῦ ὁμοίου μεταβάσει ἀπὸ τοῦ πεπειραμένου ἐπὶ τὸ ἀπείραστον).

24. As noted above, the Israelites are said to test God multiple times in the Hebrew Scriptures, and James surely knew these passages, so God could not be viewed as "untested," although we cannot be sure how James interpreted these instances of testing. We do know that despite Gen 22:1 (LXX: ὁ θεὸς ἐπείραζεν τὸν Αβρααμ; or MT נִסָּה) James states that God tests no one (πειράζει δὲ αὐτὸς οὐδένα), probably, as I pointed out in "Meaning," because he interprets this passage with reference to Job, as was common in 1st-century Jewish interpretation (cf. his use of the binding of Isaac tradition in Jas 2:21). If, however, he is aware of Israel testing God in the Pentateuch, then he must have realized that God was testable in the absolute sense. It was R. B. Ward ("The Works of Abraham: James 2:14-26," *HTR* 61 [1968]: 283-90) who first pointed out the interpretation of the testing of Abraham in terms of testing one who was hospitable like Job and connected it to James. As early as Philo we find the hospitality that was attributed to Job also attributed to Abraham (Philo, *Abr.* 167; cf. *Sobr.* 56, where the title "friend of God" is attributed to Abraham in the context of his hospitality of Gen 18:17); this is mentioned in particular with the binding of Isaac in *Gen. Rab.* LVI:V.4 (cf. LV:IV). *'Abot R. Nat.* 7 states that Abraham's hospitality exceeded that of Job (cf. *T. Ab.* 1.1-2, 5; 2.2; 4.6, which describe Abraham as righteous like Job; Job 31:32, among other places, cites Job's hospitality, but *Testament of Job* is where Job repeatedly recites his charitable/hospitable activities). While Abraham is frequently said to undergo ten tests like Israel (variously listed in *Jub.* 17:17; 19:8; *Pirqe R. El.* 26-31; *'Abot R. Nat.* 32), he is also said to be like Job in that his testing is attributed to a challenge made by Satan to God (Prince Mastema in *Jub.* 17:16, which connects this explicitly to the ten testings tradition; unlike the Job tradition in *Jub.* 18:12, Prince Mastema is said to be shamed by the outcome).

by Pieter Lalleman, who views it as written before the mid-second century.[25] However, others argue that the work comes from the early to mid-third century. This means that the work could be our earliest witness to our term after James, even though it is listed here due to controversy over its date.[26]

In *Acts of John* 57 we read, "When the elder heard this and saw that he was not unknown but that the Apostle of Christ had told him all that was in his heart [which had been unspoken criticism of John for watching a partridge play in the dust], he fell on his face to the ground and cried out, saying, 'Now I know that God dwells in you, blessed John! How happy is the man who has not tempted God in you; for the man who tempts you tempts the *untemptable*.' And he begged him to pray for him" (Νῦν οἶδα ὅτι ὁ θεὸς οἰκεῖ ἐν σοὶ μακάριε Ἰωάννη· καὶ μακάριος ὅστις οὐκ ἐπείρασεν ἐν σοὶ τὸν θεόν· ὁ γὰρ σὲ πειράζων τὸν ἀπείραστον πειράζει. Παρεκάλει δὲ αὐτὸν εὔχεσθαι ὑπὲρ αὐτοῦ). In §90 the context is that of the transfiguration in which John alone approaches Jesus, is shocked at his appearance, and cries out, "and he, turning about, appeared as a small man and caught hold of my beard and pulled it and said to me, 'John, do not be faithless, but believing, and not inquisitive.' And I said to him, 'Why, Lord, what have I done?' But I tell you, my brethren, that I suffered such pain for thirty days in the place where he touched my beard, that I said to him, 'Lord, if your playful tug has caused such pain, what (would it be) if you had dealt me a blow?' And he said to me, 'Let it be your (concern) from now on not to tempt him that *cannot be tempted*' [Καὶ αὐτός μοι εἶπεν· Σὸν λοιπὸν εἰ τὸν μὴ πειράζειν τὸν ἀπείραστον]."[27]

---

25. P. J. Lalleman, *The Acts of John: A Two-Stage Initiation into Johannine Gnosticism* (Studies on the Apocryphal Acts of the Apostles 4; Leuven: Peeters, 1998), dates the *Acts of John* between 125 and 150 C.E. (cf. 268-70).

26. K. Schäferdiek ("The Acts of John," in E. Hennecke, *New Testament Apocrypha* [ed. W. Schneemelcher; trans. R. McL. Wilson; 2 vols.; Philadelphia: Westminster, 1963-65], 2:192-93) appears to date the first clear attestation of the work in the 4th century, after discussing (188) a parallel with Clement of Alexandria and concluding that this shows a common tradition rather than dependence. Thus one would argue that the work likely arose in the 3d century and is first cited in the 4th. M. R. James, however, confidently states that it is "not later than the middle of the second century" (*The Apocryphal New Testament* [2d ed. 1924; repr. Oxford: Clarendon, 1972], 228). If so, then it is, as noted, the earliest use of our term after James in that the Ignatius quotation may be a 4th-century interpolation. Whatever the date, the use in *Acts of John* does not show the characteristics of the 3d- and 4th-century literature we will look at later, which makes me lean toward the earlier dating.

27. While I list the passages in numerical order, many scholars believe that *Acts of*

In both passages the translation "test(s)" is better than "tempt(s)," for there is no attempt to solicit either John or Jesus to sin, but rather criticism or curiosity, something much more in line with "testing" than "tempting" in English. The second passage in particular revolves around the question of whether the apostles believe yet; in the next section Jesus will say that they do not, "for they are but human beings" (*Acts of John* 92). When it comes to ἀπείραστος itself, in both cases the meaning of "ought not to be tested" fits the context best. In both cases John or Jesus was indeed tested, but in the first case the test is passed when the covert criticism is revealed, and in the second case Jesus delivers a "mild" rebuke by tugging on John's beard. The moral of both stories is to believe rather than to test, which, despite the gnostic coloring of the *Acts of John* (the large unit containing §90 concerns Jesus' appearance and notes that at times his body could not be felt and that at no time did his feet make any footprints), is in line with the Jewish testing tradition as it existed in the first century.[28] One can test God, but one ought not to, for testing God can bring negative results.

Third- and Fourth-Century Patristic Usage

Once we move past the *Acts of John* we notice a number of new features appearing in relation to our term.[29] First, we start to get quotations of Jas 1:13.[30] These occur first in Origen, *Selecta in Exodum* 12.288.55 and *Adnota-*

John 87-105 come within *Acts of John* 37. The translations are those of Schäferdiek, "Acts of John," 2:188-259.

28. See above, n. 7.

29. There is a single reference in Alciphron, *Ep.* 2.35.3.6, "For it is good to be untested by the unwilling" (καλὸν μὲν γὰρ ἀπείρα[σ]τον εἶναι τῶν ἀβουλήτων), but here the *sigma* is textually uncertain and so we cannot be sure that this is really an occurrence of our term. What is clear is that it has to do with testing, not tempting.

30. To see how the fathers typically handle Jas 1:13, one could look at Jerome, *Contra Jovinianus* 2.3.3: "The Apostle James also, knowing that the baptized can be tempted, and fall of their own free choice, says: 'Blessed is the man that endureth temptation: for when he hath been approved, he shall receive the crown of life, which the Lord promised to them that love him.' And that we may not think that we are tempted by God, as we read in Genesis Abraham was, he adds: 'Let no man say when he is tempted, I am tempted of God: for God cannot be tempted with evil, and He Himself tempteth no man. But each man is tempted when he is drawn away by his own lust and enticed. Then the lust, when it hath conceived,

tiones in Exodum 17.16.27. They continue in Epiphanius, *Haer.* 3.484.11; Chrysostom, *Synopsis scripturae sacrae* 56.362.44, *Oratio de hypapante* 70.16; Didymus the Blind, *De trinitate* 39.641.8; Cyril of Jerusalem, *Homilia in paralyticum juxta piscinam jacentem* 17.7; Cyril of Alexandria, *Commentarii in Joannem* 1.631.15, *De adoratione et cultu in spiritu et veritate* 68.148.55, and 981.32; and Ephrem Syrus 36.40.49. In other words, James is widely known and used from the third century onward, and we cannot assume that even authors who do not cite James are ignorant of the book. Interpretations of Jas 1:13 may now be influencing the semantic field of our term.

Second, we also find a very interesting phrase, ἀνὴρ ἀπείραστος ἀδόκιμος, which probably comes from James, although the two negative words never come together in that epistle. This phrase occurs from Eusebius, *Commentaria in Psalmos* 23.661.11 and 889.7 through Gregory of Nazianzus, *Epistulae* 214.1.1; Chrysostom, *De resurrectione mortuorum* 50.424.18, *Ad eos qui scandalizati sunt* 21.4.1, *In Acta apostolorum* 60.255.59; Cyril of Jerusalem, *Mystagogiae* 5.17.3; the *Constitutiones apostolicae* 1.2.8.9 (2.3[8]); and Ephrem Syrus 71.315.2 to Severianus, *Fragmenta in epistulam i ad Corinthios* 258.27. The phrase has been variously translated, from, "If, therefore, any one be slandered and falsely accused, such a one is blessed; for the Scripture says, 'A man that is a reprobate is *not tried* by God,'" in *Constitutiones apostolicae*, to, "How then is it said elsewhere, 'a man *untempted* [untested] is a man unproved'" in Cyril. The latter translation is preferable in virtually all instances, particularly since, in each of the contexts, the phrase occurs as an explanation for why tests/temptations are necessary. It is Cyril who also explicitly connects the phrase to James by citing Jas 1:2 as the grounding for the proverb.

Third, we discover a clear bringing together of ἀπείραστος and "sin," for example, in Origen, *Fragmenta in Psalmos* 118.157.32: "For he may *be untempted* by such sins" (τηνικαῦτα γὰρ τῆς ἁμαρτίας ἀπείραστος ᾖ). So also in Theodoretus, *Interpretatio in Psalmos* 80.1869.19, which shows that this was a stock phrase used in referring to Saul's persecution of David. Cyril of Alexandria could comment (*Sermon to the Alexandrians*

beareth sin: and the sin, when it is full grown, bringeth forth death.' God created us with free will, and we are not forced by necessity either to virtue or to vice." Quotation from *Early Church Fathers — Nicene/Post Nicene*, part 2 (Garland, Tex.: Galaxie Software, 1999), as are other quotations of the Nicene and post-Nicene fathers, unless otherwise noted.

32.77.469.8), "And there remained no one *untempted* by the greed of that person, but all were in sin" (καὶ λοιπὸν ἦν οὐδεὶς τῆς ἐκείνου πλεονεξίας ἀπείραστος, πάντες δὲ ἦσαν ἐν ἁμαρτίαις). The implication of sin is also there when Theodoret in *De providentia orationes decem* 83.640.30 says, "For neither would we be afraid if our nature had remained *untempted* by them" (Οὐδὲ γὰρ ἂν ἐδείσαμεν, εἰ παντελῶς ἀπείραστος αὐτῶν ἡ ἡμετέρα φύσις μεμενήκει).

Fourth, we do find that ἀπείραστος can mean "inexperienced" (or "ignorant" as a subcategory of inexperience), for example, in Gregory Thaumaturgus, *In Origenem oratio panegyrica* 14.76: "nor did he judge it proper for us to go away with any single class of philosophical opinions, but he introduced us to all, and determined that we should be *ignorant* of no kind of Grecian doctrine [πρὸς δὲ πάντας ἦγεν, οὐδενὸς ἀπειράστους εἶναι θέλων δόγματος Ἑλληνικοῦ]."

Fifth, we continue to find combinations like "testing the one who should not be/cannot be tested." For instance, Eusebius, in *Commentaria in Psalmos* 23.1316.7, writes that "When they [Israel] tested God in the desert, [the] *untested* [or 'untestable' or 'one who should not be tested'], being forgiving, not repaying them, he gave to them their request" (Ὅτε μὲν τὸν Θεὸν ἐπείρασαν ἐν ἀνύδρῳ, ἀπείραστος, ὢν ἀμνησίκακος, οὐκ ἀμειψάμενος αὐτοὺς ἔδωκεν αὐτοῖς τὸ αἴτημα αὐτῶν).[31] Likewise Gregory of Nazianzus notes in *In dictum evangelii: Cum consummasset Jesus hos sermones* 36.288.33, "It was not enough that Sadducees should tempt Him concerning the Resurrection, and Lawyers question Him about perfection, and the Herodians about the poll-tax, and others about authority; but some one must also ask about Marriage at Him who *cannot be tempted,* the Creator of wedlock, Him who from the First Cause made this whole race of mankind [Ἀλλὰ καὶ περὶ γάμου τις πάλιν ἐρωτᾷ τὸν ἀπείραστον, τὸν κτίστην τῆς συζυγίας]."[32] For some of these authors the reference is likely to be to the impassibility of God/Christ, although other writers of this pe-

---

31. This reference, like the one in Apollinaris, *Fragmenta in Psalmos* 189.1, quotes Ps 105:14-15 LXX (106:14-15 MT) and adds ἀπείραστος, or in the case of Apollinaris, ἀπείραστος ὢν καὶ ἀμνησίκακος οὐκ ἀμειψάμενος αὐτούς, expanding the psalm text by noting that God was both one who should not be tested and one who forgives.

32. See also his *In laudem Cypriani* 35.1180.23, καὶ πεῖραν προσάγει τῷ ἀπειράστῳ, where the context identifies this one as "the second Adam." Asterius Sophista, in *Commentarii in Psalmos* 18.14.1, also uses the phrase with reference to Jesus, this time with reference to the temptation narrative.

riod go into long discussions about how Christ as a human being could truly be tempted. Only the wider context will inform us whether impassibility is intended or whether the idea is the illegitimacy of putting God/Christ to the test.

Conclusions

Where, then, has this examination of ἀπείραστος led us? We can draw some significant conclusions.

1. The term may appear first in James, in that its one possible occurrence in literature earlier than James (Chrysippus) comes in a quotation by a later author (Clement of Alexandria) who uses the term himself elsewhere. If James in fact coined the term, this would explain its predominant use by Christian authors and perhaps indicate a significant circulation of James before the time of Origen. Since the term is clearly used by Onasander and Galen, however, one must be cautious in suggesting this possibility, although it is likely that the term first appeared in the first century C.E.

2. The term does appear to be distinct from ἀπείρατος and ἀπείρητος in that the last two are found in different literature (i.e., nonmedical and non-Christian). Their use in Christian literature is mainly in literature addressed to those outside the church. This reinforces the impression that the church came to view ἀπείραστος as a "religious" word.

3. In its secular uses in Onasander and Galen, the term clearly means "untested" or "untried." This meaning does not fit the context in James, so it is clear that James is bringing it into connection with his beliefs about testing/tempting. The "secular" meaning continues, however, in the phrase or proverb ἀνὴρ ἀπείραστος ἀδόκιμος.

4. It is clear that ἀπείραστος can mean "untempted." This is probably its use in Clement of Alexandria and certainly its use in some third- and fourth-century writers, who explicitly relate it to sin. In Clement it appears to have Stoic overtones in that one is to remain untouched by pleasure and pain. However, the use of our term seems to indicate that one avoids situations that would affect him or her rather than that one has totally risen above such situations.

5. Once the idea of the impassibility of God develops, ἀπείραστος can be used to express this impassibility with regard to temptation. This leads to significant discussion as to how Jesus could have been tempted. This doctrine, however, appears to have arisen after 200 C.E. and to have shifted the meaning of our term. Furthermore, not every author appears to have connected this teaching to our term. Thus each context needs to be looked at individually.

6. By the time James is frequently quoted we find that authors are aware that Abraham was tested, but they seem to relegate it to a previous era and not bring it into connection with present testing. What they focus on in Jas 1:13-15 are the passions within the human being drawing him or her into sin. In doing this they ignore the fact that James himself is well aware of the binding of Isaac.

7. We could therefore describe the semantic field of this term as follows:

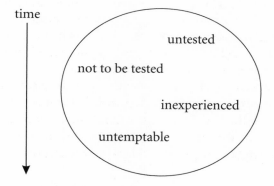

What, then, can be our conclusions about the use of ἀπείραστος in James? One could argue that James intends to say that God is "untested by evil things."[33] What this would not explain is how this idea is connected to

---

33. One could conceivably argue that James also means that God is "untestable" by evil things, meaning that he is impassible. Given that I have previously argued that James fits best into a 1st-century Palestinian setting (most recently in P. H. Davids, "Palestinian Traditions in the Epistle of James," in *James the Just and Christian Origins* [ed. B. Chilton and C. A. Evans; NovTSup 98; Leiden: Brill, 1999], 33-58), one would also need to argue that this doctrine was known in Palestine during this period. Given Philo's thought and the prevalence of Greek learning in Jerusalem itself, this is not impossible; but given the fact that James shows, at best, tangential contact with such thought, this influence is unlikely.

his not testing human beings. That is, that evil is no test for him or that it cannot affect him does not explain why God would not put a human being to the test. One could also argue, as I have done previously, that James is drawing on the Jewish testing tradition. Then the translation would be: "God should not be put to the test by evil people." This would mean that James, perfectly aware of the testing of Abraham, interprets that event like a typical Jew of his day in terms of Job or, as a Christian Jew, in terms of the testing of Jesus. And this translation makes good sense of the grammatical connections of the passage.

Thus what we have shown is that our wider study of the uses of ἀπείραστος provides interesting information about its development and the use of James in the second century and later, but it does not provide conclusive data. Such works as Ignatius and the *Acts of John* still support my original interpretation in the previous article that started this investigation, and the other works I have examined show enough development that semantic change is not only possible but probable. Thus I am again forced back on the context in James to make a decision, and given the grammar of the passage and a first-century Palestinian context, my original translation still makes the most sense of the passage. When one is put to the test by the circumstances of life, one should not turn and accuse God (i.e., in order to blame him for one's failure of the test). First, sinful human beings should not put God to the test. Second, God does not put human beings to the test. What tests them, James explains, is human desire, the יֵצֶר in us. It is only later (3:15; 4:7) that James will, in company with Job and Matthew, suggest that it is "also the devil" that puts people to the test.

Publications of Gerald F. Hawthorne

Books

Colossians and Philemon. Grand Rapids: Eerdmans, forthcoming.

The Presence and the Power: The Significance of the Holy Spirit in the Life and Ministry of Jesus. Dallas: Word, 1991.

Philippians. Word Biblical Themes. Waco: Word, 1987.

Philippians. WBC 43. Waco: Word, 1983.

Editor/Coeditor

Gerald F. Hawthorne, Ralph P. Martin, and Daniel G. Reid, eds. *Dictionary of Paul and His Letters.* Downers Grove, Ill.: InterVarsity Press, 1993.

Gerald F. Hawthorne with Otto Betz, eds. *Tradition and Interpretation in the New Testament: Essays in Honor of E. Earle Ellis for His 60th Birthday.* Grand Rapids: Eerdmans; Tübingen: Mohr (Siebeck), 1987.

Gerald F. Hawthorne, ed. *Current Issues in Biblical and Patristic Interpretation: Studies in Honor of Merrill C. Tenney Presented by His Former Students.* Grand Rapids: Eerdmans, 1975.

Articles

(and André Lamorte) "Prophecy, Prophet." Pages 960-62 in *Evangelical Dictionary of Theology.* Ed. Walter A. Elwell. 2d ed. Grand Rapids: Baker, 2001.

"In the Form of God and Equal with God (Philippians 2:6)." Pages 96-110 in *Where Christology Began: Essays on Philippians 2*. Ed. Ralph P. Martin and Brian J. Dodd. Louisville: Westminster John Knox, 1998.

"Holy, Holiness"; "Holy Spirit"; "Joy"; and "Melito of Sardis." In *Dictionary of the Later New Testament and Its Developments*. Ed. Ralph P. Martin and Peter H. Davids. Downers Grove, Ill.: InterVarsity Press, 1997.

"The Imitation of Christ: Discipleship in Philippians." Pages 163-79 in *Patterns of Discipleship in the New Testament*. Ed. Richard N. Longenecker. McMaster New Testament Studies. Grand Rapids: Eerdmans, 1996.

"Philippians, Theology of." Pages 609-12 in *Evangelical Dictionary of Biblical Theology*. Ed. Walter A. Elwell. Grand Rapids: Baker, 1996.

"The Lord's Supper." Pages 319-25, §273, in *The Biblical Foundations of Christian Worship*. Vol. 1 of *The Complete Library of Christian Worship*. Ed. Robert E. Webber. Peabody, Mass.: Hendrickson, 1993.

"Marriage and Divorce, Adultery and Incest"; and "Philippians, Letter to the." In *Dictionary of Paul and His Letters*. Ed. Gerald F. Hawthorne, Ralph P. Martin, and Daniel G. Reid. Downers Grove, Ill.: InterVarsity Press, 1993.

"Mourning"; "Peace"; "Philippians, The Letter of Paul to the"; and "Saint(s)." In *The Oxford Companion to the Bible*. Ed. Bruce M. Metzger and Michael D. Coogan. New York: Oxford University Press, 1993.

"Amen," and "Prophets, Prophecy." In *Dictionary of Jesus and the Gospels*. Ed. Joel B. Green, Scot McKnight, and I. Howard Marshall. Downers Grove, Ill.: InterVarsity Press, 1992.

"Faith: The Essential Ingredient of Effective Christian Ministry." Pages 249-59 in *Worship, Theology and Ministry in the Early Church: Essays in Honor of Ralph P. Martin*. Ed. Michael J. Wilkins and Terence Paige. JSNTSup 87. Sheffield: JSOT Press, 1992.

"The Role of the Christian Prophets in the Gospel Tradition." Pages 119-33 in *Tradition and Interpretation in the New Testament: Essays in Honor of E. Earle Ellis for his 60th Birthday*. Ed. Gerald F. Hawthorne with Otto Betz. Grand Rapids: Eerdmans; Tübingen: Mohr (Siebeck), 1987.

"The Interpretation and Translation of Philippians 1:28b," *ExpTim* 95 (1983): 80-81.

"Fable," "Hosanna," "Name," "Timothy," "Titus," "Translate," and "Tyran-

nus." In *International Standard Bible Encyclopedia.* Ed. Geoffrey W.
Bromiley. 4 vols. Grand Rapids: Eerdmans, 1979-1988.

"Canon and Apocrypha of the Old Testament," and "The Letter to the He-
brews." In *New Layman's Bible Commentary in One Volume.* Ed.
G. C. D. Howley, F. F. Bruce, and H. L. Ellison. Grand Rapids:
Zondervan, 1979; also published as *A Bible Commentary for Today:
Based on the Revised Standard Version.* London and Glasgow:
Pickering & Inglis, 1979.

"The Man Was Christ: A Second Century Easter Sermon." Excerpts from
the Paschal Homily of Melito of Sardis; translated, introduced, and
commented on by Gerald F. Hawthorne. *Christianity Today* 22
(March 24, 1978): 23-26.

"Tithe, δεκάτη." Pages 851-55 in *New International Dictionary of New Testament Theology.* Ed. Colin Brown. Vol. 3. Grand Rapids: Zondervan,
1975.

"Blessing, Cup of"; "Cross (Cross-bearing)"; "Disciple"; "Joseph the Carpenter, History of"; "Lord (Christ)"; and "Lord's Supper." In
Zondervan Pictorial Encyclopedia of the Bible. Ed. Merrill C. Tenney
and Steven Barabas. 5 vols. Grand Rapids: Zondervan, 1975.

"Christian Prophecy and the Sayings of Jesus: Evidence of and Criteria
for," Pages 105-29 in *Society of Biblical Literature Seminar Papers* 9.
Ed. George W. MacRae. Vol. 2. Missoula, Mont.: Society of Biblical
Literature, 1975.

"How to Choose a Bible," *Christianity Today* 20 (Dec. 5, 1975): 7-10.

"A New English Translation of Melito's Paschal Homily." Pages 147-75 in
*Current Issues in Biblical and Patristic Interpretation: Studies in Honor
of Merrill C. Tenney Presented by His Former Students.* Ed. Gerald F.
Hawthorne. Grand Rapids: Eerdmans, 1975.

(with F. F. Bruce, et al.) "Which Bible Is Best for You?" *Eternity* 25 (April
1974): 27-31.

A Layman's Guide: Bible Versions and Bible Enjoyment. Repr. of "Which Bible Is Best for You?" *Eternity* 25 (April 1974): 27-31. Philadelphia: Eternity Magazine, 1974.

"Christian Baptism and the Contribution of Melito of Sardis Recon-
sidered." Pages 241-51 in *Studies in New Testament and Early Christian
Literature: Essays in Honor of Allen P. Wikgren.* Ed. David E. Aune.
NovTSup 33. Leiden: Brill, 1972.

"The Letter to the Hebrews." Pages 533-66 in *A New Testament Commen-*

tary: Based on the Revised Standard Version. Ed. G. C. D. Howley, F. F. Bruce, and H. L. Ellison. Grand Rapids: Zondervan; London: Pickering & Inglis, 1969.

"Tatian and His Discourse to the Greeks," *HTR* 57 (1964): 161-88.

"The Essential Nature of the Kingdom of God," *WTJ* 25 (1962): 35-47.

"The Concept of Faith in the Fourth Gospel," *BSac* 116 (1959): 117-26.

Reviews

Review of Clinton E. Arnold, *The Colossian Syncretism: The Interface Between Christianity and Folk Belief at Colossae. JETS* 42 (1999): 157-58.

Review of James D. G. Dunn, *The Epistles to the Colossians and to Philemon: A Commentary on the Greek Text. JETS* 42 (1999): 155-56.

Review of Scott Brodeur, *The Holy Spirit's Agency in the Resurrection of the Dead: An Exegetico-Theological Study of 1 Corinthians 15,44b-49 and Romans 8,9-13. Review of Biblical Literature* 1 (1999): 354-56.

Review of Craig S. Wansink, *Chained in Christ: The Experience and Rhetoric of Paul's Imprisonments. JBL* 116 (1997): 571-73.

Review of Richard R. Melick Jr., *Philippians, Colossians, Philemon. JETS* 39 (1996): 158-59.

Review of Moisés Silva, *Philippians. Them* 16 (1990): 26-27.

Review of F. F. Bruce, *The Epistles to the Colossians, to Philemon, and to the Ephesians. Theological Students Fellowship Bulletin* 9 (1986): 34-35.

Review of *Origen: Contra Celsum* (trans. with an introduction and notes by Henry Chadwick). *Christian Scholar's Review* 10 (1981): 265-66.

Review of Joseph R. Cooke, *Free for the Taking: The Life-Changing Power of Grace. Christianity Today* 22 (Nov. 4, 1977): 37-38.

Review of Raniero Cantalamessa, *L'Omelia "In S. Pascha" dello Pseudo-Ippolito di Roma. Ricerche sulla teologia dell'Asia Minore nella seconda metà del II secolo. VC* 24 (1970): 151-52.

Contributors

David E. Aune
Professor of New Testament and Christian Origins, Department of
Theology, University of Notre Dame
B.A., Wheaton College
M.A., Wheaton Graduate School of Theology
M.A., University of Minnesota
Ph.D., University of Chicago

Peter H. Davids
Innsbruck, Austria
B.A., Wheaton College
M.Div., Trinity Evangelical Divinity School
Ph.D., University of Manchester

Bart D. Ehrman
Bowman and Gordon Gray Professor and Chair, Department of
Religious Studies, University of North Carolina at Chapel Hill
B.A., Wheaton College
M.Div., Princeton Theological Seminary
Ph.D., Princeton Theological Seminary

245

Stephen E. Fowl
Professor of Theology and Chair, Department of Theology, Loyola
College in Maryland
 B.A., Wheaton College
 M.A., Wheaton College Graduate School
 Ph.D., University of Sheffield

G. Walter Hansen
Associate Professor of New Testament and Director of the Global
Research Institute, Fuller Theological Seminary
 B.A., Wheaton College
 M.Div., Trinity Evangelical Divinity School
 Th.D., Wycliffe College and the University of Toronto

William W. Klein
Professor of New Testament and Associate Academic Dean, Denver
Seminary
 B.S., Wheaton College
 M.Div., Denver Seminary
 Ph.D., University of Aberdeen

William J. Larkin Jr.
Professor of New Testament and Greek, Columbia Biblical Seminary and
School of Missions
 B.A., Wheaton College
 B.D., Princeton Theological Seminary
 Ph.D., University of Durham

John R. Levison
Professor of New Testament, Seattle Pacific University
 B.A., Wheaton College
 B.A., University of Cambridge
 M.A., University of Cambridge
 Ph.D., Duke University

Bruce W. Longenecker
Lecturer in New Testament Studies, School of Divinity, St. Mary's
College, University of St. Andrews
B.A., Wheaton College
M.Rel., Wycliffe College and the University of Toronto
Ph.D., University of Durham

Douglas L. Penney
Associate Professor of Ancient Languages, Foreign Language
Department, Wheaton College
B.A., Wheaton College
Ph.D., University of Chicago

Jeffrey L. Staley
Adjunct Professor of Theology and Religious Studies, Seattle University
B.A., Wheaton College
M.A., Fuller Theological Seminary
Ph.D., Graduate Theological Union

Frank S. Thielman
Presbyterian Professor of Divinity, Beeson Divinity School, Samford
University
B.A., Wheaton College
B.A., University of Cambridge
M.A., University of Cambridge
Ph.D., Duke University

Tabula Gratulatoria

Thomas V. Aadland	American Lutheran Theological Seminary
Stephen J. Andrews	Midwestern Baptist Theological Seminary
David E. Aune	University of Notre Dame
David Baer Potter	President, Seminario ESEPA (Costa Rica)
David P. Barrett	Scott Theological College (Kenya)
J. Todd Billings	Harvard Divinity School
Rachel M. Billings (née Castañada)	Harvard University
Bradley Byron Blue	Monticello, Minn.
Joshua E. Bright	University of California, Riverside
Jeanette T. Brookes (née Stevens)	Fitzwilliam College, University of Cambridge
Rev. Canon William Broughton	St. George's College (Jerusalem)
James W. Bryant	The Criswell College
Michael A. Bullmore	Trinity Evangelical Divinity School
Aaron Burke	University of Chicago
Ginger Caessens (née Barth)	Jerusalem
Ronald M. Campbell	Northwestern University
J. Knox Chamblin	Reformed Theological Seminary
Frank Chan	Nyack College
Andrew D. Chignell	Yale University
Rodney Clapp	Brazos Press
Gary L. Comstock	North Carolina State University
Christopher H. Conn	University of the South

Robert E. Cooley — Gordon-Conwell Theological Seminary

Bruce Coriell — Vanderbilt University and Colorado College

William Lane Craig — Talbot School of Theology, Biola University

Peter H. Davids — Stafford, Texas

Wayne Detzler — Wingate University

Amy M. Donaldson — University of Notre Dame

William A. Dyrness — Fuller Theological Seminary

Bart D. Ehrman — University of North Carolina at Chapel Hill

James E. Eisenbraun — Founder and President, Eisenbrauns

Walter A. Elwell — Wheaton College

James D. Ernest — Andover-Newton Theological School and Boston College

C. Stephen Evans — Baylor University

†Ivan J. Fahs — Wheaton College

Hobert K. Farrell — LeTourneau University

Thomas N. Finger — Eastern Mennonite Seminary

Stephen E. Fowl — Loyola College in Maryland

Timothy E. Fulop — King College (Bristol, Tenn.)

Elizabeth A. Gaines — Mercerville, N.J.

Daniel Gallaugher — Catholic University of America and Mount St. Mary's Seminary

W. Ward Gasque — Pacific Association for Theological Studies

Timothy C. Geoffrion — Plymouth, Minn.

Michael Graves — Hebrew Union College

Gene L. Green — Wheaton College

Bruce W. Griffin — Lincoln College, University of Oxford

G. Walter Hansen — Fuller Theological Seminary

John Harrison — Oklahoma Christian University

Nathan O. Hatch — Provost, University of Notre Dame

N. Blake Hearson — Hebrew Union College

Jeffrey S. Hensley — Virginia Theological Seminary

Robert W. Herron Jr. — Lee University

John J. Herzog — Bethel College (St. Paul, Minn.)

Richard S. Hess — Denver Seminary

James K. Hoffmeier — Trinity Evangelical Divinity School

Kenneth G. Hoglund — Wake Forest University

Thomas Howard — St. John's Seminary (Boston)

Douglas Jacobsen — Messiah College

Tabula Gratulatoria

Calvin K. Katter	North Park Theological Seminary
Donald E. Keeney	Central Baptist Theological Seminary (Kansas City, Kans.)
James Kelhoffer	St. Louis University
William W. Klein	Denver Seminary
Donald M. Lake	Wheaton College
Timothy Laniak	Gordon-Conwell Theological Seminary
William J. Larkin Jr.	Columbia Biblical Seminary and School of Missions
John R. Levison	Seattle Pacific University
Donald Hans Liebert	Whitworth College
Bruce W. Longenecker	St. Mary's College, University of St. Andrews
Mark D. Luttio	St. Mary's College (Notre Dame, Ind.)
Gerald P. McKenny	University of Notre Dame
Barrett W. McRay	Wheaton College
William MacDonald	Gordon College
John C. Mellis	Queen's College, Memorial University of Newfoundland
Stanley R. Obitts	Westmont College
Robert O'Connor	Wheaton College
Dennis L. Okholm	Wheaton College
John C. Ortberg Jr.	Willow Creek Community Church (South Barrington, Ill.)
Raymond C. Ortlund	First Presbyterian Church (Augusta, Ga.)
David W. C. Pao	Harvard University
Philip B. Payne	Founder and President, Linguist's Software, Inc.
Douglas L. Penney	Wheaton College
Michael B. Phelps	Director, Ancient Biblical Manuscript Center, Claremont
John Piper	Bethlehem Baptist Church (Minneapolis, Minn.)
Don C. Postema	Bethel College (St. Paul, Minn.)
George L. Renner	Nairobi Evangelical Graduate School of Theology (Kenya)
Timothy B. Sailors	Fitzwilliam College, University of Cambridge and Eberhard-Karls-Universität Tübingen
Joel A. Scandrett	Drew University
Hermann S. Schibli	Universität Passau

Thomas E. Schmidt	Westmont College
David M. Scholer	Fuller Theological Seminary
J. Julius Scott Jr.	Wheaton College
Boyd Seevers	Northwestern College (St. Paul, Minn.)
Douglas H. Shantz	University of Calgary
Craig J. Slane	Simpson College (Redding, Calif.)
Robert W. Smid	Boston University
Gary V. Smith	Midwestern Baptist Theological Seminary
Stephanie M. Smith	St. Mary's College, University of St. Andrews
Jeffrey L. Staley	Seattle University
David Steinmetz	Duke University and Duke Divinity School
Douglas A. Sweeney	Trinity Evangelical Divinity School
Kenneth L. Swetland	Gordon-Conwell Theological Seminary
Francis C. R Thee	Northwest College (Seattle)
Frank S. Thielman	Beeson Divinity School, Samford University
Erik Thoennes	Talbot School of Theology, Biola University
Wie Liang Tjiong	School of Divinity, Regent University
Wells Turner	Baker Academic
Eldin Villafañe	Gordon-Conwell Theological Seminary
Blake Walter	Jesuit-Krauss-McCormick Library, Chicago
Catherine J. Williams	The Catholic Foreign Mission Society of America (Maryknoll)
Marvin R. Wilson	Gordon College
†Herbert M. Wolf	Wheaton College
John D. Woodbridge	Trinity Evangelical Divinity School
Robert W. Yarbrough	Trinity Evangelical Divinity School
Kent L. Yinger	George Fox University

Index of Modern Authors

Albertz, Martin, 207-8, 223

Barrett, C. K., 67-68, 76, 128, 136
Bauer, Walter, 19
Beare, F. W., 174-75
Beyer, H. W., 16
Bockmuehl, Markus, 170, 207
Brewer, Raymond R., 169, 192
Bruce, F. F., 207, 221-22
Büchsel, Friedrich, 56-57, 62-64, 67-68, 75-76
Bultmann, R., 101

Cadbury, H. J., 141-42
Carson, D. A., 32-33
Casson, Lionel, 210
Collange, J.-F., 174

Dahood, M., 47-48
Danker, Frederick, 19
Day, Peggy L., 40, 44
Deissmann, Adolf, 206-8
Duncan, George S., 207, 213

Fee, Gordon, 207, 216, 218
Feine, Paul, 206-8, 223

Ferguson, John, 214
Fitzgerald, John, 199
Fowl, Stephen, 202
French, David, 135

Geoffrion, Timothy, 192
Green, Joel, 163
Grimm, W., 16
Gunkel, Hermann, 55-56

Hauerwas, Stanley, 177-78
Hawthorne, Gerald F., 23, 55-57, 67, 77, 99, 121, 141, 167, 172-75, 178, 181, 188, 193, 204-5, 212
Hine, Stuart K., 41
Hobart, W. K., 13
Holloway, Paul A., 209
Hooker, Morna O., 93
Horsley, Greg, 183-84, 190
Hort, F. J. A., 80

Johnson, Samuel, 37

Kannaday, Wayne, 96
Kennedy, G. A., 110
Kilgallen, John J., 129

Lalleman, Pieter J., 234
Leisegang, Hans, 56-68, 75-76
Lightfoot, J. B., 216, 218
Lisco, Heinrich, 207-8
Lohmeyer, Ernst, 178-79, 205

Malherbe, Abraham J., 213
Malina, Bruce, 110
Menzies, Robert, 67
Metzger, Bruce M., 84
Michaelis, Wilhelm, 207
Miller, E. C., 169
Moulton, J. H., 228

Neyrey, Jerome H., 110

O'Brien, Peter, 203, 207
Oesterley, W. O. E., 46-48
Olyan, Saul M., 42

Painter, John, 93
Paulus, H. E. G., 205
Perelman, Chaim, 104, 110
Pervo, Richard I., 214
Peterlin, Davorin, 186
Peterman, Gerald, 184
Petersen, N. R., 163
Plummer, A., 218

Ramsay, William, 13
Robinson, J. A. T., 205
Rohrbaugh, Richard, 110

Sampley, J. Paul, 182-84
Schnackenburg, Rudolf, 101
Schweitzer, Eduard, 93
Silva, Moisés, 207, 210
Smith, Morton, 17
Spitta, Friedrich, 228
Suess, Dr., 115

Taylor, Vincent, 93
Tellbe, Mikael, 197
Turner, Max, 67

Vanhoozer, Kevin, 25
Von Baer, Heinrich, 56-57, 62, 64-68, 75-76

Wells, Louise, 12-15, 20-21
White, L. Michael, 199
Winter, Bruce, 192, 194
Witherington III, Ben, 207

Zimmerman, Reinhard, 186

Index of Scripture and Ancient Literature

OLD TESTAMENT

Genesis

1:1	114
17:9-14	105
18:17	233n.24
21:8-18	106
22:1	233
41:38	70

Exodus

4:24	51n.54
12:23	51
14:13-14	175
15:24	187
16:2	187
16:7-9	187
31:3	70
40:35 LXX	66

Leviticus

13	78-79
13:45	92
16	43

Numbers

6:24	45n.23
14:22	228n.12
16:46	51n.54
17:11 MT	51n.54
22:22	39
27:18-20	70

Deuteronomy

6:16	228n.12
6:16 LXX	231
9:22-24	228n.12
10:9	191
34:9	70

Joshua

4–6	175

Judges

3:7-11	68-69, 71
6	68
6:9	228n.12
13–16	68

1 Samuel

7:10	50n.51

10:6	69
10:10	69
11:6	69
12:17	50n.51
17	175

2 Samuel

13:17	103n.12
24:1	39, 51n.54
24:16	51

1 Kings

18:12	134

2 Kings

2:16	134
6:28	103n.12
19:35	51

1 Chronicles

21:1	39, 51n.54

2 Chronicles

18:18-22	39

Esther

8:12	170

Job

2:1	44
2:5	39
2:6	40
26:6	51n.59
27:3	70
28:22	51n.59
31:12	51n.59
31:32	233n.24
32:7-8	70
32:18	70
37:4-6	42
40:6 LXX	42
40:11	42, 51n.54

Psalms

16:8-11	128
22	175
41:4-12	175
69:22-23	49n.48
77:18	50n.51
78:18-20	227-28
78:49	42n.11, 51
88:11	51n.59
90:6-7 LXX	46
91	45-48
91:3	43n.15, 47
91:4	46
91:11-13	46
95:8-9	228n.12
104:4	42
104:7	50n.51
105:14-15 LXX	237n.31
106:14-15 MT	237n.31
106:47	130
110:1	128, 131-32
118:25-26	130
121	45n.23
146:4 LXX	42n.10
146:5 LXX	51

Proverbs

15:11	51n.59

Isaiah

7:12	228n.12
11:1-2	125
32:15 LXX	124-25
36	175
40:22	43
42:1	125
44:3	125
52:13–53:12	175
59:21	125
61:1	125
63:8	130
66:15	125

Jeremiah

3:12-13	32
17:14	130

Lamentations

2:6	90

Ezekiel

1:15	42
3:14	134
8:3	134
9	51
10:12	42
36:25-27	125
39:29	125

Daniel

4:5-6	70
4:15	70
5:11-14 MT	70
7:9	50
7:10	44
7:13	132
11:30	90

Hosea

4:19	49n.44

9:7-8	43, 49-50

Joel

2:28	125
2:32	130

Zechariah

3	40
3:1	44
3:2	45n.23
12:10	125

NEW TESTAMENT

Matthew

4:6	46n.27
4:23	12n.6
4:24	12n.6, 18, 21
8:2-3	81
8:7	12n.6, 18
8:16	12n.6, 16, 18, 21
9:30	90
9:35	12n.6
9:36	82
10:1	12n.6
10:8	12n.6, 18
12:10	12n.6
12:12-13	83
12:15	12n.6, 21
12:22	12n.6
12:22-42	87n.12
12:45	51n.58
13:39	44
14:14	12n.6, 21, 82
15:30	12n.6, 21
15:32	82
17:16	12n.6
17:18	12n.6
19:2	12n.6, 21
19:14	83
20:34	82
21:14	12n.6, 21
23:37	33

26:8	174	7:26	90n.15	8:2	13n.6, 51n.58
26:32-44 par.	175	7:31-37	19	8:30	47
26:53	47	8:2	82	8:43	17
		8:6-7	86	8:47	17
Mark		8:11-12	87	9:1	13n.6
1:1	90	8:12	89	9:6	13n.6
1:12	90n.15	8:22-26	19	9:11	21
1:13	46n.27	8:23-25	88	10:9	13n.6
1:16-20	91	9:18	90n.15	10:18	42n.10
1:25	91	9:20-25	87, 94	10:18-19	46
1:30-31	91n.16	9:22	87	10:25-37	142
1:31	88	9:22-23	82n.7, 94	10:29-37	154
1:34	13n.6, 18, 90n.15, 91	9:23	89	10:34	20
		9:27	88	11:14-32	87n.12
1:37-38	91	9:28	90n.15	11:19-20	40
1:39-45	77-97	9:38	90n.15	11:41	142, 155n.27
2:1-12	88n.13	9:47	90n.15	12:13-21	142
2:13-14	91	10:13-16	88, 94	12:16-21	155
2:13-17	88n.13	10:14	83-84, 89	12:33-34	142
2:16-17	91	11:15	90	13:14	13n.6
2:18-22	88n.13, 91	12:8	90	14:3	13n.6
2:23-28	88n.13, 91	13:25	42n.10	14:3-4	18
2:27	89	14:5	90	14:12-14	155n.26
3:1-6	88 (n. 13), 91, 94			14:16-24	142
3:2	13n.6, 18	**Luke**		16:14-31	142
3:5	82, 84, 89	1-2	66	18:16	83
3:7-12	91	1:35	61, 66	18:18-30	154
3:10	13n.6, 18	1:52-53	142	18:22	142
3:15	90n.15	2:11	129	19:8	142
3:21	91	3:16	125, 128	21:13	126
3:22-23	90n.15	4:10-11	46n.27	22:42	137
3:31-35	91	4:18	141, 156	22:69	132
5:7	48n.37	4:23	17-18, 20n.24	23:32	97
5:9	41n.9, 47, 48n.37	4:25-30	156	24:13-53	122-29
5:25-34	92	4:40	13n.6	24:46-49	138
5:40	90n.15	5:12-13	81		
5:41-42	88	5:15	13n.6, 17	**John**	
6:3	97	6:7	13n.6	1:1-4	102
6:5	13n.6, 88	6:10	83	1:17-18	102
6:12-13	20	6:18	13n.6, 17	2:1-11	116n.37
6:13	17, 90n.15	6:20-26	142	3:16	29
6:34	82	6:36	154	4:46-54	116n.37
6:41	86	7:13	82	5:10	13n.6
7:1-8	89	7:21	13n.6	5:17-20	114

5:19-47	102, 112	11:33	90	6:5	130-31
6:27-29	114	11:38	90	6:8-10	130-31
6:37	30	12:8	23	6:15	131
6:39	30	12:29	50	7:9	149n.18
6:44	30, 33	12:32	33	7:48	132
7:1–8:59	99-119	13:3-17	204	7:52	132
7:14-17	114	13:35	36	7:55-56	127, 131
7:14-53	112	14:16	45	7:55-60	139
7:15	111-12	15:13-15	204	7:59-60	132
7:15-24	104	16:8-11	130	8:7	13n.6
7:17	111-12	18:21	111	8:10	41n.9, 51
7:19-24	115			8:15-17	130
7:21	114	**Acts**		8:39	127
7:24	111n.28	1:1	131, 139	8:39-40	134
7:25-36	106-7	1:1-11	122-27, 138	9:3-4	132
7:28	111n.28	1:8	136	9:3-19	127
7:34	111n.28, 112	1:10	131	9:6	136
7:37	111n.28	1:16	122	9:15	136, 139
7:53–8:11	101, 103-4, 108,	1:21-22	136	9:15-16	127, 132
	117-18, 119	2:1-13	125	9:16	136
8:5	117	2:21	130	9:17	132
8:7	117	2:25-36	128-32	9:20	142n.3
8:11	119	2:33	126	9:22	153
8:12	111n.28, 112	2:33-36	127, 135, 138	9:34	127
8:12-59	112	2:33-38	138	9:36-38	142
8:13-30	106-8	2:36	142	10:11	132
8:18	112	2:38	124, 126	10:37-40	121
8:21	111n.28, 112	2:38-39	130	10:44-47	130
8:24	111n.28, 112	2:42-47	142	11:20-26	146n.11
8:28	111n.28, 112	3:4	131	11:29-30	142
8:31	112	3:12	131	13:1	135
8:31-32	111n.28	3:19-20	130	13:1-3	133
8:31-58	105	3:20	126	13:2	127, 133, 135, 139
8:32	114-15, 118-19	3:21	136	13:4	127, 133, 135, 139
8:36	111n.28	4:8-13	130	13:5	143
8:44	115	4:14	13n.6	13:9-12	142
8:46	111n.28	4:25	122	13:13-52	141-64
8:51	111n.28, 112	4:32-37	142, 156n.28	13:36-39	126
8:55	112	5:12-14	151	13:48	30
8:58	112	5:16	13n.6, 151	14:1	157
8:59	117	5:17	149n.18, 151	14:3	127
9:1-7	19	5:28	129	14:8-20	157
10:22-39	104	5:29	136	14:25	157
10:31	117	5:31-32	126-31, 135, 138	15:8	130

16:6	135	22:1	147	15:28	211
16:7	127, 134-35, 138-	22:6-7	132	16:4	214
	39	22:6-21	127	16:7	214
16:14	127, 144n.6	22:14-16	127, 132-33		
16:16	42n.9	22:22-23	148	**1 Corinthians**	
16:16-18	159	23:1	170	1:18	174n.25
16:20	171	23:6	148	1:18–2:5	219
16:20-21	158-59	23:11	127, 136-37, 139	2:6	219
17:4	144n.6	23:12-15	157	3:1-3	219
17:4-9	157-58	23:17-22	138	3:1-4	215
17:10-15	157-58	23:26-30	162	3:3	149n.18
17:17	144n.6	23:35	212	4:6	219
17:25	17n.24, 20n.34	24:1-9	157	4:8	215, 219
18:5-6	148	24:21	148	4:17	223n.63
18:5-17	153	24:26-27	161	4:18	215
18:7	144n.6	25:1-3	157	4:18-19	219
18:9-11	127	25:9	161	5:1-2	220
18:12-13	158	25:10-11	138	6:5	215
19:8-10	153-54	26:6-8	148	6:9	220
19:13-15	41n.9	26:13-18	127, 132-33	6:12-20	219
19:15	48n.37	26:20-23	148n.15	7:19	218n.46
19:21	127, 136, 139	26:23	126-27, 130, 135	8:1-3	219
19:22	223n.63	26:28	105n.16	8:10	219
19:23-25	160	26:32	161	10:7-10	219
19:28-29	160	27:24	136, 161n.36	10:10	51
19:32	160	27:31-35	138	10:22	149n.19
19:35-40	160	28:8-9	18	11:17	215
19:37	214	28:9	13n.6	13:4	149n.18
20:1	223n.63			15:10	220n.51
20:1-6	211	**Romans**		15:25	127
20:19	137	1:20-25	218n.46	15:29-34	220
20:21	137	3:10-11	33	15:32	212-13
20:22-24	127, 136-37, 139	3:10-12	30	15:32-33	219
20:24	132	3:25-26	173	15:42-49	220
20:35	137	4:11	218n.46	15:58	220n.51
21:2	127	8:34	127	16:5-7	211
21:4	127, 136, 139	9:18	30	16:8	221
21:11-14	127, 136-39	9:22-24	30	16:10-11	223n.63
21:17-26	217	10:19	149n.17		
21:27	158	11:9	49n.48	**2 Corinthians**	
21:28	146n.12	11:11	149n.17	1:1	223n.63
21:30-31	158	11:14	149n.17	1:8-10	214n.30
21:38	158	13:13	149n.18, 169	1:8-11	223n.63
21:39	162	15:23-24	211	1:15-24	211

2:1-4	223n.63	1:5	185, 187, 215	2:14	187-88, 200
2:12-13	223n.63	1:7	183n.11, 185, 191,	2:14-16	193-94
3:1	215		215	2:15-16	185
5:12	215	1:8	204	2:17	192, 204
6:14	190n.31	1:9	195, 199	2:18-30	168
6:14-15	51	1:12	185	2:19	223n.63
6:15	45	1:12-14	202	2:20-21	204
8:1-2	171	1:12-26	168, 177	2:22-24	211n.23
8:24	173	1:13	171n.10, 205, 213,	2:24	211, 223n.63
11:2	149n.19		221	2:25-30	185-86
11:19-20	215	1:18-26	213	2:29-30	209
12:1	215	1:19	174, 185	2:30	204
12:2	134	1:20	176	3	208, 215-21, 223
12:20	149n.18	1:24-25	211	3:2-3	196
12:20-21	215	1:26	211n.23	3:2-21	193
13:1-10	215	1:27	187, 192-95, 198	3:4-11	175, 196, 203
		1:27-30	168-71, 173, 177-	3:7-8	192
Galatians			79, 185	3:10	191, 197-98
1:6	218n.45	1:27–2:18	193-94	3:11	198
1:6-9	215	1:28	167-79, 193	3:14	192
3:1	215, 218n.45	1:28-30	197	3:15	183n.11
4:11	215	1:29-30	192	3:17	204
4:12	218n.45	1:30	211	3:19	183n.11, 197
4:15-16	215	2:1	191	3:20	170, 177, 192-93,
4:21	218n.45	2:1-2	189		196-98
4:21-31	106	2:1-5	204	3:21	198, 203
5:4	218n.45	2:2	183, 187-88, 191,	4:1	198, 215
5:6	218n.46		198	4:2	183, 186-87, 194,
5:7	215	2:3	192, 203		198
5:10-12	218	2:3-4	187-88, 196	4:3	186
5:20	149n.18	2:4	200	4:8-9	199-202
6:12-13	218	2:5	183n.11, 202-3	4:10-18	182-85, 189
6:15	218n.46	2:5-6	202	4:11	200
6:17	215	2:5-8	188	4:13	201
		2:6-8	203	4:14-16	215
Ephesians		2:6-11	168, 176, 192,	4:15-16	211
1:20-23	127		202-4, 214	4:17	183
1:21	41n.9	2:7	204	4:19	189, 201
4:1	169	2:7-8	192, 202	4:22	206
		2:9-11	202		
Philippians		2:10	41n.9	**Colossians**	
1:1	185	2:12	192, 211n.23	1:10	169
1:3-4	215	2:12-13	188	1:16	50
1:4-6	188	2:13	195		

1 Thessalonians

2:12	169
4:12	169
4:17	134

1 Timothy

1:3-7	217n.43
2:3-6	29
2:4	34
3:7	49n.47

2 Timothy

2:26	49n.47
3:3	40n.8

Titus

1:10	217n.43
2:3	40n.8

Philemon

22	211

Hebrews

1:7	42n.11
1:14	42n.11
4:14-16	127
11:28	51
12:22	47

James

1:2	236
1:2-4	227
1:12	227
1:13	225, 227, 235-36
1:13-15	227, 239
2:21	227n.8, 233
3:14	149n.18
3:15	240
3:16	149n.18
4:2	149n.18
5:14	20

1 Peter

5:8	44

2 Peter

3:9	29
3:15-16	27

1 John

2:1	45
2:1-2	30
4:3	42n.9

Jude

9	45n.23
14	47

Revelation

1:20	42n.10
4–5	127
5:11	47
7:1	42
8:5	42
8:7-12	42
9:1	42n.10
9:11	51
9:15-16	51
9:16	47
10:3-4	50
12:10	44
13:3	17
13:12	17
14:2	50n.53
14:18	42
15:1	51n.58
16:5	42
16:17-18	50n.53
19:6	50n.53

APOCRYPHA AND PSEUDEPIGRAPHA

Apocalypse of Abraham

13:6	43

Apocalypse of Elijah (C)

1:10	50n.50

4:10	50n.50

Assumption of Moses

10:1	40

1 Enoch

8:1	43
10:4	43
18:14	42n.10
42	146n.10
53:3	51
56:1	51
61:10	43
66:1	51
71:7	43
75	42
88:1-3	42n.10

2 Enoch

20:1	43, 50n.50
40	42

3 Enoch

14:4	50n.51

4 Ezra

14:40	74

Jubilees

2	42
2:2	42, 50n.51
17:16-17	233n.24
18:12	233n.24
19:8	233n.24
23:29	40
48:2	51n.54

Letter of Aristeas

31	170

Liber antiquitatum biblicarum

3:9-10	69
12:4	69

13:10	69
19:2-5	69
25:9	69
28:6-10	69-70
36:3	69
44:6-7	69

2 Maccabees
6:1	170
11:25	170

3 Maccabees
3:4	170

4 Maccabees
2:8	170
2:23	170
4:23	170
5:16	170

Sibylline Oracles
Prologue, 82-91	74

Sirach
15:11-13	227
21:27	40
38:2	16
38:6-7	15
38:7	18

Testament of Abraham
1:1-2	233n.24
1:5	233n.24

Testament of Adam
4:3	50n.51
4:8	50n.50

Testament of Benjamin
9:2-3	125

Testament of Judah
24:1-6	125

Testament of Levi
3:8	50n.50
18:1-2	125
18:5-12	125

Testament of Solomon
20:16-18	42n.10

Tobit
3:17	14
6:4	15
6:6-8	15
6:9	14
8:1-3	15
11:8-4	15
11:11-14	15
12:3	13-14, 18
12:14	14

DEAD SEA SCROLLS

1QS
IV, 12	51

4Q180
I, 7-8	43

4Q318 | | 50 |

4Q390 | | 43 |

4Q403
II, 15	43

4Q405
20-21-22 3	43
20-21-22 9	43
20-21-22 10	43

4Q511
VIII, 6	45

11QPs[a]
XXVII, 10	45

11Q13
II, 13	51

CD
V, 17	51

HELLENISTIC JEWISH LITERATURE

Philo
On Sobriety
56	233n.24

On the Life of Abraham
167	233n.24

Josephus
Antiquities
16.6.4 §§167-68	213

Jewish War
1.657	20
7.8.1 §262	226n.4

The Life
12	170